DATE DUE

The
Marketplace
of Democracy

The Marketplace of Democracy

Electoral Competition and American Politics

Michael P. McDonald

John Samples

editors

CATO INSTITUTE
Washington, D.C.

BROOKINGS INSTITUTION PRESS
Washington, D.C.

Copyright © 2006
THE BROOKINGS INSTITUTION
CATO INSTITUTE

The Marketplace of Democracy: Electoral Competition and American Politics may be ordered from:
BROOKINGS INSTITUTION PRESS
c/o HFS, P.O. Box 50370, Baltimore, MD 1211-4370
Tel.: 800/537-5487; 410/516-6956; Fax: 410/516-6998

Library of Congress Cataloging-in-Publication data
The marketplace of democracy : electoral competition and American
    politics / Michael P. McDonald and John Samples, editors.
        p.   cm.
    Includes bibliographical references and index.
    ISBN-13: 978-0-8157-5580-7 (cloth : alk. paper)
    ISBN-10: 0-8157-5580-5 (cloth : alk. paper)
    ISBN-13: 978-0-8157-5579-1 (pbk. : alk. paper)
    ISBN-10: 0-8157-5579-1 (pbk. : alk. paper)
    1. Elections—United States.   2. Representative government and representation—
United States.   3. Opposition (Political science)—United States.   4. Democracy—
United States.   I. McDonald, Michael, 1967–   II. Samples, John Curtis, 1956–
III. Title.
    JK1976.M29 2006
    324.60973—dc22   2006022353

9 8 7 6 5 4 3 2 1

The paper used in this publication meets minimum requirements of the American National
Standard for Information Sciences—Permanence of Paper for Printed Library Materials:
ANSI Z39.48-1992.

Typeset in Minion and Univers Condensed

Composition by R. Lynn Rivenbark
Macon, Georgia

Printed by R. R. Donnelley
Harrisonburg, Virginia

Contents

Part Two
Reform Mechanisms

Part Three
Reforms and Competition

Preface

The *Marketplace of Democracy* began life some years ago in conversations between the coeditors about redistricting and the lack of competition in American elections. We concluded that a conference bringing together leading scholars to examine the origins of the decline in electoral competition and putative reforms might increase public awareness and understanding of these issues. We also thought that working under the auspices of two think tanks generally associated with conflicting political outlooks might be useful. In a time of political polarization, we agree about the importance of competition and accountability for all Americans. In addition, we have agreed almost without exception about the issues and results presented herein. We would like to thank Ed Crane and David Boaz (at Cato) and Strobe Talbott and Pietro Nivola (at Brookings) for supporting this project from the start.

The project also received strong support from several foundations. For their support, we extend thanks to the Armstrong Foundation, the Carnegie Corporation of New York, the JEHT Foundation, the Joyce Foundation, and the Kerr Foundation.

The contributions to this volume were first presented at a conference held at the Cato Institute in March 2006. We would like to acknowledge several individuals who participated in the conference: Mike Bailey, Michael Barone,

Tom Brunell, Tom Mann, Michael Munger, Bradley Smith, Lance Tarrance Jr., and Amy Walter. The staff at Cato also did a great job with the more than 200 guests attending the conference. Our thanks go to Linda Hertzog, Margaret Bruntrager, and Alisa Steinberg.

The Brookings Institution Press has done a rapid, thorough, and fine job of bringing this book to the public. We would like to acknowledge the work of Larry Converse, Chris Kelaher, Janet Mowery, Janet Walker, and Susan Woollen.

Finally, we would like to thank the contributors to this volume. Their valuable data, imaginative analysis, and thorough professionalism have made editing this work a pleasure.

1

The Marketplace of Democracy: Normative and Empirical Issues

Michael P. McDonald and John Samples

The U.S. government is founded on and derives its legitimacy from the principle of the consent of the governed. Citizens can be satisfied with many forms of government, and the course of American political development might have been radically different if King George III had been responsive to the grievances of the colonies. However, history has demonstrated the long-term dangers of a government based on a short-term benevolent authoritarian regime; inevitably a despot rises to power. To protect against future despotism, the Founding Fathers renewed the ancient Roman method of expressing the consent of the governed: a representative government selected in periodic elections.

Prominent political theorists define representative democracy in terms of meaningful choices presented to voters: Joseph Schumpeter defines representative democracy as "that institutional arrangement for arriving at political decisions in which individuals acquire the power to decide by means of a competitive struggle for the people's vote."[1] Robert Dahl calls it "a system of control by competition."[2] Adam Przeworski discusses the institution as it

---

1. Schumpeter (1950, p. 269).
2. Dahl (1984, p. 113).

"defines the scope of government and establishes rules of competition."[3] The notion of competition as a necessary condition of democracy is so fundamental that it can be found in introductory election textbooks.[4]

Democratic elections are about choice between competing candidates and the issues they intend to follow if elected. Given what little political knowledge voters have, or even care to have, about complex and arcane public policy issues, there is debate over the degree to which representatives need to be delegates responsive to the public or trustees who are elected to implement policy for the public interest, even if the public does not agree. Even among those who champion a trustee view of politics, a representative should be in some measure a delegate. Why hold democratic elections otherwise?

Once elected, will representatives in the trustee role subvert the electoral process to protect themselves? America's Founding Fathers, such as James Madison, were concerned that in a democracy a majority could tyrannize a minority of the population. While we may commonly think about majority tyranny in the sphere of public policy, Madison astutely recognized that majorities, such as those in state legislatures acting through their authority to regulate elections granted by article 1, section 4 of the Constitution, would act to insulate themselves from electoral pressures that might jeopardize their majority status:

> Whenever the State Legislature had a favorite measure to carry, they would take care so to mould their regulations as to favor the candidates they wished to succeed. Besides, the inequality of the Representation in the Legislatures of particular States, would produce a like inequality in their representation in the National Legislature, as it was presumable that the Counties having the power in the former case would secure it to themselves in the latter.[5]

As J. S. Mill would later write, "In every government there is some power stronger than all the rest; and the power which is strongest tends perpetually to become the sole power."[6] In the course of American political development, the subverting of the electoral process to favor the majority has taken many forms, such as: Jim Crow laws designed to prevent African American representation; malapportioned districts that favor rural representation over urban; the partisan gerrymander devised by Gov. Elbridge Gerry in 1812; the

3. Przeworski (1991, p. 36).
4. Flanigan and Zingale (2002).
5. Quoted in Farrand (1911, pp. 240–41).
6. Mill (1991, p. 315).

adoption of restrictive ballot access laws; and others. The latter—ballot access laws designed to prevent minor-party access to elections—suggests that in certain circumstances the two political parties would form what Samuel Issacharoff terms a "bipartisan cartel" to ensure low levels of electoral competition for incumbent members of both political parties.[7]

At first blush, a concern that competition is lacking in American elections would appear to be unfounded. The presidential elections of 2000 and 2004 were among the closest in history. Republicans narrowly control both houses of Congress, but a change to the Democrats, especially in the Senate, seems possible with every congressional election. These relatively narrow majorities in Congress reflect a national electorate that divides evenly along partisan lines. Any expert would be hard pressed to say that one of the major parties dominates American politics.

A closer look, however, gives reason for concern. Incumbent members of the House of Representatives almost always win reelection. Since 1998 they have been reelected more than 98 percent of the time. As with most statistics, this rate should not be understood in isolation. In the modern political era (the years after 1945) members of Congress have won reelection over 90 percent of the time. In examining election returns in the last quarter of the twentieth century, James Campbell and Steve Jurek found that both the gross number of seats that changed hands and the net partisan gains or losses after 1970 were typically less than half of what they had been before that date.[8] Specifically, in the thirty-eight elections from 1900 to 1974, thirty-three (87 percent) involved seat swings of at least ten seats from one party to another. Of the thirteen elections from 1976 to 2000, only five (38 percent) resulted in double-digit seat shifts.[9] The 2002 House elections were on several dimensions less competitive than the "normal" elections from 1974 to 2000. Decennial reapportionments usually change some districts in ways that foment competition for some incumbents. However, the 2002 elections—the first after the 2000 reapportionment—were less competitive than the elections of 1972, 1982, and 1992.[10] Indeed, House races had fewer seats that might change hands in 2004 than in 1994.[11]

In contrast, senators have not been as consistently successful at being reelected. Since World War II, 78.6 percent of all senators have won reelection.

7. Issacharoff (2002).
8. Campbell and Jurek (2003, p. 20).
9. Campbell and Jurek (2003, p. 10).
10. Issacharoff, Neuborne, and Pildes (n.d., p. 16).
11. Irwin (2004, p. 11).

More recently, however, they have lost more often than their counterparts in the House: in 1980, for example, only 55 percent of the incumbent Senate candidates won reelection. Nonetheless, the incumbency advantage for senators has been rising and by 1992 was about the same as that of a House incumbent.[12] Those already in office also dominate state elections for legislative and executive branch offices. Competition in the United States bears a troubling resemblance to that in nations where candidates run unopposed or with token opposition, nations that American leaders condemn as lacking truly democratic or legitimate elections.

Should we be concerned about the lack of competition between incumbent officials and challengers in U.S. elections? To answer that question we need to understand why citizens of a liberal democracy such as the United States should value electoral competition. Electoral competition is not an end in itself; it is rather a means of achieving important political goals in a democracy. With those normative goals in place, we can then inquire whether the current system serves those goals as well as possible, all things considered.

Normative Arguments Favoring Electoral Competition

The literal Greek translation of "democracy" is "rule by the people." The people may rule directly by making laws through direct voting by the assembled citizens, a species of government favored by "theoretic politicians" that James Madison found that history had shown was likely to lead to instability, injustice, and confusion in government.[13] The solution to the "superior force of an interested and overbearing majority" among the people was, Madison argued, to be found in the deliberative setting of representative legislatures so "that the public voice, pronounced by the representatives of the people, will be more consonant to the public good than if pronounced by the people themselves, convened for the purpose."[14]

Competition and Accountability

Yet representation also offers dangers for democracy. In ruling indirectly the people may not rule; their agents in the legislature may betray their trust and make laws that benefit themselves or particular groups rather than a majority or the people as a whole.[15] In the language of political economy, the

12. Jacobson (2004, pp. 25, 28).
13. Madison (1960, pp. 61, 56).
14. Madison (1960, p. 62).
15. Parisi (2004, pp. 216–17).

agents (the representatives) shirk their responsibilities to their principals (the people who elect them). Elections, along with vigorous competition among candidates and parties, ensure that public officials serve the interests of those who elected them. In short, democratic theorists value electoral competition as a way to ensure that representatives are accountable to voters. As political scientist G. Bingham Powell said, "The citizens' ability to throw the rascals out seems fundamental to modern representative democracy because it is the ultimate guarantee of a connection between citizens and policymakers. It enables the citizens to hold the policymakers accountable for their performance. Such accountability is a keystone of majoritarian democratic theory."[16]

Accountability and electoral competition concern the political process. But most political struggle concerns substantive differences over policies, interests, and ideals. Conservatives have emphasized individual freedom and rights as a means to limit government. The Progressive tradition has argued that equality should counterbalance or replace liberty on the scales of public policy.[17] Naturally, both sides would want a political process that favors their substantive ideals and would fear electoral competition if accountability to voters meant realizing the ideals of their opponents. But neither side can reasonably expect the other to agree to a process that guarantees the victory of their opponents. We might, however, come to value a process for itself and not for its substantive outcomes. Substantive differences notwithstanding, both conservatives and Progressives have good normative reasons to value accountability in the political process.

Liberty and Accountability

James Madison identified the political problem of classical liberalism: "In framing a government which is to be administered by men over men, the

16. G. Bingham Powell Jr., quoted in Issacharoff (2002, p. 624). Robert Dahl wrote some time ago that "continuing responsiveness of the government to the preferences of its citizens [is] a key characteristic of democracy" (Dahl 1971, p. 1). J. M. Bessette notes, "Political accountability is the principle that governmental decision-makers in a democracy ought to be answerable to the people for their actions. The modern doctrine owes its origins to the development of institutions of representative democracy in the eighteenth century. Popular election of public officials and relatively short terms of office were intended to give the electorate the opportunity to hold their representatives to account for their behavior in office. Those whose behavior was found wanting could be punished by their constituents at the next election. Thus, the concept of accountability implies more than merely the tacit consent of the governed. It implies both mechanisms for the active monitoring of public officials and the means for enforcing public expectations." See Bessette (2001, pp. 38–39).

17. For an example of balancing the two values, see Rawls (1971). For an example of the priority of equality, see Dworkin (1978, p. 266ff.).

great difficulty lies in this: You must first enable the government to controul the governed; and in the second place, oblige it to controul itself." Madison then immediately adds: "a dependence on the people is no doubt that primary controul on government" even if history had shown the necessity of checks and balances in constitutional arrangements.[18] More generally, the classical liberal believes government possesses a monopoly on violence that is both necessary and a threat to its citizens. Economists expect that, all things being equal, a monopolist will charge higher prices to consumers than would exist under perfect or imperfect competition. Similarly, economically minded citizens should expect that those who hold a monopoly on the legitimate use of violence will use it to further their own interests at some cost to the interests of others. In the absence of some effective constraint on government, the ruled should expect to be exploited by their rulers. Hence, in studying politics, public choice scholars have sought a set of institutions that constrain the actions of government officials in light of the wants of citizens.[19] Elections and electoral competition are means to control that monopoly on violence and restrain its abuse. The classically liberal part of the American vision of politics thus values electoral competition as a way to control and limit government and thus preserve individual liberty.

Equality and Accountability

What of the egalitarian side of American liberalism? Electoral democracy begins with equality as embodied in "one person, one vote." In shirking their responsibilities, elected officials acquire unaccountable power, an inequality that undermines the basic principle of democracy. Moreover, Progressives believe that representatives who are unaccountable to their voters are likely to be responsive to the political agenda of the economically powerful. Shirking by representatives thus leads to the inequalities in the private market economy being transferred to the public sphere, contrary to the demands of democratic equality and even social justice. For this reason the Progressive might be inclined to favor more electoral competition to preclude shirking that fosters political and economic inequality.

The Community as a Whole

Beyond left and right, the commitment to representative democracy requires a commitment to a government that reflects the preferences of its peo-

18. Madison (1960b, p. 349).
19. Brennan and Hamlin (2000, pp. 101–02).

ple. If those preferences are distributed normally on a single issue, everyone is fully informed, a single representative is selected from a district, and majority rule determines outcomes, lawmakers will ultimately take policy stands that appeal to the median voter of their district.[20] Electoral competition between two viable candidates is essential to this outcome.

Yet the median voter's policy preference may not be the realized outcome. Candidates are responsive to their activists during nominations in primaries and caucuses, and activists are among the core suppliers of campaign money and volunteer time. These activists are closer to the extremes of the political spectrum than to the median voter. Candidates are not a blank slate and possess personal policy preferences too. In the general election, a candidate who wishes to gain a majority of votes must move toward the median voter of his or her district, and the winner will thus ultimately represent the greater part of the overall distribution of voters. Of course, the median of a district may differ from the national median, but if competition is lacking, a nominee need not position him- or herself separately from the party's activist base, and many voters around the middle of a district's electorate or perhaps "the community as a whole" may ultimately go without representation.[21]

Competition has other benefits to the general community besides representation. Electoral competition provides a partial solution to the problem of lack of voter information. Competition is related to more free campaign coverage by the media and more campaign expenditures aimed at informing and mobilizing voters. Competitive elections interest voters and draw them to the polls. Competition thereby fosters other indicators of a healthy democracy, such as higher levels of participation by voters and activists and stronger political parties that must evolve or perish in Darwinian political conflict.[22]

Constitutional Considerations

The Constitution of the United States does not specifically require electoral competition, and many Supreme Court decisions related to elections depend on the equal protection clause of the Fourteenth Amendment, which

---

20. Downs (1957).

21. Issacharoff (2002, pp. 628–29).

22. It is universal practice in scholarly work on voter turnout to include a measure for competition in voting analyses. These analyses uniformly find that higher turnout is related to greater levels of competition. One of the early works that ties competition and turnout together with party money allocation can be found in Cox and Munger (1989, pp. 217–31). The relationship between party strength and competition is articulated by Rosenthal (1998, p. 195).

has no obvious relevance to questions of incumbency advantage. However, three legal scholars have argued that the current dearth of electoral competition violates article 1 and the First Amendment of the Constitution.

According to the Founders, the U.S. Constitution grants enumerated powers from the people to their government. Powers that are not granted to the state or national governments are retained by the people. Article 1, section 4 of the U.S. Constitution states that the "Times, Places and Manner of holding Elections for Senators and Representatives shall be prescribed in each State by the Legislature thereof." This grant of power does not include "the power to regulate congressional elections with the aim and effect of artificially insulating members of Congress from electoral competition through state creation of overwhelmingly 'safe,' non-competitive congressional election districts."[23] Yet the evidence indicates that state legislatures have exercised just such a power, contrary to the constraints of the Constitution.

Article 1, section 2 of the Constitution states that "The House of Representatives shall be composed of Members chosen every second Year by the People of the several States." This language recognizes the sovereignty of the people and their affirmative right to elect the House. Insofar as incumbent officials manipulate the electoral system to reduce electoral competition, they might be said to abridge the ultimate power of citizens.[24] The First Amendment to the Constitution also bears on this issue. The First Amendment seeks to secure the conditions of liberal democracy, not the least of which is "the free flow of information needed to permit genuine electoral choice."[25] When incumbents create safe electoral districts, they preclude such choice and thereby contravene the fundamental purpose of the First Amendment.

Normative Criticisms of Electoral Competition

The Founding Fathers were divided on the efficacy of mass democracy. While the founding documents clearly appealed to virtues of equality and self-determination, some did not believe the masses had the capacity and temperament to make wise voting decisions. In the formative years of American political history, a debate raged over whether voting was a right or a privilege. If one were to take the Declaration of Independence to its logical conclusion, then voting was a right to be enjoyed by all. However, all of the colonies—and

23. Issacharoff (n.d., p. 9).
24. Issacharoff (n.d., p. 14ff.).
25. Issacharoff (n.d., p. 20).

later states—restricted the franchise to a certain few, most notably those with property, on the premise that only those with property were competent enough and free of others' influences to make wise voting decisions.[26]

Responsibility

The authors of *The Federalist Papers* wrote of responsibility rather than accountability. Responsible officials were to use discretion and judgment to promote the long-term well-being of the country, even though voters might not recognize their efforts for some time, if ever. Officials would be called upon to resist popular desires when the people push for prejudiced, irresponsible, or unjust measures; responsibility, not accountability, they said, is needed in such cases until reason can return to the people.[27]

Officials should thus sometimes ignore the wishes of their constituents in favor of the longer-term good of those same voters. The quintessential advocate of this position, English political philosopher and Member of Parliament Edmund Burke, stated:

> Parliament is not a congress of ambassadors from different and hostile interests; which interests each must maintain, as an agent and advocate, against other agents and advocates; but parliament is a deliberative assembly of one nation, with one interest, that of the whole; where, not local purposes, not local prejudices ought to guide, but the general good, resulting from the general reason of the whole. You choose a member indeed; but when you have chosen him, he is not a member of Bristol, but he is a member of parliament . . . our representative owes you, not his industry only, but his judgment; and he betrays instead of serving you if he sacrifices it to your opinion.[28]

Yet such cases of defensible shirking are surely exceptions to the rule of electoral accountability. If not, representatives would be free to enact their notions of the public good with few constraints, a liberty that would contravene the idea of popular government. Indeed, Burke discovered democratic accountability when he was later forced to resign from his constituency in 1780.

Along this vein, a lack of electoral competition could be interpreted as a sign of healthy representation. An exceptional representative who successfully balances the interests of the constituency and the nation, who is a masterful

26. Keyssar (2000).
27. Bessette (2001).
28. Burke (1999, p. 25).

campaigner, who runs an office that assiduously provides high-quality constituency service, and is thus loved by the voters, is a representative who engenders little competition.[29] Incumbents who are not challenged or who soundly drub their competition might not be products of a flawed electoral system, but rather indicators of effective representation.

Deliberation

Others reject the implicit link between electoral and market competition. They argue that elections, unlike markets, should concern ideals and principles rather than preferences and interests.[30] Such criticisms grow out of the theory of deliberative democracy, which demands that "people collectively shape their own politics through persuasive argument" instead of by asserting their wills or fighting for their predetermined interests.[31] Deliberative democracy thus seems to be more about arguments among citizens than about competition among candidates for votes. Much evidence in public opinion research suggests such engagement in politics contravenes the inclinations and capacities of most individuals.[32] Yet these theorists sometimes say that "ongoing accountability, not direct political participation, is the key to deliberative democracy." Accountability matters because it is said to foster deliberation, the giving of reasons, about public issues.[33] If so, and if electoral competition serves the end of accountability, competition fosters a deliberation suited for a society much larger than ancient Greece. In any case, it hardly seems likely that a lack of electoral competition will foster deliberation about public issues.

Representation

Many electoral systems and government institutions around the world are designed to center deliberation at the elite level.[34] Switzerland, in the extreme, has a national governing council with guaranteed representation for all major parties and super-majority voting rules, which forces bargaining among elites. In the electoral systems of these countries, competition is

29. Zaller (1998, pp. 125–85).
30. See Thompson (2004, p. 176). Thompson also argues that an emphasis on electoral competition detracts from other worthy goals like "making electoral reform more cooperative" and "tending to the business of government."
31. Gutmann (1993, p. 417).
32. Zaller (1992).
33. Gutmann (1993, p. 418).
34. Lijphart (1999).

secondary to representation derived through forms of proportional representation that provide for what J. S. Mill called "full representation" of all interests in a society.

Electoral competition in these countries arises in contests for votes that translate into the proportions of representation awarded to the various political parties. The U.S. government is not among these consociational democracies. Its electoral system of single-member, plurality-win districts is designed to provide rule for the majority of the electorate. Indeed, single-member districting systems tend to amplify the seats awarded to the party that wins the most votes, thereby strengthening the hand of the largest party, which sometimes may not receive a majority of the vote. Deliberation in the United States is, by design, to be conducted among the masses, not the elites.

Still, there are exceptions in the U.S. electoral system designed to guarantee representation to protected classes of citizens. The Voting Rights Act explicitly requires drawing special districts with a majority of minority populations within their borders in order to provide minorities with the opportunity to elect a candidate of their choice. Elections in these districts are not competitive, and indeed, competitive elections might erode minority representation. There are states where supporters of one party are so concentrated that it is impossible to devise district boundaries that facilitate competition; and there are regions within more competitive states where doing so would result in extremely spaghetti-like districts that combine dissimilar and removed communities. Indeed, voters prefer to have a representative who shares their culture and ideology.[35]

Summary

The case for electoral competition appears strong in the abstract. Such competition militates against shirking, fosters accountability, and informs voters. These effects notwithstanding, few people would argue that electoral competition should be maximized whatever the cost to other values. To determine the values and trade-offs at stake here, we need to answer three questions. Is the decline in electoral competition widespread and significant? If so, what has caused this decline? Finally, what if anything should be done to foster more electoral competition? By moving from abstract moral arguments to concrete analysis and policymaking, we have more hope of determining the value of electoral competition.

35. Brunell (2006, p. 80).

Empirical Issues

Liberals, conservatives, and voters in general have good reasons to value electoral competition and the political accountability that comes with it. However, electoral competition is an ideal more loved in theory than in practice.
Many people would find their interests harmed by an increase in electoral
competition. Those who already hold office would be more likely to face
defeat at the polls more often than if electoral competition remained the
same. Moreover, incumbents might well wish to be free in some degree of the
wishes of their constituents, a freedom that would be fostered by less rather
than more electoral competition.[36] The party that holds a majority in a legislature (and to some extent, the elected officials who belong to that party)
might also find themselves out of power if a sufficient number of seats
changed hands. The opposition to more competition goes beyond those who
hold power. Activists who support an incumbent official or the dominant
party might also have second thoughts about the practical implications of
more electoral competition.

Such real and potential opposition implies, of course, that challengers, the
minority party, and supporters of both have, for the time being, an interest in
more electoral competition. However, the nature of political struggles works
against this interest. Those who hold power are able in overt and subtle ways
to restrict those who would remove them from office and from power. At the
heart of electoral competition is a conflict of interest between insiders and
outsiders. Most of the people most of the time should hope for enough electoral competition to limit government or to ensure the accountability of representatives to their principals.

Those same representatives who direct that same government have an
interest in less electoral competition and have ways to act on that interest that
are not easily detected by most people most of the time. Public policy may
reduce electoral competition in several ways. Rules governing access to the
ballot can limit the choices before voters by restricting the number of candidates who appear. Gerrymanders can arrange for an electorate that is likely to
reelect incumbent officials. Campaign finance regulations can restrict and

36. "In politics, incumbents can create direct benefits by acting, not on behalf of constituents, but on behalf of themselves. By manipulating the rules of the game, incumbents can
frustrate challengers directly. Through reducing the prospect of challenge, elected officials act
as monopolists who create significant entry barriers and then exact monopoly rents. The
more secure their hold on power, the more existing officeholders are free to pursue their own
interests rather than interests of their constituents." Issacharoff and Pildes (1998, p. 709).

complicate the fundraising needed to compete for public office.[37] Do representatives act on that interest and impede electoral competition in these and other ways?

Declining Electoral Competition

Much electoral competition scholarship focuses on the advantages of incumbents in elections to the House of Representatives. In one of the first scholarly articles on incumbency as a problem for electoral competition, Robert Erickson noted that "it is commonly assumed that being an incumbent offers a considerable advantage to the congressional candidate. The incumbent candidate can use his office to do favors for individual constituents, increase his visibility among the general public, and generate additional financial support for future campaigns." He concluded that incumbency alone added about 2 percent to the vote share of sitting members of the House of Representatives.[38] In 1974, David Mayhew noted that the number of "marginal seats" in the House of Representatives—seats that might pass to the other party in the next election—had declined by half since 1956 and wondered why "it seems a lot easier now than it used to be for a sitting Congressman to win three-fifths of the November vote."[39] Time did not change these findings much. Gary King and Andrew Gelman constructed a better measure that indicated incumbency advantage had increased to more than 10 percent of the vote by 1990.[40] The number of marginal House seats also decreased significantly in the 1990s after rising in the late 1980s.[41]

It is possible that the House of Representatives is an anomaly in American politics, an island of incumbency success in a sea of vigorous competition. For this project we asked several scholars to examine electoral competition within *and* beyond the Beltway. Gary Jacobson examines the competitiveness of elections in the United States. Richard Niemi and Thomas Carsey look at competitiveness in state elections. Stephen Ansolabehere, John Mark Hansen, Shigeo Hirano, and James Snyder Jr. offer a long-range look at the competitiveness of party primaries.

The U.S. electoral system has many moving parts. Figure 1-1 presents the major causal pathways that translate the general mood of the nation into the election results. The mood of the country is filtered through the

37. Issacharoff (2000, p. 95).
38. Erickson (1971, pp. 395, 404).
39. Mayhew (1974, p. 304).
40. Gelman and King (1990, p. 1158).
41. Irwin (2004, p. 11).

Figure 1-1. The United States Election Process

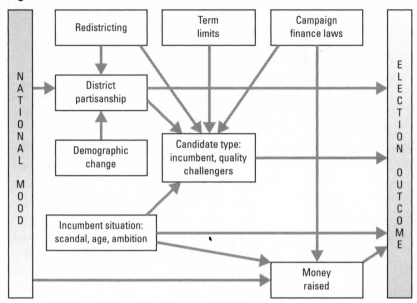

sieve of districts, which often are composed of an electorate much different than the national average. Candidates have abilities, resources, and circumstances that factor into election outcomes within their districts, and that are somewhat independent of the fate of the national parties. Incumbents are able to use the resources of their office and their knowledge of politics to raise large sums of campaign money. Most serious challengers bide their time, waiting for favorable circumstances to run, such as an incumbent retirement or a scandal. In recent elections, knowing the partisanship of a district and the party of the incumbent has been sufficient to predict the outcome with a high degree of certainty. It is this situation that motivates this project.

Each one of the causal arrows in figure 1-1 has been the study and speculation of many election scholars and political observers. Good government advocates have tended to focus their reform efforts on one of three factors: redistricting, term limits, and campaign finance reform. Redistricting reform seeks to level the playing field between candidates, term limits seek to pit equal opponents against one another by removing incumbents after a fixed number of terms in office, and campaign finance reform seeks to make sure candidates play with the same monetary resources. Often these reform efforts are strongly advocated as "the solution" at the exclusion of other possible reforms. What should be clear from figure 1-1 is that the effect of any reform cannot be understood in isolation from the others. For example, redistricting, term limits, and campaign financing all affect candidate emergence: quality challengers may strategically delay taking on an incumbent until he or she is temporarily vulnerable after a redistricting rearranges a district's constituency; similarly, a candidate may delay contesting an election until an incumbent is term-limited out of his or her seat; and campaign finance reform alters the calculus of a candidate's decision to enter a race because it may provide more (or fewer) resources to challengers relative to incumbents. In addition, under certain circumstances reforms might not have the desired effect and may even be counterproductive to electoral competition. Understanding how the reforms operate in isolation and in concert is important to understanding how reform might bring about a desired goal.

The National Mood

Walter Dean Burnham, observing historical elections, posited that the American national mood is akin to geology's plate tectonics.[42] There are stable periods of one-party dominance in elections that last for about thirty-two years; then a major event or issue arises that causes an earthquake affecting the two major parties' electoral coalitions. The parties take new positions on issues, and new party coalitions emerge that persist until the next political earthquake. During the intervening period, an election in which the dominant party wins Burnham calls a "maintaining election." But even between earthquakes, the out-party may temporarily rise to power on a change in national mood caused by a fleeting issue or a strong presidential candidate. Burnham labels these "deviating elections."

The theory of realigning elections works up to a point. The last realigning election was supposed to have occurred in the 1960s, but because of Vietnam, the civil rights movement, or Watergate—no one is sure exactly why—a violent restructuring of the party coalitions did not materialize as Burnham predicted. Instead the United States entered a protracted period of "dealignment": the party coalitions weakened as an increasing number of voters identified with neither political party. There are some indications that voter loyalty to parties may be on the rise again, but political observers would be hard-pressed to label the current political climate of intense competition at the presidential level and the narrowly balanced Congress as a period of

42. Burnham (1970).

Republican electoral dominance. The current national mood describing the maintaining elections is one of narrow competition at the national level, with the deviation around an issue or bundle of issues giving temporary advantage to one of the parties.

Incumbency as a Cue

Voters do not possess a great deal of information about politics in general or about candidates for office in particular. Research suggests many voters use shortcuts or cues to manage the cognitive challenge of casting a ballot.[43] In the past, partisan identification was the most important cue guiding voters, although incumbency certainly mattered. With partisan cues weakening in the wake of party dealignment since the 1960s, many voters are left to choose among candidates, one of whom, the incumbent, is almost always better known than the others.[44] Voters might also equate experience with candidate quality, thus utilizing the incumbency cue to make their choice. Indeed, a recent study finds that candidate quality as measured by electoral experience yielded increasing returns at the polls and can explain most of the increase in incumbency advantage, at least until 1980.[45] Incumbency advantage and diminished electoral competition thus both arise from the decline of partisanship, a development beyond the control of political players.

Incumbency Advantage and Personal Vote

Members of Congress have many resources to help them become well known to their constituents. They make frequent trips to their districts, procure federal subsidies and programs for their districts, do casework for constituents having difficulties with the federal bureaucracy, and in other ways help those who will vote on election day. In securing this "personal vote," incumbents essentially exchange services and attention for votes. A recent study indicates the personal vote accounts for perhaps 4 percent of incumbency advantage.[46] Some scholars who have studied the personal vote argue that it allows elected officials to be relatively unresponsive to their constituents and nonetheless achieve high rates of reelection. Others argue that the services associated with the personal vote compensate voters who are unhappy with the partisan positions of a member of Congress. Between par-

43. Popkin (1991).
44. Mayhew (1974, p. 313).
45. Cox and Katz (1996, pp. 478–97).
46. Ansolabehere, Snyder, and Stewart (2000, p. 30).

tisanship and the personal vote, members end up offering good representation to much of their district.[47]

The Money Advantage of Incumbents

Candidates spend money to publicize their achievements, ideas, and character in order to attract votes. Some of that money will come from the public, as the personal vote argument indicates: the staff, trips, spending on benefits, and publicity of an incumbent are generally supplied by the taxpayer. But American campaigns also involve private financing derived from campaign contributors. Incumbents on average raise much more money than challengers, thereby making contributions a plausible part of the incumbency advantage story. Incumbents also sometimes retain unspent campaign funds—so-called war chests—that might scare off challengers, leading to uncontested races or contests between incumbents and inexperienced (that is, low-quality) challengers. In short, the fundraising and spending gap between incumbents and challengers might correspond to the win-loss record of the two groups.

Redistricting and Geographic Distribution of Partisans

Members of Congress represent districts whose population often changes, as measured by the decennial census. House members and state representatives thus represent a variable constituency, the nature of which is determined through a process known as redistricting, which is controlled by state officials who may be political allies of the representative or state legislators themselves. For partisan reasons, the officials who draw the district lines will be tempted to create an electorate that is likely to reelect an incumbent or secure election for a generic party candidate. If elected officials choose their voters (rather than the other way around), electoral competition and accountability might be diminished, all other things being equal. This argument appeared early in the scholarly literature.[48] More recently, scholars have proposed that redistricting enhances the advantages of incumbency in more subtle ways. The decline of parties, together with extensive redistricting beginning in the 1960s, rewarded candidates who could build their own campaign organizations in sharply redrawn districts. Overnight the value of experienced candidate who had already won office increased; that increase in value might also

---

47. Ansolabehere, Snyder, and Stewart (2000, p. 31).
48. Mayhew (1974, pp. 306–10).

scare off challenges from the other party. For these reasons, redistricting has remained a likely suspect in the search for illegitimate sources of incumbency advantage. In this volume, Gary Jacobson and Michael McDonald examine the effects of redistricting on electoral competition.

Redistricting is constrained in some important ways by the geographic distribution of partisans. Congressional districts are apportioned to the states on the basis of their population. Some states are so overwhelmingly Democratic or Republican that any district drawn within their state lines will inevitably reflect the partisanship of the state. Even in heterogeneous states, partisans may be concentrated in communities in ways that make it impossible to draw competitive districts without violating the traditional redistricting principle of compactness. In this volume, Jacobson looks closely at the results of elections immediately after a census, when the effects of redistricting would be most evident. Michael McDonald offers an in-depth examination of redistricting and incumbency.

Two-Party Duopoly

Almost all members of Congress belong to one of the two major political parties. At the state level, independents and members of minor parties hold only a handful of elected offices. The 2004 election results suggest the difficulties third parties face in competing for office. In that year third parties ran sixty-six candidates for the U.S. Senate, 319 candidates for the U.S. House, and fourteen for the office of state governor. The Libertarian Party fielded about half the third-party candidates for the House, and two of them received over 20 percent of the vote (in Florida and Arizona). However, the median Libertarian candidate for a House seat received 1.6 percent of the vote, and those who fared well did so without the presence of a strong Republican candidate. In the Senate races, the most successful third-party candidate, running under the Constitution Party banner, received almost 4 percent of the vote in Pennsylvania. Among the elections for governor, the best showing by a third party was in Washington, where the Libertarian candidate received 2.3 percent of the total vote.[49] These results suggest that third parties face formidable barriers to seriously entering the electoral fray. Scholars have cited several reasons for the weakness of third parties. Paul Herrnson's analysis brings us up to date on the realities and possibilities of minor parties in the American system.

49. Congressional Quarterly (2005).

The Best Politicians Win

John Zaller offers a different and perhaps more optimistic interpretation of what seems to be diminishing electoral competition. He asks, "Couldn't the biggest part of what is commonly called 'incumbency advantage' be that incumbents are simply better politicians than most of their opponents and beat them primarily for that reason?" He argues that it is not what candidates do, or even the resources they have to do it with, but rather how well they do what they do. What successful incumbents have is political skill, which means doing well at "finding out what voters want and convincing them that you have given it to them."[50] Insofar as political accountability is valuable because it means voters get what they want, and insofar as voters are the best judges of whether they are getting what they want, Zaller's argument indicates the decline in electoral competition may be a sign the American political system is working well.

Shirking Not Evident

Skeptics might ask whether electoral competition is essential to political accountability. One could accept that electoral competition has diminished and yet wonder whether representatives have shirked their responsibilities to those who elected them. For some time scholars have studied whether public opinion influences policymaking. This research has found mixed results. Early research found that members of Congress were responsive to (or ideologically inclined to agree with) voters in their districts. Later research looked at shifts in policy in response to shifts in aggregate public opinion. These studies found that government responded rapidly to general shifts in public opinion.[51]

Yet this research is not conclusive, and one can easily find examples of representatives who have ignored policies that have strong public support. For example, Congress turned down Medicare legislation for many years in the 1960s and refused to pass national health insurance in the 1980s and 1990s, even though both programs had strong public support.[52] Congress also disregarded the majorities that have appeared from time to time to support more stringent gun control laws. Other studies have found a disconnection, especially in foreign policy matters, between public opinion and policy at various

---

50. Zaller (1998, p. 170).
51. See Stimson, Mackuen, and Erikson (1995, pp. 543–65) and Stokes (1999, p. 261).
52. Jacobs (1993).

times.[53] A reform discussed later, term limits, also has enjoyed wide support for many years without becoming law except through the initiative and referendum process in individual states.

Earlier research by a contributor to this volume, John Matsusaka, suggested that legislatures in states with the initiative had strayed from the wishes of the median voter to some extent and that the initiative had been used to correct that departure from the democratic mean.[54] Matsusaka has also documented a long downward trend in public satisfaction with legislatures and with government in general. Fewer and fewer people over time have said they feel they have a say in what government does, a trend consistent with the belief that elected representatives are not responsive to their constituents.[55]

Policy Changes

If incumbents benefit from the status quo, they are hardly likely to enact reforms that increase electoral competition. Of course, if voters wanted more competition, incumbents might respond if their short-term electoral concerns outweighed their larger interest in less competition. Yet voters know little about politics and policy and have few incentives to know a lot. They might assume that competition has value with the experience of markets in mind; but understanding how incumbents diminish competition and what measures might enhance their choices is difficult for experts, and voters have other matters demanding their attention. The question of competition will be raised by challengers who either have too few resources to make the issue stick or to win the election, in which case they would become incumbents with interests contrary to electoral competition (the behavior of the House Republicans and term limits comes to mind here). Samuel Issacharoff thus predicts that reforms favoring competition will not come about "without a destabilizing shock to the status quo. The difficulty comes in choosing the source of this shock. It cannot come from within. The normal workings of the political process cannot be trusted to undertake this effort any more than the normal operations of competition can be relied on to overcome monopoly power in commercial markets."[56] Can policies be changed to increase elec-

---

53. On both gun control and foreign policy, see Oskamp and Schultz (2005, p. 289).
54. Matsusaka (1995, pp. 587–623).
55. Matsusaka (2005, pp. 157–77).
56. Issacharoff (2000, p. 96).

toral competition? If so, which policies make the most sense in light of the analysis presented in the scholarly literature and this volume?

Venues

The shortcomings of internal reform raise the question of who or what might increase electoral competitiveness if the insiders cannot be expected to do so. One answer might be the Supreme Court.[57] The job of applying the law sometimes requires the judiciary to limit the actions of the other branches. Of course, restricting the power of the other branches can be difficult for the Supreme Court, whose members are not elected. Moreover, current constitutional doctrine examines political issues as a balancing of individual rights and state interests. Electoral competitiveness and political accountability are not values the Supreme Court can apply without a change in doctrine.[58] In this volume Nathaniel Persily examines the prospects for judicial intervention to enhance electoral competitiveness.

Another way to circumvent the political status quo has been the initiative and the referendum. As noted earlier, scholarly studies have found that these direct democracy devices can impose the preferences of the median voter on reluctant legislatures. In particular, the movement to limit the terms of legislators in the states succeeded only where the initiative was available. John Matsusaka, a leading analyst of the initiative and referendum, takes a look in these pages at the prospects and problems of direct democracy in increasing electoral competition. Bruce Cain and Thad Kousser take up the specific reform of term limits, which have been in effect in some states for well over a decade. Term limits are a direct attempt to increase electoral competition by limiting the careers of incumbents. How well they have achieved that goal should tell us something about the difficulty and possibilities of future efforts.

As early as 1938 the Gallup organization polled Americans about their views on publicly financed election campaigns. If private financing does not give enough challengers enough money to compete with incumbents, some experts have concluded that the public treasury might do a better job and foment more competition while perhaps reducing corruption in the bargain. At the same time, public financing has not been popular with Congress (which has never passed a serious bill to provide public campaign financing)

---

57. Issacharoff (2000, p. 98).
58. Issacharoff (n.d.) makes the case for recognizing competitiveness as a constitutional requirement.

or the public (who have shown little support for such measures in surveys). The federal presidential funding system has been in place for three decades, but there is little evidence that it has increased competition in primaries or general elections.[59] Several contributions touch on questions of money and competition. Gary Jacobson looks at the relationship between financial advantage and incumbent success in recent national elections, a topic informed by much of his earlier work on congressional elections. Some argue that incumbents will not face serious competition from challengers until taxpayers, rather than private contributors, finance campaigns. Kenneth Mayer, Timothy Werner, and Amanda Williams, as well as David Primo and Jeff Milyo, look at the electoral effects of public financing in the states. James Gimpel and Frances Lee examine the geography of campaign finance and its implications for congressional elections.

Conclusion

The contributions in this volume provide a comprehensive examination of the state of electoral competition in the United States. We selected the scholars to participate in this examination on the basis of their reputation and current research interests. As we hoped, the volume is filled with data and analysis as well as theories and conjectures. It is not, however, an expression of one point of view or political position on the origins of and solutions to the problem of declining electoral competition in this nation. In the final chapter we trace the implications of these studies for a nation dedicated to rule by the people.

References

Ansolabehere, Stephen, James Snyder Jr., and Charles Stewart III. 2000. "Old Voters, New Voters, and the Personal Vote." *American Journal of Political Science* 44: 17–34.

Bessette, J. M. 2001. "Accountability: Political." In *International Encyclopedia of the Social &Behavioral Sciences*, edited by Neil J. Smelser and Paul B. Baltes. Oxford, U.K.: Elsevier.

Brennan, Geoffrey, and Alan Hamlin. 2001. *Democratic Devices and Desires*. Cambridge University Press.

Brunell, Thomas. 2006. "Rethinking Redistricting: How Drawing Districts Packed with Partisans Improves Representation and Attitudes towards Congress." *PS: Political Science and Politics* 29:77–85.

59. Samples (2006).

Burke, Edmund. 1999. *Select Works of Edmund Burke: A New Imprint of the Payne Edition*. Vol. IV. Indianapolis: Liberty Fund.

Burnham, Walter Dean. 1970. *Critical Elections and the Mainsprings of American Politics*. New York: Norton.

Campbell, James E., and Steve J. Jurek. 2003. "The Decline of Competition and Change in Congressional Elections." In *The United States Congress: A Century of Change*, edited by Sunil Ahuja and Robert Dewhirst. Ohio State University Press.

Congressional Quarterly. 2005. *Third-Party Results*. Washington: CQ Press. Dynamically generated November 10, 2005, from CQ Electronic Library, CQ Voting and Elections Collection: http://library.cqpress.com/elections/partycontrolthirdresults.php?third_year1=2003&third_year2=2005.

Cox, Gary W., and Jonathan N. Katz. 1996. "Why Did the Incumbency Advantage in U.S. House Elections Grow?" *American Journal of Political Science* 40: 478–97.

Cox, Gary W., and Michael C. Munger. 1989. "Closeness, Expenditures, and Turnout in the 1982 U.S. House Elections." *American Political Science Review* 83: 217–31.

Dahl, Robert A. 1971. *Polyarchy: Participation and Opposition*. Yale University Press.

———. 1984. "Polyarchy, Pluralism, and Scale." *Scandinavian Political Studies* 7: 225–40.

Downs, Anthony. 1957. *An Economic Theory of Democracy*. New York: Harper.

Dworkin, Ronald. 1978. "What Rights Do We Have?" In *Taking Rights Seriously*. Harvard University Press.

Erickson, Robert S. 1971. "The Advantage of Incumbency in Congressional Elections." *Polity* 3: 395–405.

Farrand, Max, ed. 1911. *The Records of the Federal Convention of 1787*. Yale University Press.

Flanigan, William, and Nancy Zingale. 2002. *Political Behavior of the American Electorate*. 10th ed. Washington: CQ Press.

Gelman, Andrew, and Gary King. 1990. "Estimating Incumbency Advantage without Bias." *American Journal of Political Science* 34: 1142–64.

Gutmann, Amy. 1993. "Democracy." In *A Companion to Contemporary Political Philosophy*, edited by Robert E. Goodin and Philip Pettit. Oxford, U.K.: Blackwell.

Irwin, Lew. 2004. "A 'Permanent' Republican House? Patterns of Voter Performance and the Persistence of House Control." *Forum* 2: 1–20.

Issacharoff, Samuel. 2000. "The Role of Government Regulation in the Political Process: Oversight of Regulated Political Markets." *Harvard Journal of Law and Policy* 24: 91–100.

———. 2002. "Gerrymandering and Political Cartels." *Harvard Law Review* 116: 593–648.

Issacharoff, Samuel, and Richard H. Pildes. 1998. "Politics as Markets: Partisan Lockups of the Democratic Process." *Stanford Law Review* 50: 643–717.

Issacharoff, Samuel, Burt Neuborne, and Richard H. Pildes. N.d. Brief as Amici Curiae for Appellants, *League of United Latin American Citizens* v. *Rick Perry et al.*, United States Supreme Court.

Jacobs, Lawrence. 1993. *The Health of Nations: Public Opinion in the Making of American and British Health Policy*. Cornell University Press.

Jacobson, Gary C. 2004. *The Politics of Congressional Elections*. 6th ed. New York: Pearson Longman.

Keyssar, Alexander. 2000. *The Right to Vote: The Contested History of Democracy in the United States*. New York: Basic Books.

Lijphart, Arendt. 1999. *Patterns of Democracy: Government Forms and Performance in Thirty-Six Countries*. Yale University Press.

Madison, James. 1960a. "Federalist no. 10." In *The Federalist*, edited by Jacob E. Cooke. Wesleyan University Press.

———. 1960b. "Federalist no. 51." In *The Federalist*, edited by Jacob E. Cooke. Wesleyan University Press.

Matsusaka, John G. 1995. "Fiscal Effects of the Voter Initiative: Evidence from the Last Thirty Years." *Journal of Political Economy* 103: 587–623.

———. 2005. "The Eclipse of Legislatures: Direct Democracy in the 21st Century." *Public Choice* 124: 157–77.

Mayhew, David R. 1974. "Congressional Elections: The Case of the Vanishing Marginals." *Polity* 6: 295–317.

Mill, J. S. 1991. "Considerations on Representative Government." In *On Liberty and Other Essays*. Oxford University Press.

Oskamp, Stuart, and Wesley P. Schultz. 2005. *Attitudes and Opinions*. 3rd ed. Mahwah, N.J.: Lawrence Erlbaum.

Parisi, Francesco. 2004. "Public Choice Theory from the Perspective of Law." In *The Encyclopedia of Public Choice*, edited by Charles Rowley and Friedrich Schneider, Vol. 1. Boston: Kluwer Academic.

Popkin, Samuel L. 1991. The *Reasoning Vote: Communication and Persuasion in Presidential Campaigns*. University of Chicago Press.

Przeworski, Adam. 1991. *Democracy and the Market: Political and Economic Reforms in Eastern Europe and Latin America*. Cambridge University Press.

Rawls, John. 1971. *A Theory of Justice*. Harvard University Press.

Rosenthal, Alan. 1998. *The Decline of Representative Democracy: Process, Participation, and Power in State Legislatures*. Washington: CQ Press.

Samples, John. 2006. *The Fallacy of Campaign Finance Reform*. University of Chicago Press.

Schumpeter, Joseph. 1950. *Capitalism, Socialism and Democracy*. 3rd ed. New York: Harper.

Stimson, James A., Michael B. Mackuen, and Robert S. Erikson. 1995. "Dynamic Representation." *American Political Science Review* 89: 543–65.

Stokes, S. C. 1999. "Political Parties and Democracy." *Annual Review of Political Science* 2: 243–67.

Thompson, Dennis F. 2004. *Just Elections: Creating a Fair Electoral Process in the United States*. University of Chicago Press.

Zaller, John R. 1992. *The Nature and Origins of Mass Opinion*. Cambridge University Press.

———. 1998. "Politicians as Prize Fighters: Electoral Selection and Incumbency Advantage." In *Politicians and Party Politics*. Johns Hopkins University Press.

PART ONE The State of Competition

2

Competition in U.S. Congressional Elections

Gary C. Jacobson

After falling irregularly for several decades, turnover in elections to the U.S. House of Representatives has reached an all-time low. On average in the four most recent elections (1998–2004), a mere fifteen of the 435 seats changed party hands, and only five incumbents lost to challengers.[1] Net partisan swings have also been minimal by historical standards and would have been smaller still had successful Republican gerrymanders not added to the party's narrow majority in 2002 and 2004.[2] Since 1994, Republicans have won between 221 and 232 of the 435 House seats, and Democrats between 204 and 212, by far the most stable partisan balance for any six-election period in U.S. history.[3]

The historically low incidence of seat turnover and partisan change during the past decade has revived scholarly concern about the decline in competition for House seats that had been prompted by a similar period of stasis in the 1980s. It is easy to understand why. Turnover is by definition a product of competitive races. If low turnover reflects the disappearance of competitive districts and candidates rather than, say, unusually stable aggregate preferences

1. Another six incumbents lost to other incumbents after redistricting had combined their constituencies, and several more lost primaries in newly drawn districts.
2. Jacobson (2003, pp. 1–22); Jacobson (2005b, pp. 199–218).
3. Stanley and Niemi (2003, table 1-10).

among voters, then election results have become less responsive to changes in voters' sentiments. To the degree that diminished competition renders members of Congress, individually and collectively, immune to electoral retaliation, democratic accountability is impaired and elections lose their point. Thus it is important to understand why turnover has declined, and the extent to which changes in electoral competition have contributed to the decline, as a prelude to considering what, if anything, might be done about it. My purpose here is to examine the evidence for declining competition, to explore its causes, and to assess the extent to which the problem lies in the behavior of voters, in the structure of elections, or in both. I deal here mainly with House elections, the principal locus of worry about declining competition, but I also review briefly the changes in competition for Senate seats as well, for they help to make it clear that forces beyond the manipulation of district boundaries have been at work.

The Decline in Seat Turnover and Close Elections

The incidence of total partisan turnover (seats changing party control), net partisan change, and incumbent defeats produced by House elections since 1952 is displayed in figure 2-1. The data show that all of these variables have fluctuated widely over the past half-century, with some elections generating very little change, and others, including most recently 1994, producing major shifts in membership and the party balance. But they also show that low-turnover elections have become more common in the past two decades, particularly by the measure of net partisan change. The net party swing exceeded a dozen seats in eleven of the seventeen elections from 1952 through 1984; in the ten elections since then, it has done so only once—in 1994—and the average for the remaining nine elections is a mere six seats.

The proportion of marginal seats—defined as those won by a relatively narrow vote margin and thus considered competitive—has also fallen, although again the trend is by no means uniformly downward. Conventionally, seats won with less than some specified share of the major-party vote are classified as marginal; 60 and 55 percent are commonly used breakpoints. Figure 2-2a shows that, by the 60 percent standard, in elections from 1952 through 1964 about 40 percent of seats typically fell into the marginal range. This proportion then declined (albeit with interruptions) through 1988, then rose at the beginning of the 1990s to near the levels of thirty years earlier, before dropping again to exceptionally low levels in the 2002 and 2004 elections (12 and 14 percent, respectively). Notice, however, that the decline in

Figure 2-1. Turnover in House Elections, 1946–2004

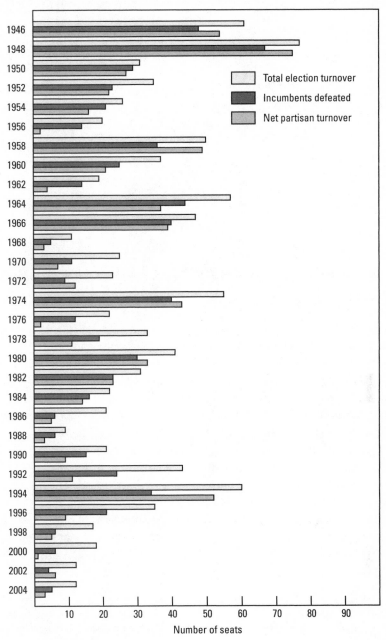

Source: Compiled by author.

Figure 2-2a. House Seats Won with Less Than 60 Percent
of the Major-Party Vote, 1946–2004

Percent

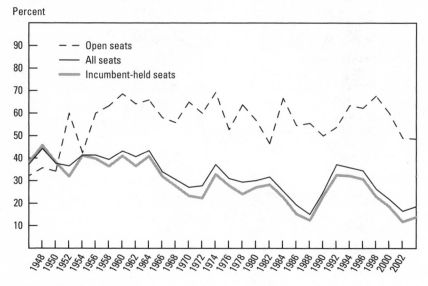

Source: Compiled by author.

marginality is confined largely to incumbent-held seats. The trend for open
seats is considerably less pronounced and, unlike the downward trend for
incumbent-held seats, is not statistically significant. The proportion of open
seats changing party control has also remained, on average, stable (with large
fluctuations but no trend). Thus the exhaustively analyzed "vanishing marginals" phenomenon is mainly a consequence of the rise in the value, in votes,
of running for the House as an incumbent.[4] Figure 2-2b displays the trends
according to the 55 percent standard, which largely parallel the trends in figure 2-2a (the observations for all seats are correlated at .81), but at a much
lower overall level of marginality.

Another index of competition, *CQ Weekly*'s pre-election estimate of the
number of House seats in play, has also trended downward, but in a cyclical
fashion. Observe in figure 2-3 that in the 1980s and 1990s, elections that fol-

---

4. The concept of "vanishing marginals" originated with Mayhew (1974, pp. 295–317). For
a general discussion of the literature on this topic, see Jacobson (2004, pp. 28–41). The same
trends appear if marginal seats are defined more stringently to include only those won with
less than 55 percent of the major-party vote.

Figure 2-2b. House Seats Won with Less Than 55 Percent
of the Major-Party Vote, 1946–2004

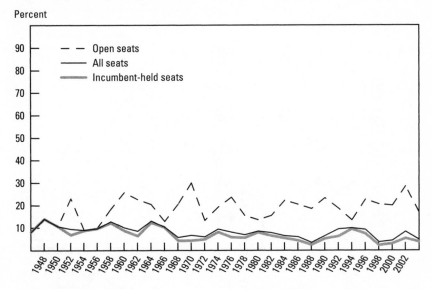

Percent

Source: Compiled by author.

lowed reapportionment (represented by darker bars) featured a relatively high number of competitive races, reflecting the opportunities and uncertainties created by the reshuffling of district lines. Competition then diminished during the rest of the decade, perhaps because parties and candidates learned from experience where challenges were likely to prove futile and gave up. The redistricting after the 2000 census, in contrast, did not produce the usual spike in competition, and in 2004 *CQ*'s count of competitive races fell to its lowest point in the series. The number of districts in which one of the major parties failed to field a candidate was also unusually high for a reapportionment year in 2002, and, after dropping sharply in the early 1990s, the incidence of such uncontested races has returned to the levels of the 1980s (see figure 2-4).

Why the Decline in Turnover and Close Contests?

Evidence of the sort presented in figures 2-2a and 2-2b points directly to an increase in the advantages of running as an incumbent as the source of declining competition. Incumbency is clearly part of the long-term story, but

Figure 2-3. Competitive House Elections, 1982–2004

Number of competitive races[a]

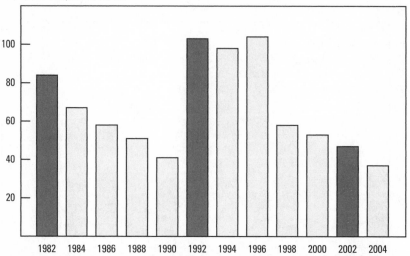

Source: The 2004 data are from www.nytimes.com/packages/html/politics/2004_ELECTIONGUIDE_GRAPHIC/
INDEX_housecq.HTML; for earlier years they are from the October election previews in the *CQ Weekly Report* and
CQ Weekly.
a. Competitive races are those classified by CQ as "tossups" or "leans Democratic (Republican)"; uncompetitive races are those classified as "safe" or "Democrat (Republican) favored."

it cannot by itself account for the unusually low frequency of seat turnovers in the most recent five elections, because by the usual measures the incumbency advantage was smaller during this period than it was in the 1970s and 1980s.[5] Moreover, because competition is endogenously shaped by the strategic behavior of potential candidates and contributors, the incumbency advantage as measured in votes is at least as much a consequence as a cause of decreased competition.[6]

A competitive election requires that both parties field competent candidates with sufficient financial resources to get their messages out to voters.

5. Jacobson (2004, p. 28). According to the "slurge" (the average of the "retirement slump" [the mean loss in vote share to a party when a seat it held becomes open] and the "sophomore surge" [the mean bonus in vote shares won by members running as incumbents for the first time]), the mean value of House incumbency, in votes, was 7.0 percent in the period 1974–80, 8.1 percent in 1984–90, and 5.7 percent in 1994–2000 and 2004 (the statistic cannot be calculated for redistricting years). Bruce Oppenheimer reports slightly different estimates that support the same point; see Oppenheimer (2005, p. 140).

6. Cox and Katz (2002).

Figure 2-4. House Candidates without Major-Party Opposition, 1952–2004

Number of candidates

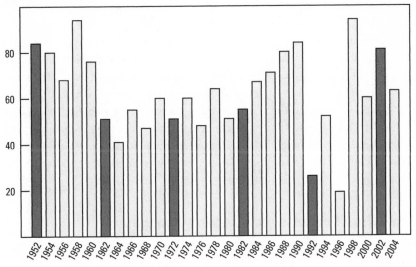

Source: Compiled by author.

But the decisions of potential candidates and donors about whether to participate depend on their estimates of the prospects of success. Politically skilled and ambitious politicians do not invest in hopeless efforts; neither do the people and organizations controlling campaign money and other electoral resources. Judgments about the prospects of success are strongly affected by incumbency—thus open seats tend to attract a much larger proportion of high-quality candidates who raise much more money than the typical challenger to an incumbent—but incumbency is not the only consideration. The underlying partisan balance in a district and national political conditions also count heavily in their decisions. Thus at least two developments unrelated to incumbency might have contributed to declining levels of competition and partisan turnover in recent years: a decrease in the number of districts where the partisan balance gives the out-party some hope of winning, and the absence of the kind of national partisan tides that raise the chances of victory for the favored party.

Insofar as a decrease in the number of seats winnable by either party is to blame for declining competition, it has two possible sources: changes in district lines, and changes in the behavior of voters. The first option has received the most attention; incumbent-friendly and partisan gerrymanders, it is argued, have increased the number of lopsidedly partisan constituencies, thus diminishing the number of potentially competitive districts.[7] There is some evidence for this claim—it is, for example, consistent with the data for 2002 in figures 2-3 and 2-4—but it is not unchallenged.[8] The second option recognizes that voters have grown more reluctant since the 1970s to vote contrary to their party identification or to split their tickets, making it increasingly rare for districts to elect House candidates who do not match the local partisan profile. A more speculative though related notion is that partisans have been voting with their feet by opting to live where they find the social (and therefore political) climate congenial, creating separate enclaves preponderantly red or blue.[9] These alternative explanations for the disappearance of competitive districts are not incompatible; indeed, the processes they entail would be mutually reinforcing.

How Have Congressional Districts Changed?

Determining the extent to which the most recent decline in competition for House seats reflects changes in the partisan makeup and aggregate voting habits of districts requires an estimate of the underlying partisan disposition of districts over several decades. Survey data are unavailable, and party registration data are missing for about half the states, so the best available approximation of district partisanship is the district-level presidential vote, normalized around the national mean for each election year to remove the effects of particular presidential contests. By this measure, the more competitive districts should be those in which the presidential vote falls closer to the national mean. Figure 2-5 shows that, according to each of three alternative cutoff points (districts with the presidential vote falling within 2, 3, and 5 percentage points of the national average), the proportion of potentially competitive districts has fallen over the past decade, reaching new lows in 2004.

What is behind this decline? Redistricting is the usual suspect, but a closer look the trend invites reconsideration. Notice that most of the drop in potentially competitive districts occurred between 1994 and 2000, a period during

7. This argument has become the conventional wisdom of editorial writers, among others; see the selection of samples in Abramowitz, Alexander, and Gunning (2005, p. 3), who argue against the claim; it was recently defended by McDonald (2006, pp. 91–94).

8. Jacobson (2003, pp. 10–11); but see ibid.

9. Oppenheimer (2005, pp. 152–54); Bill Bishop, "A Steady Slide toward a More Divided Union," *Austin American-Statesman*, May 30, 2004 (www.statesman.com/specialreports/content/specialreports/greatdivide/0530divide.html).

Figure 2-5. Competitive Districts as Measured by the Adjusted
Presidential Vote, 1952–2004

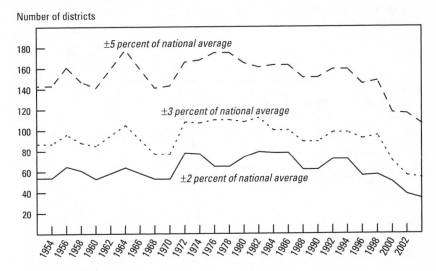

Number of districts

Source: Compiled by author.

which only a small number of districts were redrawn (and none in a way that affected these data). Most of the decrease thus had to be a consequence of changes in the behavior of district electorates. Table 2-1 displays the results when the contribution of redistricting and behavioral change are parsed out by counting changes (1) following redistricting (using the presidential vote from before and—reallocated to the new districts—after the districts were redrawn) and (2) between reapportionment years. Redistricting was clearly one source of the loss of potentially competitive districts, especially after 2000. But gerrymanders were not the most important sources of change; presidential voters were. Depending on the measure examined, between 64 and 90 percent of the falloff in the number of closely balanced districts since 1982 resulted from changes in voting patterns. Redistricting made things worse, but the trend would have occurred without it.

Changes in House Voting Patterns

The effect of the decline in the number of closely balanced House districts (insofar as partisan balance can be measured by the presidential vote) has been compounded by an even larger decline in the propensity of districts to

Table 2-1. Redistricting and Behavioral Changes as Source of the Decrease in Number of Marginal House Districts, as Measured by the Presidential Vote

Year	Number of marginal districts (defined by the degree of deviation from the average district presidential vote)		
	±2 percent	±3 percent	±5 percent
1980	74	180	165
1982 (computed from 1980 presidential vote)	79	112	161
Redistricting change, 1980–82	+5	+4	−4
1984	78	100	163
1988	62	89	151
Behavioral change, 1982–88	−17	−23	−10
1992 (computed from 1988 presidential vote)	58	97	145
Redistricting change 1988–92	−4	+8	−6
1992	72	98	159
1996	56	92	145
2000	50	70	117
Behavioral change, 1992–2000	−8	−27	−28
2002 (computed from 2000 presidential vote)	38	56	116
Redistricting change	−12	−14	−1
2004	34	54	106
Behavioral change, 2002–04	−4	−2	−10
Net redistricting change since 1982	−16	−6	−7
Net behavioral change since 1982	−29	−52	−48
Total change	−45	−58	−55
Percentage decrease	−57.0	−51.8	−34.1
Percent of decrease attributable to behavioral change	64.4	89.7	87.3

Source: Compiled by author.

elect representatives whose party does not match the district's presidential leanings. This decline is largely but not entirely a consequence of the southern realignment, in which white southerners, who had been voting Republican at the presidential level for decades, began in the 1990s to vote with nearly the same regularity for Republicans at the congressional level as well. Illustrative data appear in figure 2-6. For this figure, each seat is classified as "unfavorable," "neutral," or "favorable" for the party holding it based on the district's underlying partisanship as measured by the presidential vote in the coterminous or (for midterm elections) the immediately prior presidential election. Districts where the winner's presidential candidate ran 2 percentage points above the national average are classified as favorable, those where the

Figure 2-6. Partisan Leanings of House Districts, 1952–2004
(Based on the District Presidential Vote)

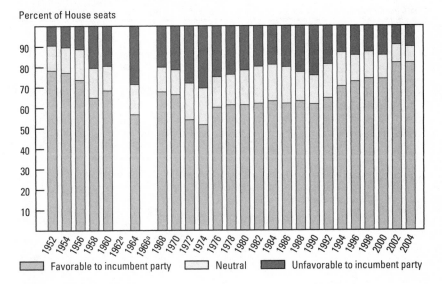

Percent of House seats

Favorable to incumbent party   Neutral   Unfavorable to incumbent party

Source: Compiled by author.
a. Data for 1962 and 1966 are missing because the presidential vote is not available for redrawn districts for those years.

presidential vote was within 2 percentage points of average are classified as neutral, and those where the winner's party's presidential vote was 2 points or more below average are considered unfavorable.

The data show a declining proportion of House seats that are either neutral or unfavorable to the incumbent party and a complementary rise in the proportion of seats held by the locally favored party. These trends are sharply different for Democrats and Republicans, however. Eighty-two percent of the reduction in seats held by the "wrong" party since 1980, and 93 percent of the reduction since 1990, occurred among Democrats. Republicans account for 70 percent of the growth in seats held by the "right" party since 1980 and 90 percent of the growth since 1990. The two critical moments were the 1994 election, when Republicans took sixteen seats from Democrats in Republican-leaning districts (thereby switching the same number from "unfavorable" to "favorable" to the incumbent party) and the 2002 election, which, with the help of Republican gerrymanders in key states, put an additional eighteen Republicans into "favorable" partisan districts.

Table 2-2. District Partisanship and House Election Results, by Decade

Partisan turnover	District party balance		
	Unfavorable	Neutral	Favorable
1950s	20.9 (14.1)[a]	12.8 (13.1)	4.1 (72.8)
1960s	13.3 (24.0)	14.7 (14.2)	3.8 (61.8)
1970s	13.7 (26.8)	10.1 (16.6)	4.9 (56.6)
1980s	8.9 (20.9)	7.9 (16.5)	3.3 (62.6)
1990s	24.4 (17.2)	13.9 (14.2)	2.4 (68.6)
2000s	18.2 (11.0)	1.5 (8.1)	0.6 (80.9)
Challengers (challenger wins)			
1950s	3.2 (72.8)	10.3 (13.4)	16.8 (13.8)
1960s	2.4 (61.7)	13.3 (14.8)	10.2 (23.5)
1970s	3.8 (57.1)	7.1 (16.4)	9.2 (26.5)
1980s	2.1 (62.4)	3.3 (16.6)	6.7 (21.0)
1990s	1.5 (69.8)	8.3 (14.0)	14.1 (16.2)
2000s	0.2 (81.6)	0.0 (8.0)	9.9 (10.4)
Open seats (Democrat wins)			
1950s	27.3 (60.8)	54.5 (10.5)	98.3 (28.6)
1960s	37.8 (52.9)	100.0 (9.7)	82.7 (37.4)
1970s	38.5 (48.9)	60.0 (17.7)	89.9 (33.5)
1980s	32.0 (53.8)	62.1 (15.6)	82.4 (30.7)
1990s	15.7 (50.6)	45.0 (15.0)	90.1 (34.4)
2000s	11.7 (60.7)	54.5 (11.9)	91.3 (27.5)

Source: Compiled by author.
a. Numbers in parentheses show the percentage of districts in this category.

The decline in the number of seats held by a party in "unfavorable" districts (along with the reduction in neutral districts) by itself depresses competition and partisan change, for these are the districts that have usually seen the most action. The first section of table 2-2 shows that partisan turnover has been highest when parties have had to defend seats where the underlying partisan balance is unfavorable to them. The decline in the proportion of such seats thus diminishes the likelihood of turnover, a problem compounded by the diminishing probability of turnover when a seat is held by the favored party. The second section isolates challengers from incumbents, showing that, not surprisingly, their prospects are best when local partisanship favors their party, and that the proportion of such seats has become quite small. The third section displays the falloff in the proportion of open seats won against the partisan grain; the share of Democrats winning seats in Republican-leaning districts ("unfavorable") has fallen, while the proportion of Democrats winning seats in Democratic-leaning districts ("favorable") has risen.

The Concentration of Competition

As House candidates have found it increasingly difficult to win in districts with unfavorable partisan balances, the proportion of districts considered vulnerable to a takeover by the out-party has naturally fallen. The combination of fewer ostensibly vulnerable seats and lower prospects for winning seats that are not vulnerable has altered the behavior of potential candidates and contributors. With the decline in the number of seats where the current party's hold seems precarious enough to justify a full-scale challenge, strategic calculations about running and contributing have led to an increasing concentration of political talent and resources in the diminishing number of potentially competitive districts at the expense of the rest.

This trend is clearest in the shifting patterns of challenges to incumbents. The proportion of challengers who have previously won elective public office—a crude but serviceable measure of candidate quality[10]—has headed downward, most notably among Democrats (see figure 2-7). Back in the 1970s, nearly 30 percent of Democratic challengers were experienced officeholders; by the 2000s, that proportion had dropped by more than half, to 13 percent; for both parties combined, the drop was from 22 percent to 14 percent.[11] But the disappearance of experienced challengers is confined to districts where the challenger's prospects were already slim because the partisan balance favored the incumbent. In districts where the partisan balance (indicated by the presidential vote) is favorable to the challenger's party, the proportion of experienced challengers has grown substantially (see figure 2-8); evenly balanced districts have seen little change. Incumbents in districts favorable to the challenger's party have also become much less likely to get a free pass; in the 1970s and 1980s, about 17 percent of incumbents defending unfriendly territory were unopposed by major-party candidates; since then, the proportion has fallen to less than 5 percent.

For similar reasons, the gap between the campaign finances of challengers in different competitive circumstances has widened. The amount of money available to challengers in districts where the incumbent enjoys a favorable partisan balance has been flat for a decade, while challengers in more competitive districts have been able to spend increasingly substantial sums (see

10. Jacobson (1989, pp. 776–78).
11. Decades in this analysis are defined by redistricting cycles; thus, for example, the 1970s cover 1972–80.

Figure 2-7. U.S. House Challengers with Experience
in Elective Public Office, by Decade

Percent

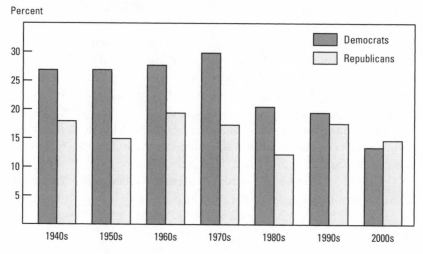

Source: Compiled by author.

Figure 2-8. The Local Party Balance and Quality of House Challengers,
by Decade

Percent of challengers with experience in elective public office

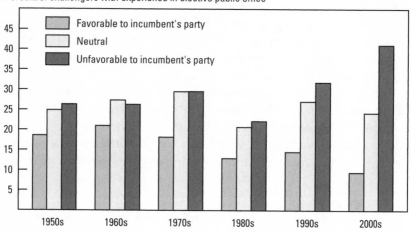

Source: Compiled by author.

Figure 2-9. Campaign Spending by Challengers, 1972–2004

Average campaign expenditures (adjusted for inflation, 2004 = 1.00)

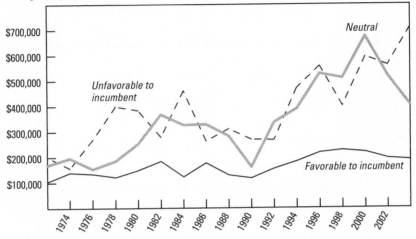

Source: Compiled by author.

figure 2-9). Campaign resources available to challengers have thus become increasingly concentrated in the relatively small number of potentially competitive districts, a pattern magnified by the additional campaign spending by party committees and other political organizations that flows very disproportionately to the same districts. Spending by and for incumbents is also heaviest in these districts, although even feebly opposed (or even unopposed) incumbents now routinely spend lavishly as well.[12] Regardless of the partisan makeup of the district, however, the incumbent's level of spending remains statistically unrelated to the results once the challenger's level of spending is taken into account.

More to the point here, high-spending challengers are as likely to win in districts where the partisan balance is favorable now as they were in the past. Notice in table 2-3 that higher-spending challengers in districts that favor their party have as good a track record in recent years as they did earlier, and even if "recent" is confined to the post-1994 period they have not done significantly worse. The real decline in challengers' prospects is thus attributable to the smaller proportion of districts favorable to the challenger's party (see

12. Jacobson (2006).

Table 2-3. Challenger Victories, by Campaign Spending
and District Partisanship

Spending by challenger[a]	District party balance		
	Favorable to challenger	Neutral	Favorable to incumbent
1972–90			
Less than $500,000	3.0	3.6	1.5
More than $500,000	32.9	15.5	25.1
1992–2004			
Less than $500,000	2.4	2.3	0.2
More than $500,000	33.6	15.7	9.1
1996–2004			
Less than $500,000	0.0	0.0	0.0
More than $500,000	25.3	9.2	6.4

Source: Compiled by author from Federal Election Commission data.
a. Spending is adjusted for inflation (2004 = 1.00).

table 2-2) and the difficulty even high-spending challengers have in over-coming an unfavorable partisan balance.[13]

The Absence of Partisan Tides

Recent discussions of declining House competition have usually ignored the dearth of strong partisan tides since the early 1980s—with 1994 the notable exception—but it deserves consideration as well. In the seventeen elections from 1952 through 1984, the major-party vote for House candidates differed by an average of 3.3 percentage points from the previous election, with the swing exceeding 3 points eight times. In the ten elections since then, the aver-age swing is only 1.9 percentage points and has been greater than 3 points only twice; if 1994 is excluded, the average is a mere 1.4 points. Aside from 1994, these were all elections when short-term partisan forces generated by national conditions were nearly neutral or offsetting, so the absence of large partisan swings is not especially anomalous.[14] The 1994 election left no doubt

13. A party's experienced candidates and campaign money have also become increasingly concentrated in those open seats with a favorable or neutral underlying partisan balance, al-though the size of the change and degree of concentration are considerably smaller than for challengers to incumbents.

14. For a discussion of national forces in the 1986, 1988, and 1990 elections, see Jacobson (1992, pp. 185–95); for 1992 through 2002, see Jacobson (2004, pp. 170–99); for 2004, see Jacobson (2005b, pp. 203–06).

that a strong surge in public sentiment favoring one party over the other could still produce a dramatic change in the House's partisan balance. This possibility has not been tested since then, however, and the data examined above suggest that, partly as a consequence of the 1994 election itself and its sorting of House districts into the "right" party's hands, a national partisan tide would have to be quite powerful indeed to have an equivalent impact today. Still, the aggregate data have yet to show that seat shifts have become significantly less sensitive to vote shifts in recent elections.

Figure 2-10 plots House seat swings against vote swings for elections from 1952 through 2004.[15] Elections since 1992 are highlighted and labeled. With the possible exception of 1996, they do not stand out much, either visually or statistically, from other elections featuring similar vote swings.[16] As it happens, the aggregate swing to the Democrats in 1996 did not include the Republican freshmen elected in 1994, reflecting not only their "sophomore surge" but also the fact that more than three-quarters of them had won Republican-leaning districts that were relatively easy to retain, and this appears to be the reason the seat swing was so unresponsive to the vote swing that year. Democrats lost seats despite gaining votes in 2004 only because of the Texas redistricting; without it, the entry for 2004 would fall very close to the fitted line.[17]

In sum, the low turnover of House seats in recent elections has multiple, mutually reinforcing causes. The favorite culprit of many critics, the creation of safe (lopsidedly partisan) districts via gerrymandering, while not absolved, is a relatively small part of the story and is significant mainly through its interaction with a more crucial change, the increasing partisan consistency and polarization of district electorates. Bruce Oppenheimer offers a telling demonstration of the importance of voter-driven polarization by comparing changes in presidential voting patterns between 1960 and 2000 in a hypothetical state consisting of the seven congressional districts in the single-

15. I use the average district-level vote change to measure the national shift; the national major-party vote shift produces a very similar picture, but I use the former measure because it is less sensitive to variations in the incidence of uncontested races and the way states count (or fail to count) votes in such races.

16. In a variety of regression models I used to estimate the effects of seat shifts on vote shifts over the twenty-seven elections in this set, the 1992–2004 observations were neither collectively nor individually distinguishable, statistically, from the rest, although the signs of coefficients were always consistent with a smaller effect in recent years.

17. The line is estimated as a third-order polynomial to fit the nonlinear relationship between seat and vote swings. On the effects of the Texas redistricting, see Jacobson (2005a, pp. 165–66).

Figure 2-10. Partisan Change in House Votes and Seats, 1952–2004

Seat swing to or from Democrats

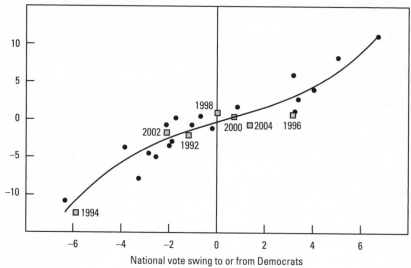

National vote swing to or from Democrats

Source: Compiled by author.

district states to changes in the twenty-seven actual states with from five to ten House districts. He finds that the degree of polarization (measured by the increase in the mean district margin above 50 percent of the presidential vote) grew more for his hypothetical state—which was not, of course, subject to redistricting—than for any of the actual states where redistricting did occur.[18]

The evidence in table 2-1 also points to behavioral change among voters as the major source of the increase in polarized districts. The depressive effect of this trend on House competition has been magnified by the growing disinclination of voters to elect representatives who do not match the district's partisan profile. The drop in the number of House candidates able to win against the partisan grain reflects the recent dearth of strong partisan tides—national conditions powerful enough to induce large numbers of voters to abandon the party they normally support—but also and more important the longer-term growth in ideological and partisan consistency in the electorate.[19] The

18. Oppenheimer (2005, pp. 150–51).
19. Jacobson (2007, chap. 2).

long odds against defeating incumbents in districts where the partisan makeup favors their side, especially in the absence of any boost from national forces, deters experienced challengers and their potential contributors, guaranteeing easy reelection for most officeholders. Efforts to take seats from the other party are thus increasingly concentrated in the diminishing set of potentially vulnerable districts.

The Republican Advantage

The increase in partisan polarization and consistency has clearly favored the Republican Party, allowing it to profit from a structural advantage it had held for decades but, until recently, had been unable to exploit. The Republicans' advantage lies in the fact that their voters are distributed more efficiently across House districts than Democratic voters are. To grasp this point, consider the distribution of the major-party vote for president in 2000. Short-term political forces were evenly balanced that year, and party-line voting was the highest it had been in decades, so both the national and district-level presidential vote reflected the electorate's underlying partisan balance with unusual accuracy.[20] The Democrat, Al Gore, won the national popular vote by about 540,000 of the 105 million votes cast. Yet the distribution of these votes across current (2006) House districts yields 240 in which Bush won more votes than Gore but only 195 in which Gore outpolled Bush. The principal reason for this Republican advantage is demographic: Democrats win a disproportionate share of minority and other urban voters, who tend to be concentrated in districts with lopsided Democratic majorities.[21] But successful Republican gerrymanders in Florida, Michigan, Ohio, Pennsylvania, and, after 2002, Texas did enhance the party's advantage, increasing the number of Bush-majority districts by twelve, from 228 to 240.[22]

The Republicans' structural advantage, though enlarged in the post-2000 redistricting, is nothing new. As figure 2-11 shows, except after the 1964 election, Republicans have consistently held more seats than Democrats in districts where their party enjoyed a partisan advantage (estimated here as having the district vote for their party's presidential candidate by at least 2 percentage

20. Jacobson (2001, pp. 5–27).
21. For example, according to the CBS News/*New York Times* poll of August 20–25, 2004, Democratic identifiers outnumbered Republicans nearly five to one in New York City. See "New York City and the Republican Convention" at www.cbsnews.com/htdocs/CBSNews_polls/nyc.pdf, November 6, 2004.
22. Jacobson (2005a, pp. 201–03).

Figure 2-11. District Partisan Advantage, 1952–2004

Percent

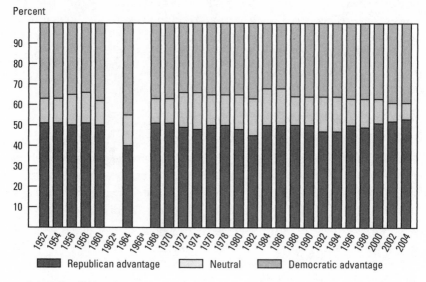

Republican advantage ▮▮▮   Neutral ☐   Democratic advantage ▮▮▮

Source: Compiled by author.
a. Data for 1962 and 1966 are not available because the presidential vote was not recalculated for redrawn districts for these years.

points above the national average).[23] In past decades Democrats were able to win a substantial proportion of these Republican-leaning seats, as much as 43 percent in the 1970s (figure 2-12). Their ability to win such seats has dropped dramatically since the 1980s, a major reason why they have been unable to retake the House since losing it in 1994. Republicans have never done particularly well in Democratic presidential territory and remain less successful than Democrats in this regard; but this is not a problem for them at present because their structural advantage would deliver Republican House majorities even if they won only Republican-leaning seats.[24]

A Note on the Senate

Senate elections have been substantially more competitive than House elections for decades and remain so today. Yet the same polarizing forces that

23. The substantive point is unchanged if the standard is 5 rather than 2 percentage points.
24. Democrats have also done worse in the dwindling number of evenly balanced districts; from the 1950s through the 1980s they won 66 percent of these districts; since 1992 they have won 53 percent.

Figure 2-12. Winning against the Partisan Grain, by Decade

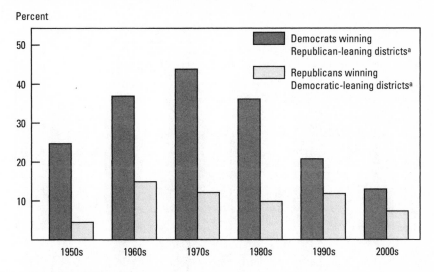

Percent

Democrats winning
Republican-leaning districts[a]

Republicans winning
Democratic-leaning districts[a]

Source: Compiled by author.
a. Leaning districts are defined as those in which the district-level presidential vote was at least 2 percentage points higher than the national average for that election.

have reduced the number of competitive House contests have also affected Senate races—another indication that redistricting is only part of the story, for Senate "districts" are of course never redrawn. States, like congressional districts, have grown more polarized in presidential voting. For example, the number of states where the major-party vote split was within 2 percentage points of the national vote has dropped from a postwar high of eighteen in 1976 to a low of seven in 2004; the number where the split was within 5 points of the national vote fell from thirty-three to eighteen over the same period. Senate and presidential results have also grown increasingly consistent (see figure 2-13), and by the 109th Congress (2005–06) the proportion of Senate seats held by the party that had won the state's electoral votes in the most recent election was, at 75 percent, the highest share in at least a half-century.[25] Like House candidates, Senate candidates have found it increasingly difficult to win states against the partisan grain. In the 1960s, 1970s, and 1980s, about 45 percent of Senate candidates managed to win in states

25. Jacobson (2005a, p. 176).

Figure 2-13. States Won by Same Party in Senate and Presidential Elections, 1952–2004

Percent

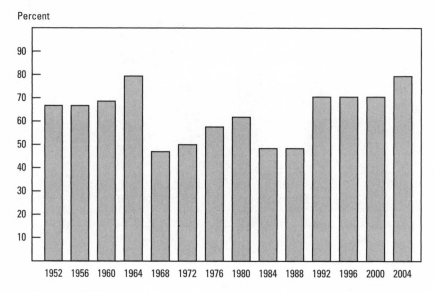

1952 1956 1960 1964 1968 1972 1976 1980 1984 1988 1992 1996 2000 2004

Source: Compiled by author.

where their presidential candidate had run 2 or more percentage points behind the national vote in the concurrent or most recent election; in the 1990s that share fell to 31 percent, and for 2002 and 2004 it was down to 20 percent. Using the 5-point partisan disadvantage standard, the comparable figures are 36 percent, 28 percent, and 12 percent, respectively, for the three periods.

Still, a substantial proportion of Senate races remain competitive. Partisan turnover, total and net, remains proportionately much higher than in House elections. Senate incumbents, while more secure than in the past, are still far more vulnerable than House incumbents.[26] The proportion of marginal contests, although somewhat lower in recent elections, remains quite high in comparison with House elections (figure 2-14). In the most recent three-election cycle, 43 percent of the Senate victors won with less than 60 percent of the vote, and 25 percent won with less than 55 percent; the equivalent fig-

26. In the 1960s and 1970s, 81 percent of senators who sought reelection were successful; since then, their success rate has risen to 89 percent overall, but it fell below 80 percent in both 1986 and 2000.

Figure 2-14. Marginal Senate Seats, 1952–2004

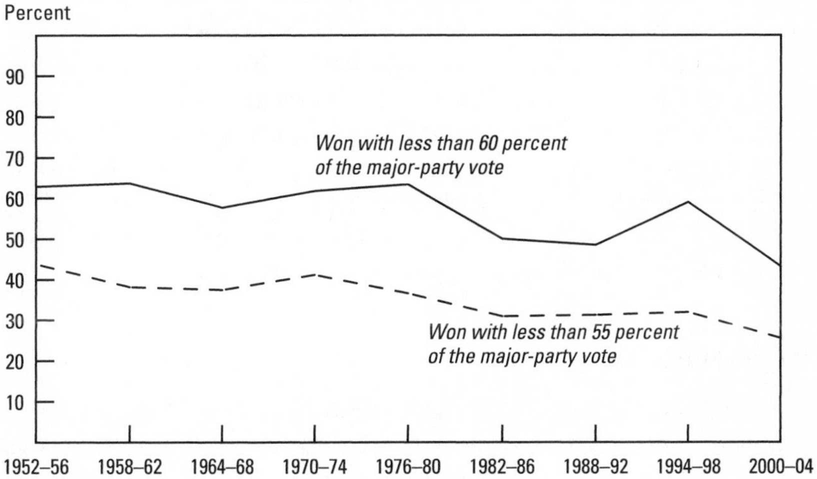

Percent

Source: Compiled by author.

ures for House elections in the three elections were 19 percent and 8 percent, respectively.

Senate elections remain more competitive for several reasons. With the exception of the seven single-district states, Senate constituencies tend to be considerably more diverse socially and economically, and therefore politically, than House constituencies. A far larger proportion of states than House districts are potentially winnable by either party. Although, in line with the national trend toward greater partisan consistency, the number of split Senate delegations (one senator from each party) has fallen from twenty-two to thirteen since 1990, no fewer than thirty-six states have nonetheless been represented by senators from both parties during this period. Because the odds are better, Senate races attract a larger proportion of experienced, politically talented, well-financed candidates. With control of the Senate at stake in every recent election, the intensity of campaigning in the more competitive races has at times reached truly astonishing levels. Competing for South Dakota's 570,000 registered voters in 2004, Republican challenger John Thune and Senate Minority Leader Tom Daschle spent a total of $34 million between them—more than $60 per voter; eight other tight contests were lavishly financed as well.[27]

27. Jacobson (2006, table 3).

Thus although the overall level of Senate competition has declined some-what, more than enough seats have been in play to leave control of the Senate up for grabs in every recent election. But as in House elections, the firming up of partisan loyalties and the deepening red-blue division has worked to the Republicans' benefit, for they enjoy a structural advantage—a more efficient distribution of their regular voters—in pursuit of the Senate as well as the House. Although Al Gore won more votes nationally than Bush in 2000, Bush outpolled Gore in thirty of the fifty states. Again there is nothing new in this, but it has become more consequential with the decline in the ability of Senate candidates to win against the partisan grain.

Implications

If this analysis is on target, feasible solutions to the problem of declining competition for congressional seats are quite limited. If redistricting were taken from legislatures and given to neutral bodies enjoined to ignore partisan interests in favor of other criteria, they might create a few more evenly balanced and therefore potentially competitive districts. But because voters are to blame for most of the recent diminution of such districts, unless map-makers sought deliberately to maximize their number through pro-competitive gerrymanders, the effect would probably be modest under the current distribution of partisans and their levels of polarization and party loyalty. And any effective scheme intended to increase the number of competitive districts would inevitably threaten the Republicans' structural advantage and control of the House and, as such, would be guaranteed to provoke adamant opposition.

Campaign finance reforms are also unlikely to have much effect on competition. No more than a handful of challengers in recent elections could make a plausible claim that they might have won but for a shortage of funds; in the past three elections, only four of the fifty-five losing House challengers who received at least 45 percent of the vote spent less than $500,000; nearly three-quarters of them spent more than $1 million. Nor did the incumbent's spending advantage seem to matter; no matter how I analyzed the data, I could detect no significant effect of the incumbent's level of spending on the results of these elections (or any others). Of the fifteen House incumbents who have lost since 2000, only four were outspent by the challenger; on average these losing incumbents outspent the opposition by more than $500,000. Experienced challengers and campaign donors do not ignore potentially competitive districts, and challengers do not lose simply because incumbents spend so much; their problem is a shortage of districts where the partisan balance offers some plausible hope. Senate races, too, have almost invariably attracted experienced and well-financed candidates whenever the competitive circumstances have warranted.

The one thing that clearly could generate a greater number of competitive races is not subject to legislative tinkering: a strong national tide favoring the Democrats. Such Democratic landslides as occurred in 1958 and 1974 put substantial numbers of Democrats into Republican-leaning seats (in addition to those they already held), thus leaving a larger portion inherently competitive. A pro-Democratic national tide would, by definition, shake up partisan habits, at least temporarily, counteracting the Republicans' structural advantage. But absent major shifts in stable party loyalties that lighten the deepening shades of red and blue in so many districts, after the tide ebbed the competitive environment would likely revert to what it had been since 1994.

References

Abramowitz, Alan I., Brad Alexander, and Matthew Gunning. 2005. "Incumbency, Redistricting, and the Decline in Competition in U.S. House Elections." Paper presented at the Annual Meeting of the Southern Political Science Association, New Orleans, January 6–8.

Cox, Gary, and Jonathan Katz. 2002. *Elbridge Gerry's Salamander*. Cambridge University Press.

Jacobson, Gary C. 1989. "Strategic Politicians and the Dynamics of U.S. House Elections, 1946–86." *American Political Science Review* 83 (September): 776–78.

———. 1992. *The Politics of Congressional Elections*. 3rd ed. New York: HarperCollins.

———. 2001. "A House and Senate Divided: The Clinton Legacy and the Congressional Elections of 2000." *Political Science Quarterly* 116 (Spring): 5–27.

———. 2003. "Terror, Terrain, and Turnout: The 2002 Midterm Election." *Political Science Quarterly* 118 (Spring): 1–22;

———. 2004. *The Politics of Congressional Elections*. 6th ed. New York: Longman.

———. 2005a. "The Congress: The Structural Basis of Republican Success." In *The Elections of 2004*, edited by Michael Nelson. Washington: CQ Press.

———. 2005b. "Polarized Politics and the 2004 Congressional and Presidential Elections." *Political Science Quarterly* 120 (Summer): 199–218.

———. 2006. "The First Congressional Elections after BCRA." In *One Election Later: 2004 Politics after the Bipartisan Campaign Reform Act*, edited by Michael J. Malbin, pp. 185–203. Lanham, Md.: Rowman and Littlefield.

———. 2007. *A Divider, Not a Uniter: George W. Bush and the American People*. New York: Longman.

Mayhew, David R. 1974. "Congressional Elections: The Case of the Vanishing Marginals." *Polity* 6 (Spring): 295–317.

Oppenheimer, Bruce I. 2005. "Deep Red and Blue Congressional Districts: The Causes and Consequences of Declining Party Competitiveness." In *Congress Reconsidered.* 8th ed., edited by Lawrence C. Dodd and Bruce I. Oppenheimer. Washington: CQ Press.

Stanley, Harold W., and Richard G. Niemi. 2003. *Vital Statistics on American Politics, 2003–2004.* Washington: CQ Press.

3 Competition in State Legislative Elections, 1992–2002

Richard G. Niemi, Lynda W. Powell, William D. Berry, Thomas M. Carsey, and James M. Snyder Jr.

A frequent theme in writings on state legislatures is the rich opportunity for comparative studies—the notion that ninety-nine chambers with "great similarities" but also "important differences" "provide legislative scholars leverage for rigorously testing important theories."[1] With respect to legislative *elections*, scholars have frequently taken advantage of this opportunity, having looked at the incumbency advantage, turnover, term limits, the relationship between elections and divided government, the role of gerrymandering, and so on. But even in the area of legislative elections, research is hampered by the lack of up-to-date information on elections in all fifty states. At this writing in 2006, it has been more than fifteen years— eight election cycles—since a comprehensive set of election data was compiled and therefore that long since a broad overview of election results has been made.

We gratefully acknowledge support from the National Science Foundation (Grants SBR-9422375, SES-0136526, and SES-0317924) for collecting and processing the state legislative election data.

1. Squire and Hamm (2005, p. 2).

With a new data set now available, we anticipate that many of the old questions will be revisited.[2] At the same time, the continuing evolution of state legislative professionalization, changes in district types and districting practices, and the shock wave brought about by legislative term limits will generate many innovative inquiries as well. Here, in the first foray into this new data set, we provide a broad overview—a look for trends, or lack of them, at a very general level. Such an overview is called for in part because of the extensiveness of the available data. Even ignoring finer institutional variations, the existence of fifty states and ninety-nine chambers provides a great deal of information to summarize and internalize. Central tendencies are important, but so too are distributions and outliers; knowing what has happened "in general" is significant, but so too is what has happened at the extremes and whether the extremes are to a greater or lesser degree than in the past made up of isolated, one-of-a-kind cases.

The purpose of this chapter, then, is to set out some basic information about state legislative elections, focusing on incumbency reelection rates, the frequency of open seats, and the level of competition. Because turnover of legislative personnel is so closely allied with election results, we also draw on turnover data for the state legislatures. We concentrate on the past decade or so, beginning in 1992—because of the importance of redistricting to legislative elections—and continuing through the 2002 elections. Because only a few states hold elections in odd-numbered years, we combine those elections with the ones held in the immediately following year, so we have six election cycles.[3] We present data separately for single-member districts (SMDs) and multimember districts (MMDs) and for lower and upper houses. We do not attempt a comprehensive explanation of the variations we

2. The data collection is a product of what was originally three independent efforts to gather legislative election data for all states and elections since 1988 in order to bring up to date the data set originally collected by Malcolm Jewell (1991) and made available through the Inter-University Consortium for Political and Social Research. The new data set, running through 2002, will be available through ICPSR as well. We should also note that Berry and Carsey (2005) recently made the original data more valuable by "cleaning" the names in the data set (that is, creating an adjusted name that is consistent across multiple instances of the same candidate, unlike the original, which might have included inconsistencies or redundancies, such as names with and without a middle initial). Their algorithm for name cleaning has been applied to the updated data.

3. States with elections scheduled in 1991 accomplished their redistricting quickly, so 1991, like 1992 in most states, is a redistricting year. Hence the decision about how to combine odd- and even-year elections.

observe, though we do often show how the varying levels are related to legislative professionalization.[4]

Incumbent Reelection Rates

We begin with incumbent reelection rates—simply the percentage of winners among incumbents running for reelection. These rates have been very high since at least the late 1960s, and we do not anticipate any significant changes during the most recent period.[5] Nevertheless, there are some variations worth noting. With so many different chambers, there is always a question about how to report the results. Tables of as many as forty to fifty rows (one for each state, plus summary rows) and seven columns (one for each election plus a summary column) can be useful, especially if one is interested in results for specific states. But such large tables can be overwhelming, containing too much information to grasp easily. Hence, we will display the results using what are variously called box plots, or box-and-whisker charts.

As an example, consider figure 3-1, which summarizes the reelection rates for incumbents in SMDs in lower houses in each of forty-four states. For each year, the thick black line is the median. Thus in 1992 half of the reelection rates across states are above .94 and half are below this value. The "box" shows the 25th and 75th percentiles for reelection rates (.92 and .97, respectively); that is, 25 percent of the cases are below the box and 25 percent are above the box, with 50 percent inside the box. The thin lines extending above and below

---

4. District type, chamber, and professionalization are used throughout the literature on state legislative elections. Carey, Niemi, and Powell (2000, p. 684) suggest that theory supports the use of term length rather than chamber (though the two are highly correlated), and that district size might also be relevant, at least with respect to incumbency advantage. We will explore these factors in later work.

A word of caution is appropriate with respect to the coverage and accuracy of the data. To the extent possible, we include all chambers. There are, however, some missing data— throughout in the case of Louisiana, and occasionally for other states in particular years due to data entry or other errors. (The data set contains Louisiana data, but its primary system makes it unclear how best to compare it with other states.) We have made numerous checks on these data, but with many thousands of elections over a decade, there are bound to be errors. A few may be in the original data transmitted to us, but others surely occurred when we entered the data. The errors are not likely to affect analyses aggregated across states, especially when states and years are combined. Nevertheless, when researchers come across cases that are far out of line with other data points or cases that they have reason to question, they should verify the information before using it to make a substantive point or creatively "explaining" it. In preparing this work, we have checked out and eliminated a number of odd cases, but some errors are likely to remain.

5. Garand (1991) provides results for 1968 through the 1980s.

Figure 3-1. Incumbency Reelection Rates, State Legislative Lower Houses, Single-Member Districts, 1992–2002[a]

Percentage reelected among incumbents who ran

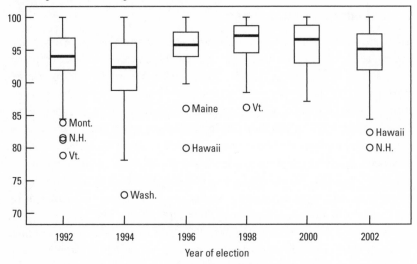

Year of election

a. *N* ≈ 42 states. Number in all figures varies slightly from year to year due to four-year terms in some states and to occasional missing data.

In figures 3-1 through 3-11, for each year, the thick black line is the median. The "box" shows the 25th and 75th percentiles: that is, 25 percent of the cases are below the box and 25 percent are above the box, with 50 percent inside. The thin lines extending above and below the box show the range—that is, the lowest and highest values. The range is modified in that "outliers"—values far from the rest of the observations—are excluded even from the range and are individually labeled. The definition of outliers can be found in Bohrnstedt and Knoke (1988, p. 88).

the box (the "whiskers") show the range—that is, the lowest and highest values. However, the range is modified in that some values are sufficiently far from the rest of the observations that they are labeled "outliers." They are excluded even from the range and most are individually labeled. These plots, especially when shown for a series of years, make it easy to grasp the main tendencies of the data.

Now, looking across the years, the median reelection rate for incumbents in lower house SMDs has been more than 90 percent since 1992 and has been 95 percent or above in four of the six election years since then (see figure 3-1).[6]

6. We combine single-member districts, multimember districts with posts, and multimember districts with staggered terms into a single category, which we refer to for short as

As one might expect, the rate is generally lower in the years immediately following redistricting, but the difference is not completely consistent and is too slight to matter anyway. There is no indication that this high rate of reelection decreased over this period, as a regression of the reelection rate on time is flat, and the rate was fractionally higher in the 2002 redistricting year than it was ten years earlier. In any given year, there are states with somewhat lower reelection rates, though only occasionally does the rate drop below 85 percent. At the high end, it is not unusual for 100 percent of the incumbents in a given state to be reelected in a given year.

In multimember districts the median percentages of incumbents reelected are slightly smaller, but still on the order of 90 percent (see figure 3-2). One extreme case exists—North Carolina in 1994—in which a particularly low percentage of incumbents was returned to office.

With medians over 90 percent and minimums typically in excess of 80 percent, it is not likely that we can explain a great deal of the between-state variation. However, one pattern stands out. Among the states with exclusively SMDs, seven small states have averages for 1992–2002 of less than 90 percent (Hawaii, 89 percent; Maine, 89 percent: Montana, 89 percent; New Hampshire, 88 percent; Vermont, 87 percent), and four of the largest states have especially high averages (Massachusetts, 98 percent; Michigan, 98 percent; New York, 98 percent; Pennsylvania, 99 percent). Because small states tend to have the least professionalized legislatures, and big states the most professionalized, the size connection may be attributable to the levels of professionalization of their respective legislatures.

Using Squire's index of professionalization (which combines legislative pay, staff per member, and average days in session), the correlation between legislative professionalization and average reelection rates is .42.[7] This moderately sized relationship may be the result of multiple factors. For one thing, in small states it may be easier to fund a successful campaign to defeat an incumbent. Though there is a smaller resource base from which to raise funds, the dollar amounts needed may be even smaller, relatively speaking. It is also likely that incumbents in more professionalized states are more eager to hold on to their jobs and thus make greater efforts to retain them. Consistent with this explanation is research showing that legislators in more

---

SMDs. In districts with posts and staggered terms, constituents are represented by more than one candidate, but candidates run for a single, specific seat.

7. For the index of professionalization, see Squire (2000).

Figure 3-2. Incumbency Reelection Rates, State Legislative Lower Houses, Multimember Districts, 1992–2002[a]

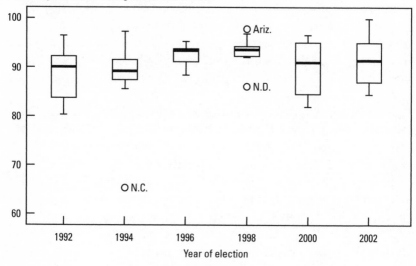

Percentage reelected among incumbents who ran

Year of election

a. *N* ≈ 7 states.

professionalized legislatures report working longer hours and putting more time and energy into keeping in touch with constituents, helping them with problems with government, and bringing projects to their districts.[8]

Turning to state Senates, we deal only with SMDs, as just two states in the 1990s had MMDs for the upper house. We anticipate that incumbent reelection rates will be slightly lower, as they are for the U.S Senate compared to the U.S. House of Representatives, presumably because the prestige of the higher office and a smaller number of seats result in more qualified candidates competing for those seats.[9] As it turns out, the overall differences between upper and lower chambers are very slight and not entirely consistent (see figure 3-3).

8. Two recent articles explore the relationship between professionalization and how legislators spend their time. See Kurtz, Moncrief, Niemi, and Powell (2006) and Carey, Niemi, Powell, and Moncrief (2006). Note that in MMDs the pattern described in the text does not hold. We do not know whether it is due to one or two unusual cases among the small number of relevant states or to some systematic difference between single-member and multimember districts.

9. Reelection rates for the U.S. House from the 1950s to the present can be found in Stanley and Niemi (2005, pp. 51–52).

Figure 3-3. Incumbency Reelection Rates, State Legislative Upper Houses, Single-Member Districts, 1992–2002[a]

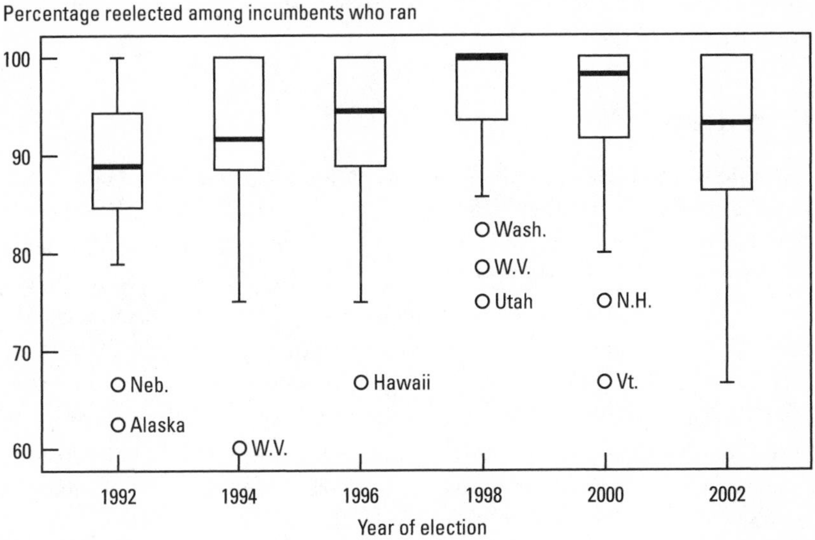

Percentage reelected among incumbents who ran

Year of election

a. $N \approx 47$ states.

Except for 1992, median reelection rates are still above .90. In two of the six years, the rate for senators is higher than for House members, and in 1998 the median state saw not a single incumbent senator defeated (that is, in half of the states, no incumbents lost). There were, however, more instances in which the reelection rate dropped below 85 percent—as many as ten such states in redistricting years.

One further difference is that, unlike in the lower houses, there is virtually no correlation between professionalization and incumbency reelection rates. Some of the least professionalized states had relatively low incumbency reelection rates (Utah, 86 percent; Vermont, 83 percent), but so too did moderately professionalized states (Iowa, 87 percent; Nebraska, 87 percent; Virginia, 85 percent). Among the most professionalized states, some had extremely high reelection rates (New York, 98 percent; Pennsylvania, 97 percent), but others did not (New Jersey, 90 percent; Wisconsin, 92 percent). An explanation for this difference between lower and upper houses may lie in the ambitions of lower house members. Even though members of the lower house in relatively professionalized states are more interested in moving up to the state Senate, the larger size of lower houses—more than twice the size of the Senate in many states—may put pressure on senators in every state.[10] Professionalized or not, upper house legislators more often than lower house members face challengers who have experience and a degree of visibility, precisely because of their service in the lower house.

Open Seats

Extremely high rates of incumbency reelection are more or less significant depending on the number of incumbents who run for reelection. In the U.S. House, this percentage has been on the order of 90 percent at least since the end of the World War II period, meaning that only about 10 percent of the races in any given year are open-seat contests.[11] In state legislatures, the median percentage of open seats is typically more than 20 percent (see figures 3-4 to 3-6).[12] The percentage of open seats is also more variable over time in the states. In redistricting years, the median percentage is above 25; that is, in half the states, more than a quarter of all races are for open seats. Even in the intervening years, 15–20 percent or more of the seats in many states do not include an incumbent.

In any given year, there is also considerable variability. This can be seen in two ways. First, there are occasional instances of very high numbers of open seats. In North Carolina in 1992 and in Oklahoma in 1994, for example, more than half of the districts had open seats (see figure 3-4) (along with a number of states later in the decade, which we shall come back to). Second, on average, some states have more open-seat races than others. Ignoring, for the moment, the effects of term limits, there is a modest connection between the average percentage of open seats in SMDs and legislative professionalization ($r = -.43$). Nonprofessionalized states tend to have higher percentages of open seats (Alabama, 26; Mississippi, 28; Montana, 27; Wyoming, 29; but also Colorado, 31; Hawaii, 36). In contrast, the most highly professionalized states have lower percentages of open seats (New York, 14; Pennsylvania, 11; Wisconsin, 15; but also Delaware, 12; Indiana, 13; Virginia, 13).

Multimember districts are again slightly different, with the median share of open seats 5–9 percentage points higher than for SMDs (compare figures 3-4 and 3-5). The large differences in 2000 and 2002 might be surprising, but recall that the very large numbers in figure 3-4 (the outliers) are excluded

10. Carey et al. (2000, p. 104).
11. Stanley and Niemi (2005, p. 51).
12. The calculations in this section are based on general elections only. A few incumbents run for reelection but are defeated in primaries.

Figure 3-4. Open-Seat Races, State Legislative Lower Houses, Single-Member Districts, 1992–2002[a]

Percentage of open seats

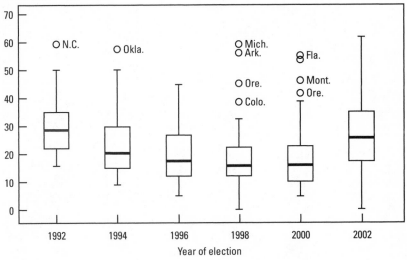

Year of election

a. N ≈ 42 states.

from the calculation of medians. As with incumbency reelection rates, the percentages of open-seat races in MMDs show no correlation with legislative professionalization.

Elections in upper houses show higher percentages of open seats on average. The median percentage for upper houses never dips below 20; it is typically 5–10 points higher than for lower houses (compare figures 3-4 and 3-6). At the same time, the ranges for upper houses are also much wider; in particular, some states have very low numbers of open seats. New York averaged only 10 percent open seats across the six elections, with several other states averaging no more than 15 percent (Connecticut, Idaho, Massachusetts). At the other extreme (again, ignoring states with term limits), there were more upper chambers in which there was a consistently high level of open-seat races. Whereas only one state (Arkansas), on average, had open-seat contests in as many as 40 percent of its lower house races, this level was reached by eleven states in their upper houses (Arkansas, California, Colorado, Florida, Hawaii, Kansas, Michigan, Montana, Ohio, Oregon, and Utah). We can speculate about factors that might explain this difference. It may be that more members of upper houses retire, believing they have served enough time in

Figure 3-5. Open-Seat Races, State Legislative Lower Houses, Multimember Districts, 1992–2002[a]

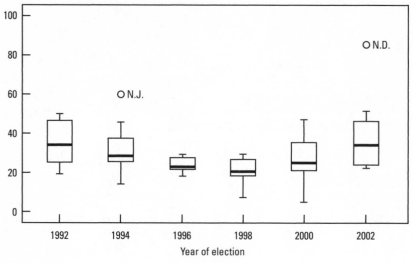

Percentage of open seats

a. $N \approx$ 8 states.

public service. Or it may be that the prestige of the upper chamber, along with the ready supply of qualified candidates (eager lower chamber members) leads to more senators choosing to retire rather than face stiff competition and possible defeat (or slightly larger numbers actually being defeated in primaries).

Turnover

Incumbency reelection rates and the number of open seats together determine turnover rates in the legislatures. If most seats are contested by incumbents, and most of them win, turnover is small. While it is true that a very large proportion of incumbents who run for reelection win (though with some variation across types of districts and states), we have seen that quite a few contests at the state legislative level are for open seats, making turnover greater than was suggested by the rhetoric of the term-limits movement. Of course, since turnover rates are relatively easy to compute, they can be calculated directly, something that has been done since the 1930s. Here we present turnover rates for 1992–2002 as a way of helping gauge how significant the

Figure 3-6. Open-Seat Races, State Legislative Upper Houses, Single-Member Districts, 1992–2002[a]

Percentage of open seats

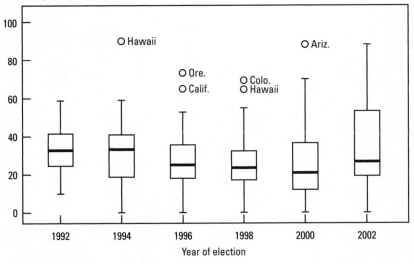

a. *N* ≈ 48 states.

information is about open seats and incumbent reelection rates. A more complete analysis is given elsewhere.[13]

Turnover is usually measured as the percentage of new legislators seated at each session. Using that measure, figures 3-7 and 3-8 show average turnover rates for each state for the period 1990–2002.[14] On average, close to a quarter of all legislators are new after any given election year. This represents a decline from around 50 percent turnover in the 1930s but a leveling off between the 1980s and 1990s, even without the greater turnover in term-limited states.[15] Unsurprisingly, turnover is higher in states with term limits, though we find that the initially very high rates that sometimes occur when term limits first take effect are not always repeated in subsequent elections in those states. In any case, among the incumbents who can and do run in term-limited states, reelection rates in those states remain very high.

13. Moncrief, Niemi, and Powell (2004).
14. In upper houses, where elections are often staggered, these numbers represent percentages of the entire body, not simply of those up for reelection.
15. Moncrief, Niemi, and Powell (2004).

Figure 3-7. Turnover in Lower Houses of U.S. State Legislatures, 1992–2002[a]

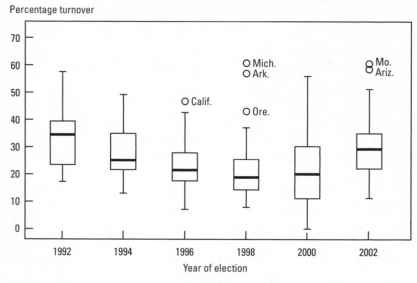

Percentage turnover

Year of election

a. *N* ≈ 50 states.

Variability in turnover rates is substantial. Over time, the greatest turnover is in redistricting years, when it averages about 30 percent in lower houses, dropping by as much as 15 percentage points later in the decade. Across states, turnover varied in the 1990s from lows of 10–11 percent (Delaware, Indiana, New York, Oklahoma) to highs of around 40 percent (Alabama, Kansas). Across district type, turnover is greater in MMDs. And owing to variations both in incumbency reelection rates and in the numbers of open seats, turnover in both houses (in non-term-limited states) is correlated with legislative professionalization (–.38 in both lower and upper SMD houses, using 1990s average turnover). Turnover differs surprisingly little between lower and upper chambers; the higher rate of incumbency defeats and open seats in Senates counterbalance the effects of staggered terms.

Competition Levels

A decline in marginal elections—that is, a decline in the number of competitive seats—has been a major, long-time concern in legislative studies, at both the congressional and state legislative levels. Fifteen years ago, Weber, Tucker,

Figure 3-8. Turnover in Upper Houses of U.S. State Legislatures, 1992–2002[a]

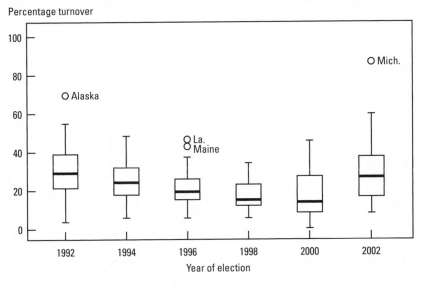

Percentage turnover

Year of election

a. $N \approx 50$ states.

and Brace analyzed data from twenty states, concluding that "marginal seats are vanishing in some U.S. state legislatures."[16] The measure of competitiveness they and others have used is whether the winning candidate received less than 60 percent of the vote. As this is a fairly generous definition of competitive, researchers sometimes also look at numbers of "very" competitive races—those in which the winning candidate received less than 55 percent of the vote.[17]

Based on the 60 percent cutoff value, percentages of competitive elections for 1992–2002 are shown in figures 3-9 to 3-11.[18] If Weber and his colleagues were disturbed by what they observed fifteen years ago (a median across

16. Weber, Tucker, and Brace (1991, p. 45).
17. A few states do not include uncontested elections on the ballots that were used to create the data set; they are excluded from these calculations.
18. Technically, we looked at the winning voter margin rather than at the winning candidate's vote percentage. That is, if the winning candidate won by less than 20 percent over the second-place candidate, we classified the district as competitive. We included minor-party votes. However, there are few independent candidates who win a significant percentage of the vote, so excluding them would change the results very little. Uncontested districts are included (as a 100–0 result or a 100-point vote margin).

Figure 3-9. Competitive Seats, State Legislative Lower Houses, Single-Member Districts, 1992–2002[a]

Percentage of competitive seats

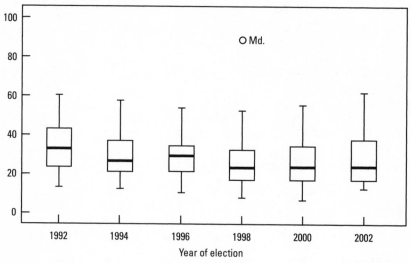

Year of election

a. $N \approx 42$ states.

twenty states of 43.6 percent competitive districts), they would be even more concerned now. In SMDs, the median percentage of competitive districts is about 25 percent in the state's lower houses (see figure 3-9). And while the median is highest in the 1992 redistricting year, the 2002 numbers increased only minimally from the lows of 1998 and 2000. At the same time, the degree of competition varies widely. In some states, 55–60 percent of the districts are competitive in a given year, while in other states, no more than 10–15 percent are competitive. Overall, there is a modest connection with professionalization ($r = -.20$). The most professionalized states tend to have low levels of competition (Massachusetts, 12; New York, 17; Pennsylvania, 14; Wisconsin, 23), and a few of the least professionalized are at the high end (Maine, 45; Vermont, 53), but there are some significant exceptions as well (Minnesota, 41; Washington, 43).

What drives this connection, of course, is the percentage of open seats. Thus, it is not surprising that competition is somewhat higher in MMDs (see figure 3-10). Given the small number of such states, the medians are more variable, but they hover in the 35–45 range, some ten points higher than for SMDs. Likewise, competition is higher in upper houses (see figure 3-11). In

Figure 3-10. Competitive Seats, State Legislative Lower Houses, Multimember Districts, 1992–2002[a]

Percentage of competitive districts

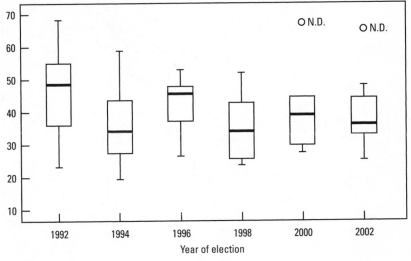

Year of election

a. $N \approx 8$ states.

both types of districts and chambers, however, rates of competition declined after 1992 and failed to rebound in 2002.[19]

The Effects of Term Limits

The term-limits debate was framed mostly in terms of turnover—that term limits would allow more people to serve in the legislature (and, of course, keep them from serving for lengthy periods). But forcing legislators out of office was expected to create more open-seat elections, and thus a secondary effect would be greater competition. Have term limits accomplished these goals?

Term limits have clearly resulted in greater turnover, though the jury is still out in several respects, including whether turnover in each state will now be higher at each election than it was before term limits, or whether very high levels will be mixed with near-normal levels.[20] With respect to incumbent

19. Patterns for *very* competitive elections are the same, though the rates are naturally lower. In SMDs, median levels of competition are 10–16 percent for 1992–2002, and are 4–5 points higher in MMDs and upper chambers.

20. Moncrief, Niemi, and Powell (2004).

Figure 3-11. Competitive Seats, State Legislative Upper Houses, Single-Member Districts, 1992–2002[a]

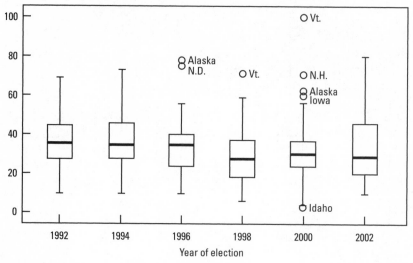

Percentage of competitive seats

Year of election

a. N ≈ 44 states.

reelection, open seats, and competition, term limits appear to have had a mix of nil, immediate, and sustained results. The nil results are for incumbent reelection rates; they are not likely to be affected—that is, incumbents are just as likely to win when they are allowed to run for reelection—and that is what we observe (see table 3-1).

Open seats, in contrast, have increased dramatically (see table 3-2). The percentage of open seats in term-limited states is, on average, roughly twice that in non-term-limited states; most within-state comparisons show substantial increases in the percentage of open seats immediately after limits came into force. As with turnover rates, there are hints that the numbers of open seats will not be consistently high (note the dropoff in 2000 in the Arkansas and Michigan lower houses and the 2000 versus 2002 results in Montana and Ohio). It is too early, however, to be certain of steady-state patterns.

Competition levels have also increased, although much less than one might expect given the rise in the number of open seats (see table 3-3). Indeed, apart from 1996, when limits were in effect in only a few chambers, the difference in the percentage of competitive seats was only three to seven

Table 3-1. Incumbency Reelection Rates in States with Term Limits Effective between 1996 and 2002

Percentage reelected among incumbents who ran

State	Year			
	1996	1998	2000	2002
Lower house				
Arkansas		98	100	85
California	96	96	100	98
Colorado		100	93	96
Florida			98	96
Maine	86	89	92	85
Michigan		100	100	98
Missouri				96
Montana			91	90
Ohio			98	95
Average in term-limited states (listed above)	91	97	96	93
Average in non-term-limited states	95	96	96	94
Upper house				
Arizona			100	100
Arkansas				100
California		89	90	100
Colorado		100	100	100
Florida			100	86
Maine	91	100	91	92
Michigan				100
Missouri				100
Montana			92	83
Ohio			100	90
Average in term-limited states (listed above)	91	96	96	95
Average in non-term-limited states	90	95	95	90

Notes: Single-member districts only. Term-limited states are those in which limits took effect by 2002. Averages for non-term-limited states do not include term-limited states before term limits took effect.

points.[21] Nor did the level of competition always move in tandem with the percentage of open seats. In the Arizona and Montana upper houses, for example, the percentage of open seats increased sharply between 2000 and 2002, yet competition dropped dramatically in the former and was almost unchanged in the latter. In the California Senate, percentages of open seats were nearly constant, but competition fell off in 2002. In addition, there are

21. Note the contrasting results of Cain, Hanley, and Kousser (in this volume), who conclude that term limits have had virtually no impact on electoral competition. We lean toward a calculation (such as ours) that looks at the percentage of close districts rather than one that relies on average margins of victory, especially when the base (the number of contested seats in Cain and his colleagues' calculation) is itself changing differently in term-limited and non-term-limited states. Pending more detailed analysis, however, we would emphasize our agreement that levels of competition have not risen as dramatically as pro-term-limits rhetoric seemed to suggest they would, and that more open seats do not always lead to greater competition.

Table 3-2. Open Seats in States with Term Limits Effective
between 1996 and 2002

Percentage of open seats

State	Year			
	1996	*1998*	*2000*	*2002*
Lower house				
Arkansas		56	33	62
California	44	33	39	44
Colorado		38	34	26
Florida			55	45
Maine	32	22	25	36
Michigan		59	19	53
Missouri				58
Montana			46	27
Ohio			54	25
Average in term-limited states (listed above)	38	42	38	42
Average in non-term-limited states	19	15	14	23
Upper house				
Arizona			33	63
Arkansas				73
California		55	50	50
Colorado		65	70	53
Florida			65	63
Maine	34	9	37	29
Michigan				87
Missouri				88
Montana			54	76
Ohio			53	41
Average in term-limited states (listed above)	34	43	51	62
Average in non-term-limited states	25	24	20	26

Notes: Single-member districts only. Term-limited states are those in which limits took effect by 2002. Averages for non-term-limited states do not include term-limited states before term limits took effect.

a number of states in which pre- and post-term-limit comparisons do not reveal noteworthy increases in levels of competition—including the California, Colorado, Florida, Michigan, Maine, and Missouri lower houses. We cannot yet account for these varying patterns, though the especially small differences noticed so far in the upper houses may have to do with the larger number of lower house members who moved up.[22]

Conclusion

In reviewing the large array of data summarized here, one might be tempted to conclude only that little has changed in state legislative elections: incum-

22. Moncrief, Niemi, and Powell (2004).

Table 3-3. Competitive Seats in States with Term Limits Effective between 1996 and 2002

Percentage of competitive seats

State	Year			
	1996	*1998*	*2000*	*2002*
Lower house				
Arkansas		31	18	62
California	41	29	20	13
Colorado		38	40	38
Florida			34	18
Maine	54	34	40	51
Michigan		25	19	25
Missouri				32
Montana			41	40
Ohio			34	23
Average in term-limited states (listed above)	48	31	31	32
Average in non-term-limited states	28	26	25	26
Upper house				
Arizona			37	10
Arkansas				67
California		25	35	10
Colorado		53	55	35
Florida			30	32
Maine	54	37	43	63
Michigan				34
Missouri				47
Montana			31	28
Ohio			12	35
Average in term-limited states (listed above)	54	38	35	36
Average in non-term-limited states	36	31	32	32

Notes: Single-member districts only. Term-limited states are those in which limits took effect by 2002. Averages for non-term-limited states do not include term-limited states before term limits took effect.

bents continue to be reelected at very high rates; open seats are more frequent than in congressional elections but typically less than one in five (at least in SMD, lower house races); and competition in the form of close election outcomes is limited. Alternatively, one might conclude simply that state legislative voting is similar to that for the U.S. Congress: over 90 percent of incumbents are reelected; less than a third of the lower house districts are competitive (the winner gets less than 60 percent of the vote); and reelection rates are lower and competition is higher in the U.S. Senate and in state upper houses.[23]

23. Even at this level of generality, some differences exist. Most important, while no more than about one-third of U.S. House districts have been competitive since the mid-1960s, some years have seen that drop to less than one-fifth (see the chapter by Jacobson in this book, figure 2-2a); average state levels have not dropped this low. In addition, at the state level, our summary statement is limited to SMDs.

While these broad generalizations are correct as far as they go, one might instead emphasize a different point. That is, though one, of necessity, characterizes a whole set of elections with simple phrases, such as "little competition," there is in fact a good deal of variability at the state legislative level. With few exceptions, the box and whisker plots show this clearly, especially when it is recalled that 50 percent of the cases are contained in the whiskers of the charts (that is, outside the boxes). Moreover, at least some of this variability is explained by factors we have identified—type of district (SMD or MMD), level of professionalization of the legislature, chamber (or term length), and the proximity of the election year to redistricting. Some of these factors are also relevant to congressional elections, but some are unique to the state legislature. In Congress there are no multimember districts, and there is no variability (other than between House and Senate) in size and level of professionalization. And recently, of course, term limits have been added to the mix at the state level, creating new bumps and perhaps new long-term patterns as well.

Unfortunately, however, from the perspective of those hoping to create more competition, these factors are not readily manipulable, except perhaps for professionalization. And in that case, it is not likely that states would (or should) starve their legislatures simply to increase competition. Thus, while "variable" may be a good catchword for describing state legislative elections, relatively little overall competition and unclear prescriptions for change are still the norm.

References

Berry, William D., and Thomas M. Carsey. 2005. "Revised Candidate-Level State Legislative Returns in the United States with Adjusted Candidate Names, 1968–1989." Data set 3938, Inter-University Consortium for Political and Social Research.

Bohrnstedt, George W., and David Knoke. 1988. *Statistics for Social Data Analysis.* 2nd ed. Itasca, Ill.: Peacock.

Carey, John, Richard G. Niemi, and Lynda W. Powell. 2000. "Incumbency and the Probability of Reelection in State Legislative Elections." *Journal of Politics* 62 (August): 671–700.

Carey, John, Richard G. Niemi, Lynda W. Powell, and Gary F. Moncrief. 2006. "The Effects of Term Limits on State Legislatures: Results from a New Survey of the 50 States." *Legislative Studies Quarterly* 31 (February): 105–34.

Garand, James. 1991. "Electoral Marginality in State Legislative Elections, 1968–1986." *Legislative Studies Quarterly* 16 (February): 7–28.

Jewell, Malcolm. 1991. "Editor's Introduction: State Legislative Elections." *Legislative Studies Quarterly* 16 (February): 1–5.

Kurtz, Karl, Gary F. Moncrief, Richard G. Niemi, and Lynda W. Powell. Forthcoming 2006. "Time, Term Limits, and Turnover: Trends in Membership Turnover in U.S. State Legislatures." *State Politics and Policy Quarterly* 31.

Moncrief, Gary, Richard G. Niemi, and Lynda W. Powell. 2004. "Time, Term Limits, and Turnover: Trends in Membership Turnover in U.S. State Legislatures." *Legislative Studies Quarterly* 29 (August): 357–81.

Squire, Peverill. 2000. "Uncontested Seats in State Legislative Elections." *Legislative Studies Quarterly* 25 (February): 131–46.

Squire, Peverill, and Keith E. Hamm. 2005. *101 Chambers: Congress, State Legislatures, and the Future of Legislative Studies.* Ohio State University Press.

Stanley, Harold W., and Richard G. Niemi. 2005. *Vital Statistics on American Politics.* Washington: CQ Press.

Weber, Ronald E., Harvey J. Tucker, and Paul Brace. 1991. "Vanishing Marginals in State Legislative Elections." *Legislative Studies Quarterly* 16 (February): 29–47.

4   The Decline of Competition in U.S. Primary Elections, 1908–2004

Stephen Ansolabehere, John Mark Hansen,
Shigeo Hirano, and James M. Snyder Jr.

A hallmark of elections in the United States is a two-stage electoral process. Candidates running under the standard of one of the major political parties must first win the party's endorsement in a primary election. Very few other countries use party plebiscites to nominate their candidates, but the United States has employed primary elections widely for nearly 100 years.[1] The primary system is relatively new in U.S. presidential elections, in which a majority of delegates were chosen by state conventions and caucuses until the 1970s. For other state and federal offices, however, almost all states have used primary elections to nominate candidates for the general election since the early decades of the twentieth century.

From their inception, primary elections have been seen as an important vehicle for political competition in the United States. Progressive reformers at the turn of the last century pushed the primary election as a way to undercut the power of local and state political machines and as a way to bring into the parties fresh candidates, new ideas, and organized constituencies, such as unions. Competition in primaries is potentially much more fluid, volatile,

---

1. See Carey and Polga-Hecimovich (2004) for a discussion of primary elections in Latin America.

and intense than competition in general elections. Unlike in general elections, the main political parties do not exert oligopoly control over access to the ballot and do not structure the choices of voters through well-established brand names. Rather, any candidate who can secure sufficient numbers of signatures or pay the appropriate filing fee can get on the ballot.[2]

Current thinking among political scientists supports the reformers' conjectures that primary elections offer an effective second electoral screen. Anthony King argues that primary elections make all candidates in the United States excessively concerned with winning elections.[3] They are, he contends, always at risk either from a challenger of the opposing party or from a challenger within their own party. Morris Fiorina, Samuel Abrams, and Jeremy Pope argue that primary elections are an important force in polarizing elite discourse in the United States. In order to get through the primary round, Democratic candidates must first run to the left and Republicans to the right.[4] John Zaller, likening politicians to pugilists, suggests that the two-round electoral system in the United States naturally selects a certain type of politician. Like boxers who must win successive fights to move up in their rankings, he argues, politicians must win successive elections to gain seniority and political power.[5] Primary elections have doubled the electoral scrutiny a typical American politician must endure, with the result that American politicians face more electoral battles than any other politicians in the world.

These accounts imagine robust primary election competition in the United States. Surprisingly, however, not much is known about primary election competition in the United States. Most research has focused on the dynamics of presidential primaries (for example, Aldrich 1980; Bartels, 1988). A handful of papers have considered the levels of primary election competition in recent U.S. House and gubernatorial elections.[6] As a general account of primary election competition, though, these studies are limited by the offices examined and by the period studied. We know little about how competition in primary elections has varied across offices and how competition has varied over time.

2. These requirements have only lessened since the 1970s, after the Supreme Court held high fees unconstitutional in two cases, *Williams* v. *Rhodes*, 393 U.S. 23 (1968) and *Jenness* v. *Fortson*, 403 U.S. 431 (1971).

3. See King (1997).

4. See Fiorina, Abrams, and Pope (2004). There is some debate in the literature concerning the differences between primary and general election electorates in the United States and how they affect candidate selection. See Ranney (1968); Polsby (1983); Crotty and Jackson (1985); Geer (1988); Kaufmann, Gimpel, and Hoffman (2003); and Abramowitz (1989).

5. See Zaller (1998).

6. See, for example, Berry and Canon (1993); Schantz (1980).

In addition to opening up the party process, a second important rationale for introducing direct primary elections was to inject political contestation into areas that lacked competition in general elections. Reformers expected primary competition to be most salient in the many states and locales dominated by one political party. As a result, the use of primary elections would increase the overall amount of competition for any given office.

The claim that primaries may be an alternative to party competition has traditionally been supported by evidence from the Democratic-dominated South.[7] Several studies provide evidence that primaries are more likely to be contested in electorally "safe" rather than competitive areas.[8] In this view, competition in primaries and competition in general elections substitute for each other: the one increases as the other declines.

The view that primaries offer an alternative to party competition does not seem to travel well outside the South. Primaries are most competitive in open-seat elections and least competitive when incumbents are present.[9] Julius Turner writes, "The comparative usefulness of the primary as a method for selecting successors for retiring incumbents does not offset the fact that the primary is not a successful alternative to two-party competition in most parts of the United States."[10] This suggests that primaries have a limited role in holding representatives accountable for their behavior in office.

The threat of primary competition might be enough to improve representation by incumbents, and open-seat races might be sufficient to select "good types." Few democratic theorists argue that latent or infrequent competition is enough for a healthy democracy.[11] Analytical models of competition suggest that the threat of entry might lead to inferior social and political outcomes as it pulls parties away from the median, and recent empirical work suggests that competition per se (not contestability) in elections produces more optimal policies resulting in higher growth.[12]

---

7. Key (1954); Jewell (1967); Ewing (1953).

8. See, for example, Key (1956); Grau (1981); Jewell and Olson (1982).

9. Schantz (1980); Grau (1981); Hogan (2003).

10. Turner (1953, p. 210). Jewell and Breaux (1991, p. 142) state that "Students of primary competition have often argued that it is likely to be more intense where the party's chances of winning the general election are greatest. . . . The fact that we have found such a high proportion of incumbents having no opposition in either election suggests that this theory does not work perfectly."

11. Ware (1987), for example, concludes with most others that competition is desirable. An exception is Sartori (1976), who argues that there can be too much competition and that contestability is sufficient.

12. Besley, Persson, and Sturm (2005).

A separate literature argues the exact contrary, that primary and general election competition should be positively correlated. Candidates who face primary competition are likely also to face more stringent competition in the general election. At the level of individual races, some contend, contested primaries wound nominees and make closely fought November elections more likely.[13] At the level of the political system, moreover, primary competition and general election competition are two parts of the same phenomenon. Daniel Elazar, for example, argues that state political cultures create conditions that either facilitate or retard competition in all elections.[14] Seymour Martin Lipset and Stein Rokkan's classic study of social diversity and political competition also suggests a positive correlation.[15] Polities with more diversity, they argue, are bound to have more competition throughout the political system. The evidence for a positive correlation between primary and general election competition, like the evidence for a negative correlation, is mixed.[16]

All told, then, most research holds that primary and general election competition should be correlated. There is, however, considerable disagreement about whether the correlation should be negative or positive, and the evidence is at best conflicting, or limited to a particular time or region.

Here we examine the effectiveness of primaries as instruments for electoral competition. First, we ask, how much competition exists in primaries, and how has that changed over time? Second, how much do primary elections contribute to the quantity of electoral competition, and specifically are primaries a substitute or a complement for general election competition? To examine these questions, we document the changes in primary and general election competitiveness in all U.S. states throughout the twentieth century. To our knowledge, there are no previous studies that examine primary competition in all states for so many elective offices and over such a long period of U.S. history. We are able to do this using a new data set of statewide and federal primary election returns that extends back to the initial primary elections in each state.

---

13. Born (1981) and others argue the general election competition can affect the degree to which primaries will be competitive.

14. Elazar (1966).

15. Lipset and Rokkan (1967).

16. See Born (1981); Bernstein (1977); Hacker (1965); Herrnson and Gimpel (1995); Jewell and Olson (1978); Johnson and Gibson (1974); Kenney and Rice (1984); Lengle (1980); Piereson and Smith (1975). Further complications arise with the form of the primary election. Whether there exists such a positive correlation may depend on the use of run-off elections (see Canon 1978; Berry and Canon 1993) or multimember districts (Jewell and Breaux 1991), or the use of preprimary endorsing conventions.

Data and Measures

American state and federal primary elections have been rarely studied owing to the elusiveness of the data. Most of the data available in state reports have not been compiled. In some states, especially before the 1950s, primary election returns are available only from newspaper reports because the primaries in those states were treated as activities of private clubs and thus not part of the official state election process. Several projects over the years have assembled parts of the whole picture. Richard Scammon and Ben Wattenberg's *America Votes* provides primary election returns for governor, U.S. House, U.S. Senate, and president from 1956 to the present. Several studies have examined trends in primary election competition for just one of these offices.[17]

We have compiled the primary and general election returns for all statewide offices and for the U.S. House and Senate from 1900 to 2004 using official state election reports, state manuals, newspapers, and almanacs.[18] We measure electoral competition using three sets of statistics: the fraction of contested races, the defeat rate of incumbents, and the division of the vote. In general elections, the division of the vote is the share of the two-party vote won by the Democrats. This quantity itself consists of the underlying partisan division of the state, or normal vote; the personal votes of candidates, including incumbency advantages and challenger quality; national party tides, which take the form of year effects; and idiosyncratic variation.[19]

General election competition may be considered broadly or strictly in partisan terms. The absolute value of the Democratic share of the two-party vote that deviated from 0.5 captures the broadest sense of competitiveness. When considering the competitiveness of states we classify elections as being either competitive or firmly aligned with one party. We classify states in a given year as competitive if the average Democratic share of the two-party vote across all statewide offices is between 60 and 40 percent for the ten-year period before

17. On the U.S. House see Alford and Arceneaux (2000) and Gerber and Morton (1998); on the U.S. Senate see Westlye (1991); on governors see Berry and Canon (1993); on state representatives see Grau (1981).

18. The sources for individual states are listed in appendix table 4A-1. Data on general election competition in statewide elections come from the MIT State Elections Database. For further information on and discussion of the general election data, see Ansolabehere and Snyder (2002).

19. See Ansolabehere and Snyder (2002) for a decomposition along these lines.

and including the year of interest.[20] Alternatively, one might use a narrower interval of between 55 and 45 percent of the vote. Using a narrower interval did not affect our results. We prefer the wider interval because it reflects the argument of Anthony King and others that even an officeholder with a comfortable margin of support may not be or feel safe in an election.

Measuring primary election competition raises several additional issues. As with general elections, turnover occurs primarily when incumbents lose. One complication emerges when one considers the number of contestants. As in general elections, in party primaries incumbents can stand for renomination without facing opposition. It is also possible that no one runs in the primary for the nomination of the opposing party; that is, many primaries have zero candidates. We classify primaries in which one candidate runs or in which no candidate runs as uncontested. The modal primary is uncontested. The inclusion of "empty" primaries uncontested by any candidate has no substantive effect on our analysis. The same conclusions hold for primaries entered by only one candidate.

Other primaries involve more than two candidates. In Oklahoma, for example, the average number of candidates running in the Democratic gubernatorial primary over the past 100 years is just over seven. The varying numbers of primary election candidates mean that the "two-candidate" vote share is not a natural measure of the closeness of the election. Orienting the data to measure the "normal vote" proves particularly difficult in primary elections, even if all of the races involved just two candidates. Researchers cannot identify the ideological position or factional identification of each candidate using aggregate election data alone.

We have experimented with various measures of electoral competitiveness, such as the winning candidates' share of all votes, the difference between the top two candidates' vote shares, the winner's share of the top two candidates' votes, and the incumbents' share of the vote. All track each other closely, as we discuss in the next section. In analyzing the relationship between general and primary election competition, we classify as competitive those races where the winner received less than 60 percent of the total votes cast.

20. Rising incumbency advantages might make party competition seem less intense. A more precise estimate of partisan competition, then, subtracts out the estimated incumbency effect, which equals the expected share of the two-party vote in the absence of an incumbent. The results provided here are qualitatively similar using the definition of competition that does not include incumbency effects.

Trends in Primary Election Competition

Primary elections in the United States rose out of two distinct historical conditions. In the South, primaries were integral to the constellation of electoral rules and institutions designed to disenfranchise African Americans and to sustain the solid Democratic Party hold on the states of the former Confederacy. Most southern states prohibited African Americans, often explicitly, from voting in primaries. And given the Democrats' advantage in the general election, the Democratic nomination was tantamount to election. Within the Democratic primaries, though, historians and political scientists describe robust competition, with shifting factions, coalitions of convenience, and political machines built around personalities, families, and friends and neighbors.[21]

Outside the South, primary elections were the cornerstone of Progressive reforms. States that adopted the direct primary early, such as Wisconsin, California, and North Dakota, were strongholds of the Progressive movement within the Republican Party.[22] (The package of political reforms called the "Wisconsin idea," including the direct primary, was the handiwork of Progressive Republican senator Robert M. LaFollette.) The direct primary, its advocates argued, promised to turn out of office politicians long out of touch with the typical voter and to renew the Republican Party with a healthy dose of competition. In the South too, Progressives called for direct primaries as a means of weakening the hold of particular factions or organizations over state politics. Where the target of reform in the North was the business plutocracy and immigrant machines, in the South the target was courthouse cliques and plantation bosses.

Figures 4-1 and 4-2 display the history of primary electoral competition in the North and South, respectively. Throughout this article, we refer to the Northeast, Midwest, and West as the North. To be sure, there are interesting differences among these regions, such as the strength of Progressivism in the Midwest and West but not in the Northeast. But these differences pale in comparison with the distinctiveness of the South from the rest of American political culture. Each figure contains four panels, corresponding to four dif-

---

21. See Key (1949).

22. Primary elections of other kinds antedate the Progressive reforms. In the nineteenth century, some states allowed and a few required parties to conduct "indirect primaries" to elect delegates to party caucuses or conventions. The hallmark of the Progressive program was direct primaries to decide nominations by a plebiscite of party voters. For a history, see Merriam and Overacker (1928).

ferent measures of competition: the fraction of races with no competition, 1 minus the winner's vote share, the fraction of races in which the winner received less than 60 percent of the vote, and the fraction of incumbents who lost. The winner's vote share is the vote share of the total vote but excludes those winners who ran unopposed. The fraction of races in which the winner received less than 60 percent of the total vote includes the uncontested races. The figures also distinguish between races including incumbents and races for open seats. We classify both parties' primaries as incumbent-versus-challenger races if there was an incumbent running in either party's primary.

The northern, midwestern, and western states showed a modest amount of electoral competition in primaries in the 1910s and 1920s, and a steady decline in primary election competition over the succeeding decades. Given the rapid adoption of this reform and the expectations of the early advocates, we expected more competition in the early primaries. But in fact, between 40 to 50 percent of all primary elections in the northern states were *uncontested* during the early decades of the twentieth century. Competition spiked briefly during the decade of the New Deal, as both parties repositioned themselves, but then the chronic lack of contestation returned. Over the entire course of their history the northern states have sustained rates of uncontested primaries of around 60 percent.

Among the contested primaries, the winners' vote share further illustrates the decline in primary competition. In the 1910s through the 1930s, the primary election winner received less than 60 percent of the vote in 35 percent of the elections. The typical winner in this early period captured around 55 percent of the vote. After 1940, though, competition steadily eroded. By the 1990s, primary winners won less than 60 percent of the vote only 20 percent of the time, and the average winner's vote share rose to over 60 percent of the vote.

Incumbents rarely lost a primary election, even in the early period. During the Progressive era, incumbents lost less than 3.5 percent of their primary elections. This fraction dropped to about 1 percent in the 1950s and has stayed at about 1 percent ever since.

Figure 4-2 illustrates the pattern of primary competition in southern states. During the first decades of the twentieth century, primary elections were more competitive in the South than in the North. Candidates ran without primary opposition in around 35 percent of the primary races, much less often than incumbents ran unopposed in the North, Midwest, and West.

Winners' vote shares and incumbents' reelection rates provide further evidence that primary elections were more competitive in the South than the North during the first decades of the twentieth century. In this period, the

Figure 4-1. Trends in Competition and Contestation in Northern States

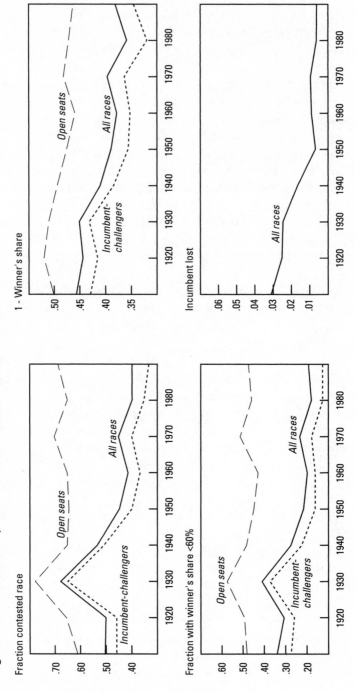

Figure 4-2. Trends in Competition and Contestation in Southern States

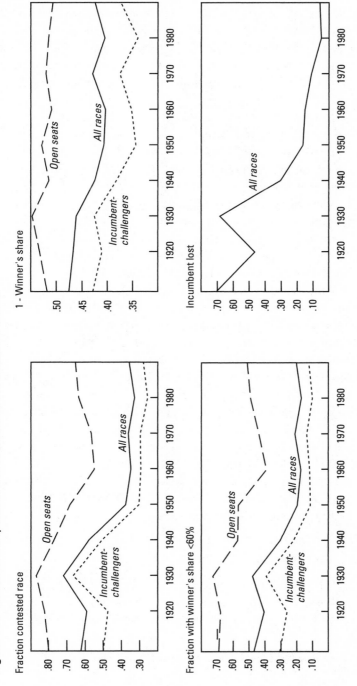

winners in roughly half of the primary elections received less than 60 percent of the vote. The winning candidate's vote share on average was less than 55 percent. Incumbents had less security in primaries in the South, with more than 5 percent of incumbents turned out of office during the early period.

The Supreme Court cracked open this closed world of southern politics in a series of cases from the 1920s into the 1940s, especially *Nixon v. Herndon*, *United States v. Classic*, and *Smith v. Allright*.[23] In the final chapter of *Southern Politics*, V. O. Key wondered aloud what the South would look like after the 1944 decision in *Smith v. Allright* effectively ended the white primary.

Our data reveal what occurred next. After 1940, southern primaries rapidly became less competitive, to the point that competition in southern primaries strongly resembled competition—or lack of it—in northern primaries. The number of uncontested primaries rose dramatically, and by the 1990s, less than 60 percent of southern primaries were contested. The average vote share of winners topped 55 percent, and the winner received more than 60 percent of the vote in more than 80 percent of the elections. Furthermore, less than 1 percent of incumbents failed to win renomination in a primary election.

Over the course of a century, then, the competitiveness of primary elections across the regions of the country has converged. The North showed modest levels of primary competition in the 1910s and 1920s, and very little incumbent turnover. The South, by contrast, began the twentieth century with relatively high levels of primary election competition. Today, however, the North and the South hardly differ. This pattern, interestingly, mirrors the trends in general election competition. The South began the twentieth century under the domination of a single party, the Democrats. The West and the Midwest had more interparty competition, but the Republicans dominated many states, especially in New England. Over the course of the twentieth century, general elections in all states became increasingly competitive. Just as the regions have converged in their levels of general election competition, so have they converged in their levels of primary election competition.

Primary and General Election Competition

How has the decline of primary election competition affected the overall level of electoral competition in the United States? The answer depends in part on the relationship between primary and general election competition.

---

23. *Nixon v. Herndon*, 273 U.S. 536 (1927); *United States v. Classic*, 313 U.S. 299 (1941); *Smith v. Allright*, 321 U.S. 649 (1944).

To illustrate how the impact of declining primary competition on overall competition may depend on the distribution of primary and general election competition, we can consider a highly stylized situation with three types of general elections. Suppose that in a given election one-third of the seats are safe Democratic, one-third are safe Republican, and one-third are competitive. In a competitive race, the candidates from both parties have an equal chance of winning the general election.

One possible distribution of primary election competition is that the seats that are competitive in the primaries are also competitive in the general elections. In this case, declining primary election competition by itself would not alter the overall competitiveness of the system. The competitive seats would remain highly competitive in both the primary election and the general election, and the safe seats would remain uncompetitive in both the primary and general elections.

A second possibility is that primary election competition substitutes for general election competition: the safe Democratic and Republican seats have stiff primary election competition, while the candidates in the seats with intense general election competition face no challenges in the primary elections. In this scenario, if primary election competition declines without a compensating increase in general election competition, then roughly two-thirds of the elections (primary plus general) that were competitive become uncompetitive. This, of course, is an extreme version of the argument put forward by V. O. Key and tested by Julius Turner using U.S. House data from the 1940s.[24]

These hypothetical cases highlight the possibility that declining primary election competition has either substantially reduced the competitiveness of the electoral system in the United States (the second case) or has had little practical consequence (the first case). Of course, the real world does not look like either of these circumstances. It is a mix of these idealized examples. But these hypothetical situations do depict a version of the world that has considerable currency (Key's hypothesis), and they do help to focus the empirical question of interest: What is the empirical relationship between primary and general election competition?

To address this question we classified primary elections as competitive or not and general elections as competitive or not. We use whether a candidate wins less than 60 percent of the vote in a given race as our measure of com-

24. See Key (1949) and Turner (1953).

petitive elections.[25] The classification of primary and general elections as competitive, in turn, yields four different cases: (1) competitive primary election and competitive general election, (2) competitive primary election but uncompetitive general election, (3) uncompetitive primary election but competitive general election, and (4) uncompetitive primary election and uncompetitive general election. We then computed the fraction of *officeholders* whose races fell into each of these categories. This procedure, of course, omits the amount of competition in the party of the general election loser. We follow the literature in examining the electoral test that the officeholders faced. Including the primary election competition of the party that did not win the seat inflates the number of elections in which there is no primary election competition by introducing a large number of cases in which no primary was held (for example, the southern Republican Party did not regularly hold primaries during the first half of the century).[26]

Table 4-1 presents the proportion of elections in each of the four categories listed above. We present the statewide elections (including U.S. Senate) and U.S. House races separately, as these offices show different levels of competition but similar trends. To simplify the presentation of time trends we divided the twentieth century into three periods: (1) 1910–38, (2) 1940–58, and (3) 1960–2000. These correspond roughly to the Progressive era and the years of the "Solid South," the years of transition in the South, and the current era of high incumbency advantages and established voting rights.[27]

There are two quantities of particular interest in table 4-1. The first is an indicator of the overall competitiveness of the system, which can be measured by the fraction of races in which the winner received in excess of 60 percent of the vote in the primary and the general election (case 4 above). The second is an indicator of the importance of primary elections per se, which can be measured by the fraction of elections in which the winner received less than 60 percent of the vote in the primary but more than 60 percent of the vote in the general election (case 2 above). This is the case in which the primaries were competitive even though the general elections were not.

25. We have examined other thresholds for competitiveness (for example, 55 percent and 65 percent), and the patterns are similar. We have also considered raw correlations in vote shares. However, owing to the very large number of uncontested races, these correlations are sensitive to missing data.

26. The patterns of electoral competition do not change significantly when the primaries of those who did not win the primary election are included.

27. See Aldrich and Niemi (1996) on the last era.

Table 4-1. Primary versus General Election Competition in Statewide and U.S. House Elections, 1910–2000

	Statewide offices					
	1910–38		1940–58		1960–2000	
All seats	Competitive primary election					
Competitive general election	No	Yes	No	Yes	No	Yes
No	26.8[a]	24.5	33.2	16.6	33.1	7.7
	(794)[b]	(728)	(795)	(397)	(1,252)	(292)
Yes	22.9	25.8	32.2	18.0	42.1	17.1
	(679)	(765)	(770)	(431)	(1,590)	(644)
	$X^2 = 7.85$		$X^2 = 1.76$		$X^2 = 48.16$	
	$(p = .01)$		$(p = .18)$		$(p = .00)$	
	U.S. House elections					
	1910–38		1940–58		1960–2000	
	Competitive primary election					
Competitive general election	No	Yes	No	Yes	No	Yes
No	39.3	12.2	49.7	8.6	63.7	4.7
	(1,005)	(313)	(1,302)	(225)	(6,233)	(460)
Yes	31.9	16.6	33.9	7.8	25.3	6.3
	(816)	(425)	(888)	(204)	(2,476)	(613)
	$X^2 = 34.33$		$X^2 = 7.24$		$X^2 = 364.16$	
	$(p = .00)$		$(p = .01)$		$(p = .00)$	

Source: Data compiled by authors.
a. Percent.
b. Number of races.

Table 4-1 illustrates a familiar story of steady decline in the overall level of competition in U.S. elections. In statewide elections the fraction of races in which the winner captured better than 60 percent of the vote in both stages of the election rose from 26 percent to 33 percent—a 7 percentage point drop in this measure of the overall level of competitiveness. In U.S. House elections competition plummeted over the course of the twentieth century. From 1900 to 1938, 39 percent of House candidates won their seats with more than 60 percent of the vote in both the primary and general elections. From 1960 to 2000, 64 percent of House candidates cleared the 60 percent mark in both elections.

Is declining primary election competition per se to blame? The fraction of cases in which the primary election was competitive but the general election was not suggests that the primaries contributed to the decline. However, the differing patterns in primary competition for statewide and U.S. House offices also suggest that the overall decline in electoral competition cannot simply be determined by the decline in primary election competition.

Primary competition did contribute to the higher level of competition in the early period from 1910 to 1938. In the primary elections for statewide offices, 25 percent of the winners faced competition in the primaries but not the general elections in the early period. Similarly in the primary elections for the House, 12 percent of winners faced competition only in the primaries during this period.

The drop in primary competition in statewide elections far exceeds the drop in overall competition. The fraction of races without serious competition rose 7 percentage points, from 26 percent to 33 percent, as noted above. However, the change in the fraction of races in which there was a competitive primary but an uncompetitive general election far exceeds the decline in the overall level. The fraction of statewide officeholders who only faced primary competition dropped from 25 percent in the first period, to 17 percentage points in the 1940s to 1950s, to just 8 percent in the final decades of the century.

In contrast, for U.S. House elections the drop in primary competition can account for only a small fraction of the drop in overall competition. Over the course of the twentieth century, the fraction of U.S. House candidates facing competition in at least one stage of the process dropped from 61 percent to 36 percent. During this period, the fraction of House members who faced a serious primary challenge but no general election challenge dropped from 13 percent to 5 percent. The fraction of House members who faced significant competition fell by 25 percentage points, but the drop in competitive House primaries can account for, at most, only an 8 percentage point decline.

The difference between statewide and House elections suggests that changes in the overall level of competition cannot be explained simply by the decline in primary competition. In the statewide elections, decreasing primary competition was offset by increasing general election competition. In the House elections, decreasing general election competition far exceeded the decline in primary election competition.

The declines in competitiveness in both primary and general elections for the House and the fall in competitiveness in primaries coupled with the rise in competitiveness in general elections for statewide offices suggests a possible connection between primary and general election competition. We wondered whether there was any evidence that primary and general election competition are correlated, or that general election competition increases when primary election declines. Or do these factors operate independently?

The data suggest that primary and general election competition are largely independent, at least within periods. The change in overall competition appears to stem from changes in the marginal distributions of primary and general election competition, rather than a substitution between primary and general election competition.

Consider again the statewide races. In the first period, roughly half of all primary elections are classified as competitive, and 51 percent of all general elections are classified as competitive. The hypothesis that primary and general election competition are substitutes predicts that the joint distribution of these two variables deviates from what is predicted under independence. Under independence we would expect roughly one-quarter of all cases in the first period to fall into each category of competition. The fraction of observed cases differed from levels predicted under independence by only about 1 percentage point in each category of competition. Although the chi-squared test rejects the statistical independence of the two variables, which is not surprising given the large number of cases, the observed distribution is substantively very close to what we would expect if primary and general election competition were independent.

A similar pattern of independence between statewide primary and general election competition appears in the 1940 to 1958 period and the 1960 to 2000 period. The observed levels of competition differ from those predicted under independence by less than 3 percentage points in each of the four categories in both periods. In the second period the chi-squared test even fails to reject the null hypothesis of independence despite the large number of cases.

The rise in the number of elections in which there was only a competitive general election and the fall in the number of elections in which there was only a competitive primary is consistent with what we would expect if the changes in primary and general election competition were independent. This finding matches prior studies, which have found little relationship between primary and general election competition.[28] We find that in statewide elections the two do not appear to act as substitutes over the very long run of the twentieth century.

What did change was the incidence of general and primary election competition. In statewide elections, primary election competition fell over the course of the past century, while general election competition rose. In the first decades of the century, half of all general and primary elections for statewide office were competitive. By the end of the century, the fraction of

28. See, for example, Turner (1953).

competitive general elections for statewide office rose to 59 percent and the fraction of competitive primary elections dropped to just 25 percent. These appear to operate independently (at least in the aggregate), and the separate changes in the marginal distributions of primary and general election competition for statewide office are sufficient to explain the change observed in the patterns of competition. Because primary election competition declined and general election competition rose, the fraction of cases in which primary elections were the only screen plummeted, the fraction of cases in which general elections were the only electoral screen surged, and the overall level of competition dropped somewhat. Declining primary election competition in statewide elections thus did not alter the overall level of competition much, but it did sharply reduce the role of primaries in generating that competition.

In U.S. House elections, we confront a different puzzle. At first glance it appears that declining primary competition contributed little to the decline of competition in U.S. House elections. But in fact, competition in elections to the House tracks the same pattern as competition in elections to statewide offices, albeit with a much lower starting level of primary competition and a decrease in general election competition. As in the statewide offices, primary and general election competition for the House are not strongly correlated. Consider the first period in table 4-1. Roughly half of all House members won their seats in competitive general elections from 1900 to 1938, but just under 30 percent faced a serious primary election challenge. If primaries and general elections operate independently, then we would expect 14 percent of all House members to have won less than 60 percent of the primary and general election vote; 15 percent to have won less than 60 percent in the primary but more than 60 percent in the general; 35 percent to have won less than 60 percent in the general but more than 60 percent in the primary; and 37 percent to have won more than 60 percent in both rounds. As in the statewide offices, the observed fraction of cases for each category of competition deviates from the fraction predicted under independence by less than 3 percentage points. Similar calculations for the 1940 to 1958 and the 1960 to 2004 periods yield similar conclusions. Although the marginal distributions had changed, the joint distribution of primary and general election competition appears consistent with the notion that the two variables operate independently.

In short, the changing patterns of competition in House elections are likely to be attributed to independent changes in the rates of general and primary election competition. The aggregate rate of competitive primaries fell from 29 percent to 11 percent of all House races. General election competition declined as well. These two forces yielded a dramatic decline in overall

competition in U.S. House elections. Competition for statewide offices followed a different trajectory than competition for the U.S. House because of
the increase in general election competition for senator, governor, and other
state executive offices. Had House elections witnessed a rise in general election competition comparable to the rise in statewide elections, a very different pattern would have emerged. Suppose the fraction of U.S. House seats
won by less than 60 percent in the general election equaled the statewide figure of 59 percent, instead of 32 percent. In that case, the changes in patterns
of competition for the House would have resembled the pattern in competition for statewide offices. Fifty-three percent of House candidates would have
won in competitive general elections and uncompetitive primary elections.
The different patterns of changes in primary and general election competition in elections for the House and for statewide offices can be attributed
entirely to different trajectories in *general* election competition.

Three conclusions are abundantly clear from this analysis. First, primaries
once often served an important screening role, but now they very rarely do.
From 1900 to 1938, one-quarter of all statewide officers and one-eighth of all
House members faced only primary competition. By the last part of the century, from 1960 to 2000, primary competition affected just one in twelve in the
statewide offices and only one in twenty in the House. Second, the overall competitiveness of the electoral system has fallen. Only one-third of all statewide
officeholders win with at least 60 percent of the vote in both the general and
primary elections, while just under two-thirds of all House candidates face no
serious general or primary competition. Third, primary and general election
competition appear to make relatively independent contributions to the total
level of competition in U.S. elections. Primary and general election competition
do not act as substitutes. The declining rate of primary election competition
meant that primaries served much less as a screen. Whether they also contributed to declining rates of overall competition depended on changes in general election competition. Where general election competition increased, overall competition changed only modestly. Where general election competition
also fell, as in elections for the House, the drop in primary election competition
contributed to a dramatic drop in the total amount of electoral competition.

Incumbents and Parties

A puzzle emerges from table 4-1. Why did general election competition
strengthen in statewide elections but weaken in House elections? Primaries
show less competition across the board, but the differential trends in general

election competition suggest two very different electoral systems at work—one at the level of U.S. House districts and the other at the level of the state. In addition, these distinct trends raise the possibility that there may be a strong connection between primary and general election competition that is masked by some other important factor—whatever explains the differential trends in general election competition over the 100-year span.

Two obvious suspects identified by the literature on political competition in the United States are incumbency and party. Andrew Gelman and Gary King, Steven Levitt and Catherine Wolfram, and others document a large increase in the incumbency advantage in U.S. House elections beginning in the late 1950s or early 1960s.[29] Stephen Ansolabehere and James Snyder document a substantial rise in the incumbency advantages in all statewide offices, as well as a clear narrowing of the party divisions within states.[30] In the analysis in table 4-1, we combined open and incumbent-contested seats, and we did not control for the underlying party division within the states.

Table 4-2 isolates the effects of incumbency. For statewide and U.S. House races, we present the competitiveness of primary and general elections over time in incumbent-contested and open seats. We use the same measure of competitiveness as in table 4-1.

The data summarized in table 4-2 reveal that incumbency was not likely to have masked an underlying correlation between primary and general election competition. For each period and for each type of election (such as open, statewide), we computed the expected results under the hypothesis that the variables are independent. As in the foregoing analysis, in no category of competition in table 4-2 did the fraction of cases we would expect under independence differ from the fraction of cases observed by more than 3 percentage points. More than half of the chi-squared tests cannot reject the null hypothesis of independence at the 1 percent significance level.

The evidence in table 4-2 also suggests that the differential trends in competition in statewide and House elections are attributable to incumbency. In both sorts of elections, incumbents enjoyed rising electoral security in the general elections, but the fraction of all races contested by incumbents was much lower in statewide elections than in House elections.

Consider, first, the open-seat races. These serve as a baseline against which to contrast the races contested by incumbents. Open-seat races show relatively little change or even growing competitiveness. In open-seat races for

29. See, for example, Gelman and King (1990) and Levitt and Wolfram (1997).
30. See Ansolabehere and Snyder (2002).

Table 4-2. Primary versus General Election Competition, Controlling for Incumbency in Statewide and House Elections, 1910–2000

	Statewide offices					
	1910–38		1940–58		1960–2000	
Open seats	Competitive primary election					
Competitive general election	No	Yes	No	Yes	No	Yes
No	17.7[a]	32.9	18.3	26.0	13.0	15.5
	(201)[b]	(201)	(135)	(192)	(155)	(184)
Yes	16.7	32.8	24.9	30.9	37.9	33.6
	(189)	(372)	(184)	(228)	(450)	(400)
	$X^2 = 0.22$		$X^2 = 0.85$		$X^2 = 5.05$	
	$(p = .64)$		$(p = .36)$		$(p = .03)$	

	U.S. House elections					
	1910–38		1940–58		1960–2000	
Incumbent versus challenger	Competitive primary election					
Competitive general election	No	Yes	No	Yes	No	Yes
No	32.4	19.4	39.9	12.4	42.4	4.2
	(593)	(355)	(660)	(205)	(1,097)	(108)
Yes	26.8	21.5	35.4	12.3	44.0	9.4
	(490)	(393)	(586)	(203)	(1,140)	(244)
	$X^2 = 9.43$		$X^2 = 0.91$		$X^2 = 41.19$	
	$(p = .00)$		$(p = .34)$		$(p = .00)$	

Source: Compiled by authors.
a. Percent.
b. Number of races.

the House, the subtables for the period 1910 to 1938 and for 1960 to 2000 are nearly indistinguishable. In both eras, 12 percent of the winners faced no serious primary or general election competition. There was a slight drop in the fraction of cases in which the winners received less than 60 percent of the vote in both the general and primary elections, but it was substantively unimportant. Statewide races show more change, and in the direction of increased competition. Overall general election competition rose considerably. Half of all open-seat winners received less than 60 percent of the vote in the general election in the first period; 71 percent of all open-seat winners faced serious general election competition in the third period. Primary election competition fell slightly in these seats, and overall competition rose.

Races contested by incumbents show a drop in competition in both statewide and House elections. In statewide elections, the fraction of incumbents who won reelection with at least 60 percent in the primary and general elections rose from 32 percent in the first period to 42 percent in the third period. House elections show a somewhat larger gain. The fraction of incumbents who won reelection with at least 60 percent in the primary and general elections rose from 42 percent in the first period to 69 percent in the third period. Primary election competition fell substantially for both the House and the statewide offices. Competition in statewide general elections did not change appreciably between these periods. House general election competition dropped dramatically. Forty-seven percent of House incumbents won by less than 60 percent of the general election vote through the first half of the twentieth century; just 28 percent did in the second half of the century.

Trends in overall competitiveness mask contrary trends in open seats and incumbent-contested seats. The open seats show little trend, or, in the case of statewide elections, some increase in competition. Incumbent-contested seats, especially in the primary elections, show significant weakening in competitiveness. Statewide elections show a slight increase in competition because half of all statewide offices are selected in open seats, and that fraction rose somewhat over the twentieth century. The higher frequency of open seats in statewide elections traces to one feature of state electoral laws: term limits on most statewide officeholders.[31] U.S. House elections show a significant weakening in competitiveness because 90 percent of all House races are contested by incumbents. That trend dominates in the House series.

Incumbency explains much of the difference in overall competition between House and statewide offices. It does not, however, affect the underlying relationship between primary and general elections. Competition in these two stages appears to operate independently.

These facts suggest that many of the fundamentals in the election system changed little. Open seats are as competitive as ever. Thus the decline in overall competitiveness appears to be a consequence of rising incumbency advantages and a greater number of incumbents running for reelection.[32]

Partisan divisions in the states also changed dramatically over the course of the twentieth century. Southern states shifted from Democratic dominance to strong two-party competition today. Likewise, many northern states that were once dominated by the Republican Party have today also become very competitive. As a final slice at the connection between primary and general election competition, we consider whether the rise of party competition within states correlated with less primary election competition.

31. See Ansolabehere and Snyder (2004).
32. Owing to complicated measurement issues, we consider the growth of the incumbency effect in primary elections in a separate paper.

We classified all states according to their degree of general election competition. To do this, we used the measure of the normal vote produced by the analysis of state election returns, as discussed above. The normal vote for a given state in a given election year is the average general election vote share across all statewide offices for the ten-year period prior to and including the election year of interest. We call states competitive if the normal division of the two-party vote calculated for that year was less than 60 percent or more than 40 percent Democratic. Strongly Democratic states are those where the normal two-party vote exceeds 60 percent, and strongly Republican states are those where the normal two-party vote falls below 40 percent. We coded each party primary election as competitive if the winner received less than 60 percent of the total vote.

Over time, American state elections have become much more competitive. From 1900 to 1938, 49 percent of all statewide officers were elected in states where the normal division of the two-party vote was closer than 60 to 40. From 1962 to 2004, 64 percent of all statewide elections occurred in competitive states.

The change in the competitiveness of states, however, is unlikely to explain the decline in competitiveness of primary elections. Even within the competitive states the fraction of both Republican and Democratic primaries in which the winner's vote share exceeded 60 percent rose by more than 15 percentage points.

The difference between the primary competition for a dominant party in a "safe" state and for that same party in a competitive state is less than 10 percentage points for the Democrats and less than 7 percentage points for the Republicans (see table 4-3). From 1900 to 1938, 52 percent of Republican party primaries were competitive in Republican-dominated states; by contrast 46 percent of Republican primaries were competitive in competitive states. Fifty-one percent of Democratic primaries were competitive in Democratic-dominated states; by comparison, 45 percent of Democratic primaries were competitive in two-party competitive states. From 1940 to 1960, 31 percent of Republican primaries were competitive in Republican-dominated states, 32 percent in the competitive states. In this same period, 39 percent of Democratic primaries were competitive in Democratic-dominated states, 33 percent in the competitive states. From 1962 to 2004, 37 percent of Democratic primaries were competitive in the handful of Democratic-dominated states, 28 percent in the competitive states; the proportion of competitive GOP primaries was virtually the same: 24 percent in Republican states and 27 percent in closely contested states. While the differences between the proportion of

Table 4-3. Primary Competition by Party in U.S. Senate
and Statewide Races, 1908–2004

Period	Democratic primary competitive		Republican primary competitive	
	No	Yes	No	Yes
1908–38				
Democratic states	48.6[a]	51.4	80.9	19.1
	(444)[b]	(469)	(89)	(21)
Competitive states	55.5	44.5	54.3	45.8
	(748)	(599)	(695)	(586)
Republican states	81.4	18.6	48.0	52.0
	(674)	(154)	(417)	(451)
1940–60				
Democratic states	60.6	39.4	88.6	11.4
	(579)	(377)	(364)	(47)
Competitive states	67.3	32.7	69.0	31.0
	(755)	(367)	(778)	(350)
Republican states	80.2	19.8	67.6	32.4
	(276)	(68)	(240)	(115)
1962–2004				
Democratic states	62.9	37.1	88.2	11.9
	(748)	(442)	(1,093)	(147)
Competitive states	71.9	28.1	75.9	24.1
	(1,853)	(724)	(1,976)	(626)
Republican states	85.2	14.8	73.2	26.8
	(213)	(37)	(180)	(66)

Source: Compiled by authors.
a. Percent.
b. Number of races.

competitive elections in the one- and two-party states are found to be statistically significant using a *t* test, these differences are substantively small.

The partisan balance does have a large and negative effect on the degree of competition in the primaries of the disadvantaged party. In a state dominated by one party, there is much less competition in the out-party's primaries than in the in-party's primaries, and also much less competition than in two-party competitive states. This surely is a disincentive to run in a competitive primary when there is little hope of winning in the general election. Thus, if a one-party state becomes a two-party state, the competitiveness of the formerly subordinate party's primary is likely to increase the competitiveness of the formerly subordinate party's primary. As states become more competitive, greater competitiveness in the out-party's primaries has the potential to offset the decline in competitiveness of the in-party's primaries.

To account for potential differences between states with dominant Democratic parties in the South and states with dominant parties in the North, we also compared electoral competition in one-party and two-party states in the South and the North.[33] Differences in the patterns between the South and North depend on whether Oklahoma is coded as southern or northern. When Oklahoma, which is known to have very competitive primaries, is excluded from the analysis, any substantive difference between the southern and northern states in the trends in one-party and two-party primary competition disappears.

Conclusions

Primary elections in the United States today fall far short of achieving the goal for which they were introduced. Primaries were conceived as a way to open up the parties and increase electoral competition in the United States, and they served as an alternative to general election competition in states that were dominated by one party. According to the simplest indicator, they seem to have served this function at the beginning of the twentieth century. Approximately one in four statewide elections would not have had significant electoral competition during the first four decades of the twentieth century were there no primary elections. However, over the whole century, the screening function of primary elections appears to have weakened dramatically. Today only about 25 percent of statewide candidates face serious primary opposition, and less than 8 percent win after competitive primaries but uncompetitive general elections.

The historical record also suggests that primary elections are not a substitute for general election competition; nor do they reflect different cultures of competition within states. Our expectation at the beginning of this inquiry was that we would find a strong correlation between primary and general election competition and, following Key's seminal work, that this correlation would be negative. However, we have discovered that primary election competition is not associated with general election competition. Rather these appear to operate independently of one another. The weakening primary election screen is not balanced out by more general election competition. The result of declining primary election competition, then, is less competition overall in the U.S. electoral system.

We have, of course, compared primaries today with primaries 100 years ago. We have not compared primaries with caucus and convention nomination systems or the system of rotation. Nineteenth-century nomination politics is

33. These results are available from the authors upon request.

almost completely undocumented. It may be that the very institution of primaries profoundly alters the politics of nominations. We have focused on the politics within one sort of institution—primary elections—which their advocates sought in order to produce a very competitive electoral system in the United States. We have documented the long-term decline in competition in primaries.

It is ultimately a normative matter whether the decline of primary election competition, and the corresponding decline in overall electoral competition, is good or bad. However, the atrophy of primary election competition raises doubts about many theoretical arguments about American politics today. We are skeptical that primary elections can be a major source of polarization in elite discourse in the United States. With so few competitive and contested primaries it is unclear to us why politicians would not be more attentive to the median voter and less attentive to the primary electorates. Also, these findings raise doubts about arguments, such as those of John Zaller and Anthony King, that primary elections contribute to incumbent vulnerability and incumbency advantages. If elections are like single-elimination tournaments, then almost all incumbents draw a bye in the first round. Given the utter lack of competition in primary elections it seems unlikely that incumbents are "running scared" that they might lose the next primary. That being said, the overall decline in competition is driven primarily by incumbency. There has been a slight decline in competition in open seats. There has been a very marked decline in competition when incumbents run.

Finally, we are concerned by the very fact that electoral competition in the United States is waning. Political science takes virtually as given that electoral competition is good. It improves accountability of government and representation; it is the venue for deliberative democracy. It may be that we, as a discipline, are wrong about this conjecture. Careful consideration of why and how electoral competition has declined might help in understanding the conditions under which competition matters. However, it seems more plausible that the conjecture is right—that more competition is usually better. With the decline of primary election competition, Americans have lost an important instrument of electoral accountability.

Appendix Table 4A-1. Elected Offices in Each State

State	Offices elected in one or more years	State	Offices elected in one or more years
Alabama	LG, SS, AG, Tr, Au, E, Ag, PU, Gm	Montana	LG, SS, AG, Tr, Au, E, PU, Ck, J
Alaska[a]		Nebraska	LG, SS, AG, Tr, Au, E, PU, Ld, J
Arizona	SS, AG, Tr, Au, E, Co, M, Tx, J	Nevada	LG, SS, AG, Tr, Au, E, M, Ld, Ck, Pr, Rg, J
Arkansas	LG, SS, AG, Tr, Au, E, Ag, Ld, PU, J	New Hampshire[a]	
California	LG, SS, AG, Tr, Au, E, I, Ld, Pr, Ck, J	New Jersey[a]	
		New Mexico	LG, SS, AG, Tr, Au, E, Ld, Co, J
Colorado	LG, SS, AG, Tr, Au, E, Rg, PU, J	New York	LG, SS, AG, Tr, Au, Ld, J
Connecticut	LG, SS, AG, Tr, Au	North Carolina	LG, SS, AG, Tr, Au, E, Co, Ag, Lb, I, J
Delaware	LG, AG, Tr, Au, I		
Florida	SS, AG, Tr, Au, E, Ag, PU, J	North Dakota	LG, SS, AG, Tr, Au, E, Ag, PU, Lb, I, Tx, J
Georgia	LG, SS, AG, Tr, Au, E, Ag, PU, Lb, I, Pn, J	Ohio	LG, SS, AG, Tr, Au, E, Ag, Ck, PW, J
Hawaii	LG	Oklahoma	LG, SS, AG, Tr, Au, E, Co, Ag, Lb, Ld, I, M, CC, Ck, J
Idaho	LG, SS, AG, Tr, Au, E, M, J		
Illinois	LG, SS, AG, Tr, Au, E, Ck, Rg	Oregon	SS, AG, Tr, E, Ag, PU, Lb, Pr, J
Indiana	LG, SS, AG, Tr, Au, E, Ld, Ck, St, J	Pennsylvania	LG, SS, AG, Tr, Au, J
Iowa	LG, SS, AG, Tr, Au, E, Ag, Cm, Ck, J	Rhode Island	LG, SS, AG, Tr
		South Carolina	LG, SS, AG, Tr, Au, E, Ag, PU, Aj
Kansas	LG, SS, AG, Tr, Au, E, I, PU, Pr, J	South Dakota	LG, SS, AG, Tr, Au, E, PU, Ld, Lb, J
Kentucky	LG, SS, AG, Tr, Au, E, Ag, Ld, Ck	Tennessee	PU, J
Louisiana	LG, SS, AG, Tr, Au, E, I, Ag, Ld, El	Texas	LG, AG, Tr, Au, E, Ag, PU, Ld, J
Maryland	LG, AG, Au, Ck	Utah	LG, SS, AG, Tr, Au, E, J
Maine	Au	Vermont	LG, SS, AG, Tr, Au
Massachusetts	LG, SS, AG, Tr, Au	Virginia	LG, SS, AG, Tr, E, Ag
Michigan	LG, SS, AG, Tr, Au, E, Ag, Ld, Rg, Hy, J	Washington	LG, SS, AG, Tr, Au, E, Ld, I, Pr, J
Minnesota	LG, SS, AG, Tr, Au, PU, Ck, J	West Virginia	SS, AG, Tr, Au, E, Ag, J
Mississippi	LG, SS, AG, Tr, Au, E, Ag, Ld, I, Ck, Tx, J	Wisconsin	LG, SS, AG, Tr, E, PU, I, J
Missouri	LG, SS, AG, Tr, Au, E, PU, J	Wyoming	SS, Tr, Au, E, J

Source: Compiled by authors from state documents and election returns.

a. Governor is the only state-elected officer.

Abbreviations: Ag = Commissioner of Agriculture, Agriculture & Industry, Dairy, etc.; AG = Attorney General; Aj = Adjutant General; Au = Auditor, Controller, Comptroller; CC = Charities & Corrections Commissioner; Ck = Court Clerk, Court Reporter; Cm = Commerce Commissioner; Co = Corporation Commissioner; E = Commissioner of Education, Superintendent of Schools, etc.; El = Elections; Gm = Game Commissioner; Hy = Highway Commissioner; I = Insurance Commissioner; J = Supreme Court Justice, Appeals Court Judge; Lb = Commissioner of Labor; Ld = Land Commissioner, Surveyor, Inspector, Geologist; LG = Lieutenant Governor; M = Commissioner of Mines, Mine Inspector; Pn = Prison Commissioner; Pr = Printer; PU = Public Utility Commissioner, Public Service Commissioner, Railroad Commissioner, Railroad & Public Utility Commissioner, etc.; PW = Board of Public Works; Rg = University Regent, Trustee; SS = Secretary of State; St = Statistician; Tr = Treasurer; Tx = Tax Commissioner, Tax Collector.

References

Abramowitz, Alan I. 1989. "Viability, Electability, and Candidate Choice in a Presidential Primary Election: A Test of Competing Models." *Journal of Politics* 51 (4): 977–92.

Aldrich, John H. 1980. *Before the Convention: Strategies and Choices in Presidential Nomination Campaigns*. University of Chicago Press.

Aldrich, John H., and Richard G. Niemi. 1996. "The Sixth American Party System." In *Broken Contract*, edited by Stephen Craig. Boulder, Colo.: Westview Press.

Alford, John R., and Kevin T. Arceneaux. 2000. "Isolating the Origins of the Incumbency Advantage: An Analysis of House Primaries, 1956–1990." Paper presented at the annual meeting of the Southern Political Science Association.

Ansolabehere, Stephen, and James M. Snyder. 2002. "The Incumbency Advantage in U.S. Elections: An Analysis of State and Federal Offices, 1942–2000." *Election Law Journal* 1: 313–38.

———. 2004. "Using Term Limits to Estimate Incumbency Advantages When Officeholders Retire Strategically." *Legislative Studies Quarterly* 29: 487–515.

Bartels, Larry M. 1988. *Presidential Primaries and the Dynamics of Public Choice*. Princeton University Press.

Bernstein, Robert A. 1977. "Divisive Primaries Do Hurt: U.S. Senate Races, 1956–1972." *American Political Science Review* 71 (2): 540–45.

Berry, William D., and Bradley C. Canon. 1993. "Explaining the Competitiveness of Gubernatorial Primaries." *Journal of Politics* 55 (2): 454–71.

Besley, Timothy, Torsen Persson, and Daniel Sturm. 2005. "Political Competition and Economic Performance: Theory and Evidence from the United States." London School of Economics.

Born, Richard. 1981. "The Influence of House Primary Election Divisiveness on General Election Margins, 1962–76." *Journal of Politics* 43 (3): 640–61.

Canon, Bradley C. 1978. "Factionalism in the South: A Test of Theory and Revisitation of V. O. Key." *American Journal of Political Science* 22: 833–48.

Carey, John M., and John Polga-Hecimovich. 2004. "Primary Elections and Candidate Strength in Latin America." Manuscript. Dartmouth College.

Crotty, William J., and John S. Jackson III. 1985. *Presidential Primaries and Nominations*. Washington: CQ Press.

Elazar, Daniel J. 1966. *American Federalism: A View from the States*. New York: Crowell.

Ewing, Cortez A. M. 1953. *Primary Elections in the South: A Study in Uniparty Politics*. University of Oklahoma Press.

Fiorina, Morris P., Samuel J. Abrams, and Jeremy C. Pope. 2005. *Culture War? The Myth of a Polarized America*. New York: Pearson Longman.

Geer, John G. 1988. "Assessing the Representativeness of Electorates in Presidential Primaries." *American Journal of Political Science* 32 (4): 929–45.

Gelman, Andrew, and Gary King. 1990. "Estimating Incumbency Advantage without Bias." *American Journal of Political Science* 34: 1142–64.

Gerber, Elizabeth R., and Rebecca B. Morton. 1998. "Primary Election Systems and Representation." *Journal of Law, Economics, and Organization* 14 (2): 304–24.

Grau, Craig H. 1981. "Competition in State Legislative Primaries." *Legislative Studies Quarterly* 6 (1): 35–54.

Hacker, Andrew. 1965. "Does a 'Divisive' Primary Harm a Candidate's Election Chances?" *American Political Science Review* 59 (1): 105–10.

Herrnson, Paul S., and James G. Gimpel. 1995. "District Conditions and Primary Divisiveness in Congressional Elections." *Political Research Quarterly* 48 (1): 117–34.

Hogan, Robert E. 2003. "Sources of Competition in State Legislative Primary Elections." *Legislative Studies Quarterly* 28 (1): 103–26

Jewell, Malcolm E. 1967. *Legislative Representation in the Contemporary South.* Duke University Press.

Jewell, Malcolm E., and David Breaux. 1991. "Southern Primary and Electoral Competition and Incumbent Success." *Legislative Studies Quarterly* 14 (1): 129–43.

Jewell, Malcolm E., and David M. Olson. 1978. *American State Political Parties and Elections.* Homewood, Ill.: Dorsey.

Johnson, Donald, and James Gibson. 1974. "The Divisive Primary Revisited." *American Political Science Review* 68: 67–77.

Kaufmann, Karen M., James G. Gimpel, and Adam H. Hoffman. 2003. "A Promise Fulfilled? Open Primaries and Representation." *Journal of Politics* 65 (2): 457–76.

Kenney, Patrick J. 1988. "Sorting Out the Effects of Primary Divisiveness in Congressional and Senatorial Elections." *Western Political Quarterly* 41 (4): 765–77.

Kenney, Patrick J., and Tom W. Rice, "The Relationship between Divisive Primaries and General Election Outcomes." *American Journal of Political Science* 31 (1): 31–44.

Key, V. O. 1949. *Southern Politics.* New York: Vintage Books.

———. 1956. *American State Politics: An Introduction.* New York: Alfred A. Knopf.

King, Anthony S. 1997. *Running Scared: Why America's Politicians Campaign Too Much and Govern Too Little.* New York: Free Press.

Lengle, James I. 1980. "Divisive Presidential Primaries and Party Electoral Prospects 1932–1976." *American Politics Quarterly* 8: 261–77.

Levitt, Steven D., and Catherine D. Wolfram. 1997. "Decomposing the Sources of Incumbency Advantage in the U.S. House." *Legislative Studies Quarterly* 22: 45–60.

Lipset, Seymour Martin, and Stein Rokkan. 1967. "Cleavage Structures, Party Systems, and Voter Alignments: An Introduction." In *Party Systems and Voter Alignments: Cross-National Perspectives,* edited by Seymour Martin Lipset and Stein Rokkan. New York: Free Press.

Merriam, Charles E., and Louise Overacker. 1928. *Primary Elections.* University of Chicago Press.

Piereson, James E., and Terry B. Smith. 1975. "Primary Divisiveness and General Election Success: A Reexamination." *Journal of Politics* 37: 555–62.

Polsby, Nelson W. 1983. *Consequences of Party Reform.* Oxford University Press.

Ranney, Austin. 1968. "Representativeness of Primary Electorates." *Midwest Journal of Political Science* 12: 224–38.

Sartori, Giovanni. 1976. *Parties and Party Systems.* Cambridge University Press.

Schantz, Harvey L. 1980. "Contested and Uncontested Primaries for the U.S. House." *Legislative Studies Quarterly* 5: 545–62.

Turner, Julius. 1953. "Primary Elections as the Alternative to Party Competition in 'Safe' Districts." *Journal of Politics* 15 (2): 197–210.

Ware, Alan. 1987. *Citizens, Parties, and the State.* Princeton University Press.

Westlye, Mark C. 1991. *Senate Elections and Campaign Intensity.* Johns Hopkins University Press.

Zaller, John. 1998. "Politicians as Prize Fighters: Electoral Selection and Incumbency Advantage." In *Politicians and Party Politics,* edited by John G. Geer. Johns Hopkins University Press.

5 Minor-Party Candidates in Congressional Elections

Paul S. Herrnson

Minor-party and independent candidates (hereafter referred to as "minor-party" candidates) face long odds in their bids for public office in the United States. American political institutions, legal arrangements, voter preferences, and the strategic decisions of political elites provide significant barriers to minor-party success. Nevertheless, thousands routinely run for public offices ranging from city councilor to state legislator to U.S. Representative to president. Despite the fact that hundreds of minor-party candidates run for the House every election season, few have succeeded in modern times. Indeed, in recent years only Rep. Bernie Sanders of Vermont successfully first ran as an independent. A few others, such as Rep. Virgil Goode (R-Va.), began their House careers as members of one major party (in this case as a Democrat) and then became independents on their way to joining the other major party.

Given that so many minor-party candidates have run for the House and so few get elected, it makes little sense to assess the impact of minor parties on the legislative process. However, it does seem reasonable to address some questions related to their candidacies and the impact of those candidacies on

I wish to thank James Kelley for assisting me with this research.

the electoral process. Following a short overview of the roles of minor parties in American politics and a discussion of the obstacles minor-party candidates must overcome to compete in elections, I address several questions related to minor-party candidacies for the House. First, which minor parties field the largest number of House candidates? Second, what influences these candidates' decisions to run for the House? Third, what types of campaign strategies do they employ? And finally, what impact did they have on the outcomes of House elections?

The Roles of Minor Parties in American Politics

Minor parties have historically performed many of the same functions as the major parties.[1] These include providing symbols for citizen identification and loyalty, educating and mobilizing voters, selecting and campaigning for candidates, aggregating and articulating interests, raising issues, advocating and helping to formulate public policies, holding opponents accountable for their performance in office, institutionalizing political conflict, and fostering political stability. Of course, minor parties are less adept than major parties at performing many of these roles.

Minor parties also have some important additional roles. They broaden or refocus the political dialogue by raising issues that the two major parties have ignored or kept off the political agenda. They help voters more effectively voice their discontentment with the two major parties and government more generally. By providing alternatives and channeling political frustrations into sanctioned outlets, minor parties loosen the ties that bind voters to the major parties, function as safety valves for the political system, and may pave the way for political realignments.[2]

Minor parties also introduce innovation to political institutions and processes. Because minor parties are born and die with some frequency, they are more prone to experimentation and innovation than are their more stable major-party counterparts. In 1831, for example, the National Republican Party introduced a major change in the presidential selection process when it held the first national nominating convention.[3] During the 1990s, H. Ross Perot's independent candidacy, and the Reform Party it later spawned, aired the first televised political infomercial, held the first national presidential primary, and allowed voters to participate in the primary via the Internet.

1. Parts of this section are drawn from Herrnson (2002).
2. Freie (1982); Burnham (1970); Sundquist (1983).
3. Ranney (1975).

Of course, not every contribution that minor-party candidates make to the political system is positive. The presence of one or more minor-party candidates can make it difficult for voters to hold the major-party candidates in an election accountable for their issue stances or performance in office. This is most likely to be the case in an incumbent-challenger contest where a major-party candidate and one or more minor-party opponents divide the anti-incumbent vote, allowing the incumbent to win with less than a majority of the vote. Also, when a strong minor-party candidate participates in an election, that individual can muddy the waters between the two major-party contestants. That candidate might argue that the Democratic and Republican candidates hold the same positions on the issues, even when there are important differences in their policy stances.

Obstacles to Minor-Party Candidacies

Minor parties work to expand the marketplace of ideas and options presented to citizens. They can drastically alter that marketplace when they replace a major party as one of the dominant parties in the two-party system. Also, through their innovations, minor parties have historically altered some aspects of the operation of that market.[4] Nevertheless, minor parties operate in an environment that is generally hostile to them. Political institutions have had a major role in perpetuating two-party hegemony in the United States.

Perhaps the biggest obstacle to minor parties is the U.S. Constitution. Federalism, the separation of powers, and bicameralism provide a strong foundation for candidate-centered politics and impede party-focused election efforts, especially those of parties that do not enjoy a broad constituent base. To compete in a presidential election, the Electoral College requires a candidate to develop both broad-based and deep support. Few contemporary minor-party nominees are capable of amassing either, and none have proved capable of developing both. Although more minor parties compete in presidential than in congressional elections, these parties' struggles at the top of the ticket do little to help them vie for congressional, state, or local offices. Lacking a competitive national standard-bearer to attract or inspire supporters, minor-party candidates for other offices are rarely able to turn to large networks of donors and activists for campaign support.

Laws that mandate single-member simple-plurality elections also make it very difficult for minor parties to have a widespread impact on elections or

---

4. Ranney (1975).

policymaking.[5] This winner-take-all system deprives any elected offices to candidates or parties that do not place first in an election, even when the party wins a significant share of the vote or many of its candidates run a close second. This is especially harmful to minor parties, which are usually considered successful when one of their candidates is the runner-up. By depriving minor parties of seats in Congress and most other offices, the electoral system discourages these parties' institutional development and growth. Most minor parties in the United States survive for only a relatively short time because of their inability to play a significant role in governing. Some minor parties have prospered in Canada, Great Britain, and a few other countries by developing enough regional strength to win elections at national and subnational levels.

Minor parties also are disadvantaged in that they do not enjoy the institutional recognition afforded to their major counterparts. Such recognition brings important benefits in terms of ballot access. The nominees of the Democratic and Republican parties are automatically placed on the ballot, freeing them to concentrate on raising issues and campaigning for public support. But many minor-party candidates have to overcome substantial hurdles to gain ballot access. In many states, minor-party candidates are granted automatic ballot access only if their party exceeded a threshold of votes in the previous election. Parties that fail to meet that threshold are considered "new" parties, even if they have existed for some time. These parties and independent candidates must meet the requirements set forth by each state to qualify for a place on the ballot. These requirements vary both in substance and in the amount of effort needed to meet them. Three states allow minor-party candidates to pay a filing fee to get on the ballot. Candidates who ran in thirty-seven House districts in 2002 were subject to these requirements (see figure 5-1).

Six states, comprising seventy-five congressional districts, require new minor parties, not candidates, to meet some organizational prerequisites in order for their candidates to qualify for a position on the ballot. Such organizational hurdles can be burdensome because they require the coordinated efforts of many individuals. Mississippi law stipulates a new minor party must hold a single organizational meeting; Vermont law dictates that a new minor party be organized in at least ten towns; and Washington State specifies that a new minor party must hold nominating conventions of at least twenty-five persons in each congressional district.[6] California, Colorado, and

5. Duverger (1954).
6. Winger (2001).

Figure 5-1. Requirements for Ballot Access for New Parties

Number of states or House districts

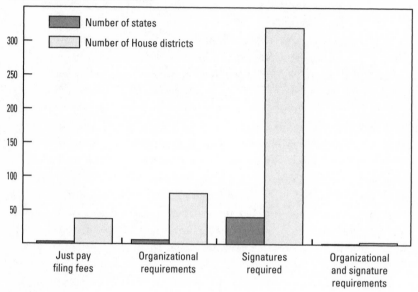

Source: Winger (2001).

Delaware require new minor parties to register some minimum number of citizens as "affiliated" voters (as opposed to independents or voters affiliated with some other party) in order for their candidates to appear on the ballot.

Forty states stipulate that minor-party candidates who are affiliated with a new party must collect signatures in order to be listed on the ballot. There are 300 House seats located in these states. Collecting signatures can be one of the most onerous requirements for achieving ballot access, depending on the number that must be collected. Georgia has the most demanding signature requirements, specifying that a candidate from a new minor party must collect 14,846 signatures in order to qualify to have his or her name appear on the ballot. Tennessee lies at the opposite extreme, requiring candidates affiliated with a new party to gather a mere 300 signatures.[7] In 1996, a minor party needed to pull together more than 1.6 million signatures to place its House candidates on the ballot in all 435 congressional districts.[8] Given that some

7. Winger (2001).
8. Jost (1995).

states base the number of signatures required on the size of their population, independent candidates and minor-party candidates affiliated with a new party who sought to run for the House in 2002 probably had to collect even more signatures. Finally, New Mexico makes it especially challenging for candidates affiliated with new parties to appear on the ballot; it requires both a party and its potential nominees to collect signatures.

The campaign finance system also hinders minor-party candidates. Under federal law, candidates can make unlimited contributions to their own campaigns, but are restricted in the amounts they can accept from others. Limits on contributions from individuals, interest-group-sponsored political action committees (PACs), and political parties apply to all candidates equally. Nevertheless, because candidates belonging to minor parties cannot turn to an established partisan or bipartisan donor pool for support, they are more likely to be handicapped by such limits. Moreover, minor parties historically have been unable to finance the expenditures that the major parties routinely make in coordination with or independently of their most competitive candidates' campaigns. As will be demonstrated later, campaign finance regulations make it virtually impossible for minor-party candidates to compete financially in House elections.

Somewhat ironically, regulations governing some of the internal operations of the two major parties serve to undercut the abilities of minor parties to build support among political activists, even in times of significant voter unrest. Participatory nominations enable the major parties to absorb protest and discourage the formation of minor parties.[9] State-regulated caucuses and state-administered primaries give dissident groups from outside or inside the party the opportunity to run candidates for a major-party nomination, thereby robbing minor parties of the ability to entice the support of some groups of disaffected voters. This discourages the growth of existing minor parties and the formation of new ones.

The mass media are usually not considered a formal political institution, but they are an important part of the strategic environment in which campaigns are conducted. Positive media coverage can improve a candidate's name recognition and credibility, whereas negative coverage or an absence of press attention can undermine a candidate's prospects. Although many major-party candidates complain about the media, virtually all of them are treated better than their minor-party counterparts. Minor-party candidates, especially for low-level offices such as the House, receive less coverage because the media are preoccupied with the horse-race aspects of elections, focusing

9. Epstein (1986).

most of their attention on the probable victors, who are almost always Democrats and Republicans.[10]

Sometimes the media are openly hostile to minor parties. The coverage afforded to the New Alliance Party, the Socialist Workers Party, and other contemporary minor parties is often distorted and rarely favorable.[11] For example, a *New York Times* article on the 2000 presidential election ran under the headline "For Third Parties, a Chance to Play Spoiler or Also-Ran."[12] Sometimes media coverage of minor parties consists solely of ridicule. Coverage of minor-party standard-bearers in the Style section of the *Washington Post* in 1996 compared their potential running mates to Prince Charles of Great Britain, Jack Kevorkian (known as "Doctor Death" because of his involvement in physician-assisted suicides), and BINTI (the gorilla who rescued a toddler who had fallen into her cage).[13] Although this coverage did not appear in the newspaper's main section, it provides insight into the treatment minor-party candidates often receive.

Public opinion and the behavioral norms of voters add to the impediments that American political institutions pose for minor parties. Most voters identify with one of the two major parties, and their socialization to politics encourages most of them to consider minor parties outside the mainstream and unworthy of support. Some voters believe that casting a ballot for a minor-party candidate could contribute to the election of the major-party candidate they least prefer.[14] This lesson was driven home in the 2000 presidential election, in which Green Party candidate Ralph Nader siphoned off enough liberal, and presumably Democratic, votes in key states such as Florida and New Hampshire to enable George W. Bush to win those states and the election. The relative ideological homogeneity of the electorate also deprives minor parties of bases of support that exist in more ideologically diverse nations. Because of Americans' moderate views, trying to outflank the major parties by occupying a place to the far left or the far right of the political spectrum rarely succeeds in capturing votes.

The career paths of the politically ambitious also explain the weakness and short-term existence of most minor-party movements in the United States.

10. Clarke and Evans (1983); Graber (1993).

11. Goodwyn (1978); Schmidt (1960); Rosenstone, Behr, and Lazarus (1984).

12. Adam Clymer, "For Third Parties, a Chance to Play Spoiler or Also-Ran," *New York Times,* August 12, 2000.

13. "There's the Ticket . . . A Selection of Running Mates for Ross Perot," *Washington Post,* September 7, 1996.

14. Brams (1978); Riker (1982).

Budding politicians learn early in their careers that the Democratic or Republican Party can provide them with useful contacts, expertise, financial assistance, and an orderly path of entry into electoral politics. Potential candidates also may be recruited to run for office by a party committee, labor union, or some other organization that promises to support their candidacy financially and strategically.[15] These factors give the two major parties tremendous advantages over minor parties in attracting and fielding the most talented candidates.

Mainstream politicians' responses to real and potential minor-party successes are an additional set of hindrances to those parties. Major-party officials often subject minor parties to court challenges to keep them off the ballot, and major-party nominees often refuse to debate minor-party candidates. By labeling minor-party candidates as extremists, irrelevant, or "spoilers," they reinforce many voters' initial skepticism. Moreover, when a minor-party candidate introduces an issue that becomes popular with voters, Democratic and Republican leaders quickly co-opt it, expanding their own constituencies, and attracting votes at the expense of the minor-party candidate who originally placed the issue on the political agenda.[16]

The anti-minor-party bias of American elections stands in sharp contrast to elections in other countries. Multimember proportional representation systems, used in most other democracies, virtually guarantee at least some legislative seats to any party—no matter how small, transient, or geographically confined—that wins a threshold of votes. Public funding provisions and government-subsidized broadcast time ensure that minor parties have a reasonable amount of campaign resources at their disposal.[17] The media provide significant and respectful coverage to many minor parties and their candidates. The distribution of public opinion in some nations provides constituencies for more than two parties, and this in turn encourages voters and politicians to affiliate with them.

The Rise of Minor-Party Candidates

The strength of minor parties has waxed and waned over the course of American history. Minor parties tend to perform best during periods of voter discontent, difficult economic times, and when the major parties fail to address

15. Herrnson (1988, 2004).
16. Eldersveld (1982).
17. Nassmacher (1993).

polarizing issues.[18] In 1978, 174 minor-party and independent candidates ran for the House. In 1992, during a period of substantial public hostility toward Congress, the number reached 536. The number of nonincumbent minor-party candidates who sought to claim a seat in Congress peaked at 675 in 2000, and then dwindled to 387 in 2002.[19] Clearly, many minor-party candidates believed that Americans' dissatisfaction with their government at the turn of the twenty-first century provided them with opportunities to try to influence policymaking at the national level by running for office and raising their favorite issues.

Nevertheless, not all of the parties were in a position to capitalize on these opportunities equally. Independents dominated the ranks of non-major-party House candidates in 1992 and 1994 (see figure 5-2). However, the Libertarian Party has steadily increased the number of congressional candidates it has fielded since the early 1990s. In 2002, the Libertarian Party became the major source of minor-party candidates, accounting for almost half of them. According to Terry Savage, a member of the executive committee of California's Libertarian Party, the Libertarians' progress was the result of an ambitious program of party-building in which he and other leaders made a conscious decision to sacrifice some ideological purity to improve their ability to win votes and raise funds, and for other pragmatic reasons.[20] The Green Party also enjoyed modest improvement between 1996 and 2002. The Reform Party, spurred on by the candidacy of their standard-bearer Perot, accounted for one-quarter of all candidates in 1996, the first year of its existence as a formal political party. However, its numbers declined as a result of changes in the party's leadership and the deep fissures that developed among both the party's leaders and its rank-and-file members. The Natural Law Party also saw the number of its candidacies rise and fall during this period.

The Impact of Strategic Ambition

Minor-party candidates bring a variety of experiences to their bids for Congress. Very few have ever held elective office, about half typically have had some experience working on a political campaign, fewer than one-tenth have held an appointive position in government, and about 5 percent have worked on the staff of an elected official. These percentages pale in comparison with

---

18. Ranney and Kendall (1956); Sundquist (1983).
19. Figures compiled from Federal Election Commission data.
20. Savage (1997).

Figure 5-2. House Candidates Affiliated with Minor Parties or No Party, 1992–2002

Percent

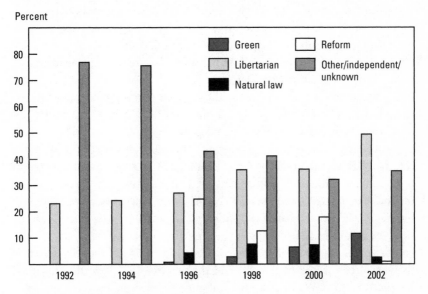

Source: Compiled from Federal Election Commission data.

those for Democrats and Republicans.[21] Obviously, relatively few minor-party candidates can be classified as highly qualified or "quality" candidates, regardless of which measure is used.

Given that minor-party candidates are overwhelmingly political amateurs, one might ask what motivates them to run. Most minor-party candidates are policy-driven; more than two-thirds state that their candidacies are inspired by ideology, issues, or a sense of duty to their party. In addition to these "policy amateurs," another 18 percent can be classified as "experience-seeking" or "hopeless" amateurs because they run for reasons of civic duty. Most of the remainder state that they run out of a sense of ambition.[22] Although some major-party nonincumbents might be considered policy-oriented or experience-seeking amateurs, a substantially larger portion of the amateurs are ambitious, and a significant number are regarded as quality candidates by virtue of having held elective office or having had significant nonelected

21. Francia and Herrnson (2002); Herrnson (2004).
22. The data are from Collet (1997). The terms "ambitious," "policy," and "experience-seeking" or "hopeless" amateurs are from Canon (1990).

experience, such as serving as a political aide, party official, political consultant, or political appointee.[23]

Despite their overall lack of political experience and largely policy-driven motives, minor-party candidates may be acting strategically when making their decisions to run for Congress. Strategic politicians generally weigh the benefits and costs of running for political office before committing to a race. Some of the factors they consider include the intrinsic value of holding the office, their prospects for success, and the effects that a successful or unsuccessful bid for office could have on their political career, their ability to advance in their chosen profession, and their family life.[24]

In deciding whether to run, strategic politicians examine a variety of institutional, structural, and subjective factors.[25] The institutional factors comprise filing deadlines, campaign finance laws, nomination processes, and other election statutes and party rules. The structural factors include the economic, social, and partisan composition of the seat; its geographic compactness; the media markets that serve it; the overlap between the district and the constituencies of lower-level elected offices, including constituencies they may have represented previously; and the possibilities for election to some alternative office. Whether an incumbent plans to run for reelection is a structural factor that greatly affects the strategic calculations of many nonincumbents, and it is prone to fluctuate more often than many of the others.

Potential candidates also assess the political climate before deciding whether to run. Local circumstances are particularly relevant to the decisions of strategic politicians. As already noted, seat status is very important. Strategic politicians are most likely to run when a seat will be vacant or when the results of the previous election, scandal, illness, or some other factor suggest that an incumbent is vulnerable.[26] A heavily redrawn election district also may encourage a strategic politician to run for Congress. National conditions, such as a public mood that favors Democrats or Republicans or challengers or incumbents, are usually of secondary importance. However, the convergence of local and national forces can have a major impact on the decisions of potential candidates. The widespread hostility the public directed at Congress and its members is believed to have played a key role in

23. Canon (1990); Herrnson (2004).
24. Schlesinger (1966); Jacobson and Kernell (1983); Bianco (1984); Canon (1990); Maisel, Stone, and Maestas (2001).
25. See, for example, Maisel and others (1990); Fowler and McClure (1990).
26. See, for example, Canon (1990).

Table 5-1. Nonincumbents Running for Open Seats or Incumbent-Held Seats in the 2002 Elections

Percent

Seats	Minor-party candidates[a]	Democrats	Republicans
Open seats	10.2	33.8	32.8
Incumbent-held seats	89.8	66.2	67.2
Total number of seats	383	465	545

Source: Compiled from Federal Election Commission data.
a. Minor-party candidates include independents.

influencing who ran in the 1994 and 1996 elections. These forces motivated numerous House incumbents to retire and encouraged nonincumbents of many partisan stripes to believe that a seat in Congress was within their grasp.[27] Favorable national and local circumstances, and these candidates' positive self-assessments of their chances, encouraged their thinking they could win the support of local, state, and national political elites, raise the money, build the name recognition, and generate the momentum needed to propel them into office. In 1998 and 2000 the nation's overall prosperity and the public's positive feelings toward incumbents had the opposite effect. The same is true of pro-incumbent redistricting and other national and local factors in 2002.

Are minor-party politicians as strategically ambitious as their major-party counterparts? The answer is no. In 2002, almost nine-tenths of all minor-party candidates ran for seats held by congressional incumbents, as opposed to only two-thirds of all major-party candidates (see table 5-1). Their decision not to wait until a House seat became open suggests that most minor-party nonincumbents do not entertain the same sense considerations that their major-party counterparts do.

Further evidence of the differences in the candidacy decisions of minor-party and major-party politicians can be garnered by comparing the number of minor-party, Democratic, and Republican House candidates who run for various House seats. One might formally hypothesize the following:

H1. More candidates run for seats that are not held by Democratic or Republican incumbents (that is, open seats).

27. Groseclose and Krehbiel (1994); Jacobson and Dimock (1994).

H2. Fewer minor-party candidates run against major-party candidates who are ideological extremists (because most minor-party candidates also occupy a position to the far right or left on the political spectrum).[28]

H3. More candidates run for more competitive than for uncompetitive seats.[29]

H4. More minor-party candidates than major-party candidates run in districts comprising more independent (and minor-party) voters, whereas more major-party candidates run in districts comprising more voters who identify with a candidate's specific party.[30]

These hypotheses were tested using negative binomial regression. Unlike ordinary least squares regression, negative binomial regression is an appropriate statistical technique for count models, such as those that count the number of nonincumbent candidates running for a congressional seat.[31] The results of a test of the first three hypotheses are shown in table 5-2. They strongly suggest that the decisionmaking of minor-party candidates differs considerably from that of their major-party counterparts. None of the independent variables are statistically significant in the equation for the number of minor-party candidates who decide to contest particular House seats. The lack of statistical significance for the coefficients for Democratic and Republican incumbents suggests that just as many minor-party nonincumbent candidates are willing to run against a Democratic or Republican incumbent or for an open seat. This contrasts sharply with the behavior of major-party nonincumbents. In the equation for Democrats, the coefficient of –2.13 for Democratic incumbents shows that significantly fewer Democratic nonincumbents will run for a seat held by a Democratic incumbent who is seeking reelection, and the coefficient of –.87 for Republican incumbents suggests that more Democrats will run for a seat held by a Republican incumbent, but that this number is still significantly smaller than the number who will run for an open seat. The findings for Republican nonincumbents show they are

28. This measure is operationalized as a folded version of the first dimension of D-nominate scores (for example, Poole and Rosenthal 1999) during the previous congressional session for incumbents seeking reelection. The data for open-seat contests consist of folded scores for the leading candidate and eventual winner of the race. Data were downloaded from www.voteview.com (January 17, 2006).

29. Seats that the Cook Political Report (2001) rated as a toss-up or leaning in January 2001, a full eighteen months before the 2002 elections, were coded competitive and the rest were coded as uncompetitive.

30. Estimates provided by candidates and campaign aides who competed in the 2002 House elections (Herrnson 2004).

31. Lawless (1987).

Table 5-2. The Impact of Incumbency, Ideological Extremism, and District Competitiveness on the Number of Nonincumbents Who Ran in a Congressional District in 2002[a]

Factor	Nonincumbent minor-party candidates	Nonincumbent Democrats	Nonincumbent Republicans
Democratic incumbent	.04	−2.13***	−.88***
	(.19)	(.16)	(.13)
Republican incumbent	.12	−.87***	−2.33***
	(.19)	(.13)	(.16)
Ideological extremism	.34	.62*	−.14
	(.33)	(.31)	(.30)
Competitiveness	−.06	.55***	.31*
	(.18)	(.14)	(.14)
Constant	−.35	.82	1.35
	(.22)	(.17)	(.16)
Number of races	434	434	434
Pseudo R^2	.002	.148	.166

a. Figures exclude Vermont's at-large congressional district, represented by Bernie Sanders (the House's sole minor-party incumbent). Coefficients were generated using negative binominal regression.
*** $p < .001$.
* $p < .05$ one-tail tests.

just as disinclined as Democratic nonincumbents to run against a House member from the opposite party, and even slightly more disinclined to consider electoral fratricide. In other words, major-party nonincumbents are overwhelmingly drawn to open-seat contests, whereas minor-party nonincumbents are not. Similarly, the competitiveness of the seat has no impact on the candidacies of minor-party politicians, but it has a positive impact on the numbers of major-party candidates who run in House districts. The results show mixed support for hypothesis 3. Ideological extremism has no impact on the number of Republican or minor-party nonincumbents who run in a congressional race, but more Democratic politicians enter races where a sitting incumbent or the leading candidate for an open seat does not represent the political center.

Table 5-3 introduces data relevant to hypothesis 4, which implies that the partisan composition of a House seat should influence the number of candidates who run for it. Because this measure is based on survey data, significantly fewer observations are included in the analysis.[32] The findings suggest that minor-party candidates, unlike their major-party counterparts, do not

32. The data are from the 2002 Congressional Campaign Study, a survey of congressional candidates and campaign aides (see Herrnson 2004).

Table 5-3. The Impact of Incumbency, Ideological Extremism, District Competitiveness, and Partisanship on the Number of Nonincumbents Who Ran in a Congressional District in 2002[a]

Factor	Nonincumbent minor-party candidates	Nonincumbent Democrats	Nonincumbent Republicans
Democratic incumbent	.40*	−2.08***	−.56***
	(.23)	(.20)	(.15)
Republican incumbent	.17	−.67***	−2.09***
	(.25)	(.16)	(.19)
Ideological extremism	.18	.39	.36
	(.46)	(.40)	(.38)
Competitiveness	−.22	.47**	.35*
	(.23)	(.16)	(.15)
Percent independents	.004	…	…
	(.005)		
Percent Democrats	…	.01*	…
	(.005)		
Percent Republicans	…	…	.01**
	(.006)		
Constant	−.52	.48	.48
	(.30)	(.31)	(.34)
Number of races	242	242	242
Pseudo R^2	.012	.158	.175

a. The figure for percent independent voters also includes voters registered with minor parties. Figures exclude Vermont's at-large congressional district, represented by Bernie Sanders (the House's sole minor-party incumbent). Coefficients were generated using negative binominal regression.

*** $p < .001$.
** $p < .01$.
* $p < .05$ one-tail tests.

appear to respond to district partisanship. That is, more minor-party candidates do not contest congressional seats that have many minor-party voters or independent voters (whose political behavior is unconstrained by partisanship), whereas slightly more Democratic and Republican politicians do run for Congress in districts where many voters identify with their party.

Of course, not all minor parties are the same, and their candidates may entertain different strategic considerations in deciding whether to run for Congress. Given the Libertarian Party's recent strategic move toward greater pragmatism in the electoral arena, it makes sense to ask whether the party's congressional candidates behave more similarly to minor-party candidates or major-party candidates when it comes to running for Congress. Because no more than one Libertarian candidate usually runs for the House in a given district, the dependent variable for the analysis in table 5-4 is whether a Lib-

Table 5-4. The Impact of Incumbency, Ideological Extremism, District Competitiveness, and Partisanship on the Candidacies of Libertarian Candidates for Congress in 2002[a]

Factor	Partial model	Model with district partisanship
Democratic incumbent	−.47	.06
	(.35)	(.41)
Republican incumbent	.24	.37
	(.34)	(.42)
Ideological extremism	1.45**	1.34
	(.62)	(.84)
Competitiveness	−.16	−.64
	(.34)	(.42)
Percent independents	...	−.01
		(.01)
Constant	−.89	−.86
	(.40)	(.52)
Number of races	434	242
Pseudo R^2	.013	.023

a. The figure for percent Independent voters also includes voters registered with minor parties. Figures exclude Vermont's at-large congressional district, represented by Bernie Sanders (the House's sole minor-party incumbent). Coefficients were generated using negative binominal regression.

** $p < .01$.

ertarian runs for an individual House seat, making logit analysis an appropriate statistical technique for the analysis.[33] The independent variables are the same as those used to test hypotheses 1 through 4. The results demonstrate that Libertarians appear to be no more strategic in their decisions than other minor-party candidates. That is, they are just as likely to run against a Democratic or Republican incumbent as for an open seat, and they do not need to consider the competitiveness or partisan composition of a district when deciding whether to run. Moreover, Libertarians show a tendency to run for House seats held by ideologues, particularly very conservative Republicans, which may help explain their poor performance at the polls. In short, the decisionmaking of Libertarian candidates for the House has little in common with that expected of candidates who possess strategic ambition.

Minor-Party Candidates' Campaigns

Given that minor-party House candidates have qualifications and motives that differ somewhat from those of Democratic and Republican candidates,

33. Long (1997).

Table 5-5. Average Amounts of Money Raised by Minor-Party, Democratic, and Republican Candidates in the 2002 House Elections[a]

U.S. dollars

Type of contribution	Minor-party candidates	Democrats	Republicans
Challengers			
Candidate contribution	1,440	128,917	41,182
Individual contribution	1,025	124,659	113,849
Party contribution	0	1,434	3,833
Party-coordinated expenditures			
PAC contribution	36	46,213	22,150
Total	2,478	311,479	187,922
Number of candidates	364	155	159
Open-seat candidates			
Candidate contribution	7,871	259,044	207,493
Individual contribution	2,580	511,804	602,409
Party contribution	0	6,914	22,160
Party-coordinated expenditures			
PAC contribution	167	280,175	315,828
Total	11,014	1,101,384	1,195,985
Number of candidates	18	48	47

Source: Compiled from data provided by the Federal Election Commission.

a. Figures are for general election candidates only. Candidate contributions include loans the candidate made to the campaign.

face greater impediments to their candidacies, and respond to different strategic opportunities than major-party candidates, it would be reasonable to expect they wage relatively distinctive campaigns. Indeed, they do. First, minor-party candidates raise substantially less money than their major-party counterparts. During the 2002 elections, minor-party general election candidates who sought to contest a seat held by an incumbent raised an average of $2,478 (see table 5-5). This figure pales in comparison with the $311,479 raised by the typical Democratic challenger and the $187,922 raised by the typical Republican challenger. Minor-party candidates relied largely on their own funds and those of individuals, usually family members and friends, to finance their campaigns. Contributions from political parties and PACs were virtually invisible on most of their campaign finance reports, whereas funds from these sources played a significant role in at least some major-party challengers' campaigns.

The financing for House open-seat contests shows even greater disparities. Minor-party candidates who ran for these seats in 2000 raised an average of $11,000, relying almost exclusively on contributions from individuals and their own resources. By contrast, Democratic and Republican candidates in these races typically raised in excess of $1 million, including substantial funding from individuals, parties, and PACs. In addition to financial assistance, most major-party open-seat candidates and competitive challengers benefit from organizational assistance provided by party committees and interest groups. This assistance is rarely, if ever, offered to similarly positioned minor-party contestants.

Given the huge disparities in wealth, it is little surprise that minor-party candidates use different approaches to campaigning. Whereas many major-party candidates assemble substantial campaign organizations that include paid campaign aides, professional consultants, and small and not-so-small armies of volunteers, minor-party candidates often wage amateur campaigns that rely on the goodwill of family, friends, and others they can attract to their cause. Well over half of all major-party challengers and candidates for open seats typically disseminate their campaign messages using television, direct mail, radio, mass telephone calls, billboards, and Internet websites, but very few minor-party candidates are able to employ most of these resources.[34]

Reflecting their insurgent tendency and ideological foundations, the content of most minor-party campaigns differs from those of major-party candidates. Minor-party candidates are more likely to seek the support of young and disaffected voters, whereas major-party candidates target their fellow partisans and senior citizens, who routinely turn out at high levels. Minor-party campaign communications also are primarily issue-oriented.[35] Major-party candidates, on the other hand, focus more on candidate qualifications and image.[36]

The Impact of Minor Party Candidates on Election Outcomes

Given their goals and limited resources, what impact, if any, do the minor-party candidates have on congressional elections? The 2002 congressional elections provide an interesting case study of electoral competition. Minor-party nonincumbent candidates ran for a total of forty-seven seats where their major-party opponent faced no major-party opposition in the general election. All of those seats were controlled by incumbents, and all but one of the open-seat House general election contests in 2002 featured a candidate from each of the two major parties (several faced minor-party opposition).

34. Herrnson (2004); Francia and Herrnson (2002).
35. Francia and Herrnson (2002).
36. Herrnson (2004).

The lone exception was Florida's 17th congressional district, where Democratic candidate Kendrick Meek, son of retiring representative Carrie Meek, was unopposed in the general election to succeed his mother. Thus, with the exception of one contest, minor-party candidates provided voters with an alternative choice on the ballot in every 2002 House race where two-party competition was absent.

Although minor-party nonincumbent candidates provided the only opposition in forty-seven House races, the level of competition they provided in most of these contests was weak at best. This is not surprising given the limited resources available to their campaigns. The candidates who won by the slimmest margin of victory in these races, Rep. Ellen Tauscher (D-Calif.) and Rep. Frank Lucas (D-Okla.), each won by a 51 percent vote margin. The average victory margin for major-party candidates competing solely against a minor-party nonincumbent opponent was 79 percent. If one adds the Vermont Independent Rep. Bernie Sanders into the calculations, the major-party candidates' margin of victory is still a healthy 78 percent.

Though most minor-party candidates lose by a large margin, even when they constitute the only opposition in a House race, they may still influence an election outcome. As noted earlier, major-party candidates often refer to their minor-party opponents as "spoilers." A minor-party candidate can play the role of spoiler in tangible and intangible ways. An intangible effect could consist of inserting issues into the campaign that change the dynamic of the race and put the front-runner at such a disadvantage that he or she ultimately loses. A more tangible and easily measurable effect occurs when a minor-party candidate siphons off a percentage of votes that is greater than the winning candidate's victory margin—as Ralph Nader did during the 2000 presidential elections. Thus the effect a minor-party candidate has on an election outcome depends on the level of visibility and support that candidate has in the race.

There were three House races in 2002 where minor-party candidates won a sufficient number of votes to have potentially changed the outcome of the election. That is, the number of votes won by minor-party candidates constituted a greater percentage than the winner's margin of victory over the second-place finisher (see figure 5-3). Although they spent a mere fraction of the amounts distributed by their major-party opponents, the funds minor-party candidates expended in two of these elections—$39,600 in Florida's 5th and $49,500 in Colorado's 7th district contests—may have been enough to attract the media coverage and voter attention needed to win sufficient votes and thereby change the outcome of the election. Moreover, sitting House members won in all three contests, suggesting that had minor-party candi-

Figure 5-3. The Impact of Minor-Party Candidates on Electoral Competition[a]

Number of races decided by minor-party candidate's impact

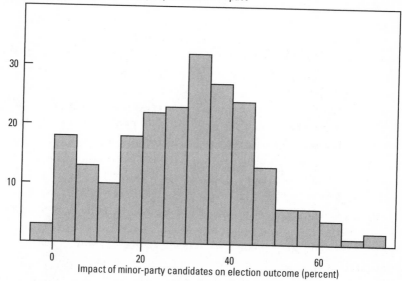

Impact of minor-party candidates on election outcome (percent)

a. The figures represent the major-party victory margin minus the total percentage earned by third-party candidates.

dates not divided the opposition vote in those races the incumbents might have lost.

In an additional thirty-one elections, minor-party candidates won between 1 and 10 percent fewer votes than the winner's victory margin over the runner-up. It is possible that some of these candidates had a significant enough presence in the race to influence the outcome. Minor-party candidates in five of the districts each raised between $109,000 and $168,000, and the receipts of minor-party candidates in another ten districts ranged from $21,000 to $36,000. These candidates also might have been able to influence the campaign agenda or the major-party candidates' tactics enough to affect the ultimate election outcome.

Conclusion

Minor-party and independent candidates have made important contributions to American politics, despite existing in a political environment that is relatively hostile to them. In particular, minor parties must overcome significant obstacles to appear on the ballot in many states. Minor parties have had different records of gaining ballot access. The Libertarian Party was particularly successful between 1992 and 2002, and the Green Party also enjoyed increasing success. However, a minor party that seeks to strengthen its presence on the ballot may need to make compromises elsewhere. In the case of the Libertarians, the party's leadership made a conscious decision to moderate the party's voice in order to attract more voters, raise more money, and generally improve its political prospects.

Another challenge that minor parties often encounter is that the potential candidates who affiliate with them are less well qualified in the traditional sense than politicians associated with the Democratic and Republican parties. Minor-party and independent candidates typically run for office for different reasons than their major-party counterparts. They generally entertain different strategic calculations when deciding whether to contest a House seat.

Of course, when minor-party candidates resolve to run for Congress, they have substantially fewer resources than major-party contestants. Their campaigns are often without significant funds, lack the benefit of a professional organization and the advice of political consultants, and can rely only on extremely limited assistance, if any, from party committees and interest groups. Because they tend to be uncompetitive, articulate issues that most voters consider somewhat extreme, and target the young and disaffected, most minor-party candidates receive very little media coverage.

Ultimately, extremely few minor-party candidates are usually in contention to win a seat in the U.S. House of Representatives, and a relatively small number are in a position to influence the outcome of a House election. Nevertheless, minor-party and independent candidates make important contributions to American politics. They broaden the dialogue in some elections, and they may influence the outcomes of some close contests. Historically, they have played an important role in ushering change into American politics. For this reason, it probably makes sense to categorize the United States as having a two-plus party system instead of just a two-party system.

References

Bianco, William T. 1984. "Strategic Decisions on Candidacy in U.S. Congressional Districts." *Legislative Studies Quarterly* 9 (1984): 360–62.

Brams, Steven J. 1978. *The Presidential Election Game*. Yale University Press.

Burnham, Walter Dean. 1970. *Critical Elections and the Mainsprings of American Politics*. New York: W. W. Norton.

Canon, David T. 1990. *Actors, Athletes, and Astronauts*. University of Chicago Press.

Clarke, Peter, and Susan Evans. 1983. *Covering Campaigns: Journalism in Congressional Elections*. Stanford University Press.

Collet, Christian. 1997. "Taking the 'Abnormal' Route: Backgronds, Beliefs, and Political Activities of Minor Party Candidates." In *Multiparty Politics in America*, edited by Paul S. Herrnson and John C. Green, pp. 103–24. Landover, Md.: Rowman and Littlefield.

Cook Political Report. 2001. "2002 Competitive House Race Chart." www.cookpolitical. com. January 20.

Duverger, Maurice. 1954. *Political Parties*. London: Methuen.

Eldersveld, Samuel J. 1982. *Political Parties in American Society*. New York: Basic Books.

Epstein, Leon D. 1986. *Political Parties in the American Mold*. University of Wisconsin Press.

Flood, Emmet T., and William G. Mayer. 1996. "Third-Party and Independent Candidates." In *In Pursuit of the White House: How We Choose Our Presidential Nominees*, edited by William G. Mayer. Chatham, N.J.: Chatham House.

Fowler, Linda L., and Robert D. McClure. 1990. *Political Ambition: Who Decides to Run for Congress*. Yale University Press.

Francia, Peter L., and Paul S. Herrnson. 2002. "Running against the Odds: Minor-Party Campaigns in Congressional and State Legislative Elections." In *Multiparty Politics in America*, edited by Paul S. Herrnson and John C. Green, pp. 79–98. Landover, Md.: Rowman and Littlefield.

Freie, John F. 1982. "Minor Parties in Realigning Eras." *American Politics Quarterly* 10: 42–63.

Goodwyn, Lawrence. 1978. *The Populist Movement*. Cambridge University Press.

Graber, Doris A. 1993. *Mass Media in American Politics*. Washington: CQ Press.

Green Party of California. 1996. *Green Party of California Policy Directions*. San Francisco: Green Leaf Publishing.

Greenblatt, Alan. 1996. "Reform Party's Chief Rivals: David and Goliath?" *CQ Weekly*, July 27.

Groseclose, Timothy, and Keith Krehbiel, "Golden Parachutes, Rubber Checks, and Strategic Retirements from the 102nd House." *American Journal of Political Science* 38 (1994): 75–99.

Hazlett, Joseph M., II. 1992. *The Libertarian Party and Other Minor Political Parties in the United States*. Jefferson, N.C.: McFarland.

Herrnson, Paul S. 1998. *Party Campaigning in the 1980s*. Harvard University Press.

———. 2002. "Two-Party Dominance and Minor-Party Forays in American Politics." In *Multiparty Politics in America*, 2nd ed., edited by Paul S. Herrnson and John C. Green, pp. 9–30. Landover, Md.: Rowman and Littlefield.

———. 2004. *Congressional Elections: Campaigning at Home and in Washington*. Washington: CQ Press.

Jacobson, Gary C., and Michael Dimock. 1994. "Checking Out: The Effects of Bank Overdrafts on the 1992 House Election." *American Journal of Political Science* 38: 601–24.

Jacobson, Gary C., and Samuel Kernell. 1983. *Strategy and Choice in Congressional Elections*. Yale University Press.

———. 1990. "National Forces in the 1986 U.S. House Elections." *Legislative Studies Quarterly* 15: 65–87.

Jost, Kenneth. 1995. "Third-Party Prospects." *CQ Researcher*. Washington: Congressional Quarterly.

Keith, Bruce E., David B. Magleby, Candice J. Nelson, Elizabeth Orr, Mark C. Westlye, and Raymond E. Wolfinger. 1992. *The Myth of the Independent Voter*. University of California Press.

Lawless, J. F. 1987. "Negative Binomial and Mixed Poisson Regression." *Canadian Journal of Statistics* 15: 209–25.

Long, J. S. 1997. *Regression Models for Categorical and Limited Dependent Variables*. Thousand Oaks, Calif.: Sage.

Maisel, L. Sandy, Walter J. Stone, and Cherie Maestas. 2001. "Quality Challengers to Congressional Incumbents: Can Better Candidates Be Found?" In *Playing Hardball: Campaigning for the U.S. Congress*, edited by Paul S. Herrnson, pp. 12–40. Saddle River, N.J.: Prentice Hall.

Maisel, L. Sandy, Linda L. Fowler, Ruth S. Jones, and Walter J. Stone. 1990. "The Naming of Candidates: Recruitment or Emergence?" In *The Parties Respond: Changes in the American Party System*, edited by L. Sandy Maisel. Boulder, Colo.: Westview Press.

Nassmacher, Karl-Heinz. 1993. "Comparing Party and Campaign Finance in Western Democracies." *Campaign and Party Finance in North America and Western Europe*. Boulder, Colo.: Westview Press.

Poole, Keith T., and Howard Rosenthal. 1999. D-NOMINATE after 10 Years. http://voteview.com/prapsd99.pdf. January 17.

Ranney, Austin. 1975. *Curing the Mischiefs of Faction*. University of California Press.

Ranney, Austin, and Willmore Kendall. 1956. *Democracy and the American Party System*. New York: Harcourt and Brace.

Riker, William H. 1982. "The Two-Party System and Duverger's Law: An Essay on the History of Political Science." *American Political Science Review* 76: 753–64.

Rosenstone, Steven J., Roy L. Behr, and Edward H. Lazarus. 1984. *Third Parties in America: Citizen Response to Major Party Failure*. Princeton University Press.

Savage, Terry. 1997. "The Libertarian Party: A Pragmatic Approach to Party Building." In *Multiparty Politics in America*, 2nd ed., edited by Paul S. Herrnson and John C. Green, pp. 141–45. Landover, Md.: Rowman and Littlefield.

Schlesinger, Joseph A. 1996. *Ambition and Politics: Political Careers in the United States*. Chicago: Rand-McNally.

Schmidt, Karl M. 1960. *Henry A. Wallace: Quixotic Crusade*. Syracuse University Press.

Stratmann, Thomas. 2005. "Ballot Access Restrictions and Candidate Entry in Elections." *European Journal of Political Economy* 21: 59–71.

Sundquist, James L. 1973. *The Dynamics of the Two-Party System*. Washington: Brookings.

———. 1983. *The Decline of American Political Parties, 1952–1998*. Harvard University Press.

Winger, Richard. 2001. "Ballot Access for New Party U.S. House Candidates for 2002." *Ballot Access News*.

The Geography of Electioneering: Campaigning for Votes and Campaigning for Money

James G. Gimpel and Frances E. Lee

Campaign: **1** obs: a tract of open country; **2a** obs: the time during which an army is in the field; **b**: a connected series of military operations forming a distinct phase of a war.

—*Webster's Third New International Dictionary, Unabridged*

Organized efforts to win elections have been referred to as "campaigns" for so long that it is easy to forget that the word originally referred to tracts of open country or armies in the field conducting military operations. But electoral contests involve "campaigns" in a far more than metaphorical sense. They are not merely a set of plans executed with the sustained intensity of battle; they are also campaigns in the original sense: they involve being "in the field," traversing geographic space. As Pitney observes, just as "[g]eography shapes combat . . . [l]ocational choices are especially crucial in election campaigns."[1] Despite the advances in communication technology, party activists and candidates must still travel thousands of miles over the course of an election cycle. Campaign travel is time-consuming, expensive, exhausting, and inescapable, even in an era of Internet connections, cell phones, satellites,

1. Pitney (2000, p. 146).

and television. In this sense, campaign strategy is as much about geography as it is about message and media.

Electoral campaigns are always waged on two fronts: the battle for votes and the battle for funds.[2] Integral to both efforts are strategic considerations of geography, travel, and the location of available electoral and financial resources. The campaign for votes involves decisions about *where* to set up turn-out-the-vote operations, *where* to direct advertisements, and *where* to hold rallies and other campaign events. Efforts to win "free" media coverage involve multiple trips, often to the same locations, with the candidate auditioning different messages to reach subsets of the electorate.

The campaign for funds involves no less attention to geographic location. People who make substantial campaign contributions will not typically do so in response to a direct mail solicitation. Potential donors need to be asked, preferably in person, preferably by candidates themselves.[3] There is no substitute for the face-to-face meeting, and so fundraisers have no choice but to meet people on their own turf. Parties and candidates must decide *where* to hold the many receptions, coffees, meet-ups, socials, dinners, and other gatherings that are necessary to spur contributions. Given constraints of time, money, and candidate energy, choosing where to target fundraising efforts involves careful strategy.

In this chapter, we examine the geography of electioneering. First, where is the campaign for dollars fought? Although scholars have studied how parties and candidates mobilize contributions and the factors that lead individuals to donate to campaigns, they have given little attention to the geography of fundraising.[4] Where do contributors live? What parts of the country are most important for fundraising? Studies of individuals' propensity to contribute are important for understanding political behavior, but they may not tell us much about the strategic situations that parties and candidates face when they campaign for funds. Isolated campaign contributors may be helpful, but they cannot be the focus of fundraising campaigns. To focus resources effectively, parties and candidates must attend to how potential contributors are situated geographically. In this paper, we hope to advance scholarly understanding of campaign finance by studying the aggregate fundraising landscape rather than the behavior of individual contributors.

2. Herrnson (2003).
3. Brown, Powell, and Wilcox (1995, pp. 57, 62–64); Alexander (1992, p. 50).
4. See, for example, Brown, Hedges, and Powell (1980); Brown, Powell, and Wilcox (1995); Francia and others (2003); Mutz (1995); Verba, Schlozman, and Brady (1993; 1995).

Second, what is the relationship between the campaign for votes and the campaign for funds? Scholars and commentators have given a lot of attention recently to the rivalry between "red" and "blue" electorates and the extent to which the parties have either distinctive or intersecting bases of mass support. If the major parties have dissimilar geographic bases of electoral support, do they also have different bases of financial support? To what extent do the campaigns for votes and funds overlap? Do parties raise money in the same places where they target voters? Are voters more likely to contribute when local party competition is fierce?

We examine the geographic distribution of individual donors' contributions to parties and campaigns for each election year between 1998 and 2004, drawing on official contribution data from the Federal Election Commission.[5] We find that the two major parties, Democratic and Republican, draw on financial bases of support that are quite similar geographically despite differences in the distribution of the parties' mass support. Donors to both parties reside primarily in densely populated affluent areas, and each party successfully taps these bases even when they are located in local or state contexts that are electorally inhospitable to the party.

The campaigns for money and votes follow different strategic logics, even if their ultimate goal is the same. We find that the competitiveness of local elections bears little relationship to a party's fundraising success in particular areas. Hotly contested local campaigns for votes do not spark higher levels of giving. In fact, the areas that parties and candidates target in their quest for votes are not the same areas where they wage their campaign for funds. Instead, fundraising occurs in places where the electoral campaign would never go. That the two major parties draw their financial support in different locations from their electoral support is likely to have important implications for mass-elite linkages in contemporary American politics.

Two Geographic Logics of Electioneering

Electoral competition in the United States is structured at all levels by the system of single-member districts and winner-take-all rules. The key to winning elections is not just who votes, but where voters live. Parties routinely win control of Congress without gaining a majority of the total two-party

5. The analysis includes contributions both to the two major-party organizations (the Democratic National Committee and the Republican National Committee) and to candidates aligned with them.

vote, and presidents are often elected without winning a majority of the popular vote.[6] Although Republicans and Democrats today claim about equal proportions of the general public in party affiliation and have won nearly equivalent numbers of votes nationally in recent presidential elections, there are relatively few competitive elections, either by absolute or historical standards.[7] Most House and Senate races are decided by wide margins, with outcomes never in doubt. Similarly, most states voted lopsidedly for one party's candidate in recent presidential elections.

Campaign strategists thus target resources toward winning votes in competitive jurisdictions. Presidential elections are contested in the minority of states that become the "battleground," with most voters residing in "blackout" states where neither campaign devotes resources to marshal or sway voters.[8] Within competitive areas, parties and candidates focus their efforts on the most voter-rich locations.[9] A solid plurality of a statewide electorate can usually be found in just a handful of counties, and both political parties will often focus on these locations. But because genuine voter persuasion is difficult, campaigns also prioritize locations in competitive jurisdictions where friendly partisans can best be mobilized.

While the campaign for votes focuses on activating voters in competitive jurisdictions, the campaign for money has an entirely different geographic logic. Donors are free to contribute to anyone, anywhere. Voters cannot cast multiple votes or exercise their franchise in another state. But donors can make multiple contributions to candidates locally or across the country, up to a regulated limit. They can even give money to candidates of both parties in the same contest, though few individual contributors do so. This makes the campaign for money a truly national effort, unshackled by state borders and other electoral jurisdictions.

Unlike the campaign for votes, campaign fundraising is not a winner-take-all game. All dollars are helpful, regardless of where they come from, even though not all votes are. Parties and candidates have no reason to concede areas that are more financially generous to the other party. If Republicans can raise $4 million in San Francisco during an election cycle, it does not matter if Democrats raise three times as much there. Republicans will still find it profitable to hold fundraising events and cultivate donor networks in

---

6. Amy (2002); Campbell (1996).

7. For recent data on party identification in the U.S. electorate, see Pew Research Center for the People and the Press (2005).

8. Gimpel and Kaufmann (2005).

9. Shaw (1999); Gimpel and Schuknecht (2002; 2003).

that city, even if it would not be worthwhile for them to campaign for votes there. With respect to geography, fundraising is a positive sum game: both parties can win in the same locations.

Since the vast majority of voters cannot afford to contribute to parties and candidates, the campaign for funds must follow the geographic distribution of income, first and foremost. As a result, the fundraising campaign is pursued on a comparatively tiny battlefield. Contributions will be sought in places where there are few friendly voters and in locations where the noncompetitive nature of the terrain would make an electoral campaign useless. In fact, the most highly urbanized areas of the country, the areas with the greatest concentrations of wealth, tend to have little two-party competition and to lie within states that are uncompetitive in presidential elections. As a result, campaign contributions to both parties are likely to come disproportionately from locations that the two major parties have already either written off or chalked up in electoral terms.

Parties and candidates cultivate a base of donors who can be relied upon to contribute, regardless of local electoral competitiveness. While there is such a creature as a swing voter, there is little evidence for the existence of "swing contributors." Candidates go back to the same contributors to ask for contributions year after year, rather than spend valuable time persuading nondonors to become donors. New-donor prospecting does occur, of course, but it pays fewer dividends than returning to established donors to ask for contributions.

The geographic logic of fundraising, however, is not merely incidental to the geographic distribution of wealth. In related work, we have shown that the geography of campaign contributions is not solely an artifact of the geographic distribution of individuals with the resources and inclination to give.[10] Individual contributors commonly act as part of a local network; their campaign contributions are a consequence of social influences that prompt higher levels of giving.[11] Campaigning and fundraising always involve a search for local social, party, governmental, and professional-occupational networks, including physicians, lawyers, teachers, students, community groups, and labor unions.[12] How potential givers are situated in space thus affects their propensity to contribute. When new donors do emerge, they do not come from out of nowhere, but are usually associated with the expansion

10. Gimpel, Lee, and Kaminski (forthcoming 2006).

11. Brady, Schlozman, and Verba (1999); Verba, Schlozman, and Brady (1995, chap. 5); Cho (2003).

12. Hinckley and Green (1996).

of existing donor networks. Money begets more money. Evidence from Texas shows that small contributions, not reported to the Federal Election Commission, generally come from the same affluent areas where large contributions are mined.[13]

Data and Approach

Our data originate from the U.S. Federal Election Commission (FEC), the official agency charged with monitoring and regulating campaigns in U.S. federal elections. The FEC maintains separate data collections for individual contributions and for corporate and political action committee (PAC) contributions. For this analysis, we examined only the individual contribution files, not the PAC/corporate donation files. FEC files include data on individual contributions of at least $200 to all campaign committees for federal office and to national, state, and local parties if they make significant contributions in federal elections. The files report both hard- and soft-money contributions.

Because the FEC files contain information on the location of each contributor, we were able to aggregate contributions to their counties of origin.[14] Counties are our principal unit of observation, presenting the advantages of greater variation and much finer granularity than the state. For every county we totaled contributions to a party's organizations (at all levels) and contributions to candidates of that party to create two primary variables of interest, *county-level Democratic contributions* and *county-level Republican contributions*.

To analyze the relationship between the campaign for votes and the campaign for funds, we collected data on congressional campaign competitiveness and seat status (incumbent present or open seat). If a county contained more than one congressional district, we calculated the proportion of those districts (whether fully contained or only partly contained within the county) in which incumbents sought reelection for each year. Similarly, we calculated the proportion of seats that were evaluated as competitive. We also use the county's presidential vote as our indicator of its political tilt, providing a sense

13. Gimpel and Cho (2006).

14. The information on contributors' zip code location available in the FEC files was largely complete and of high quality, missing from less than 2 percent of all contributors, but cleaning these files nevertheless took several months. In the cleaning process, we were eventually able to reduce the number of unreported zip codes to less than 1 percent of the file for each year. This was manageable because often we found multiple contributions had come from the same individuals, but only one contribution report contained that individual's zip code. Using contributor zip codes, we were then able to use Geographic Information System (GIS) boundary files to aggregate contributions to the county level.

for whether its contributors are embedded in a county context that is predominantly Republican, Democratic, or competitive between the two parties.

In analyzing the geography of campaign contributions, we account for how county-level differences in income, urbanization, education, race, and the presence of particular economic interests affect fundraising patterns. Fortunately, the U.S. Census Bureau makes a great deal of such information available at the county level for 1990 and 2000, with intercensal years interpolated. A description of all the economic, political, and demographic variables used in the study is provided in appendix table 6A-1.

The goal of this study is to account for basic geographic patterns in campaign contributions to both parties in order to compare and contrast the campaign for votes with the campaign for funds. After exploring the data at a descriptive level, we estimate spatial regression models of campaign contributions to each party for 1998, 2000, 2002, and 2004. Our analysis shows quite convincingly that the two campaigns follow different logics and operate on different terrains.

The Two Parties' Bases of Financial Support

Figure 6-1 is a county-level map of the 2004 presidential vote (Alaska's scale has been reduced to fit the map). The counties shown in red voted lopsidedly Republican, the counties shown in blue voted lopsidedly Democratic, and those in purple are counties in which the margin of victory was 10 percentage points or less. For purposes of comparison, figures 6-2 and 6-3 are maps of the spatial distribution of contributions to each party during the 2004 campaign.[15] [See color plates following page 136.]

Comparing the map of the geographic distribution of electoral support for the two parties (figure 6-1) with the maps showing the geographic distribution of financial contributions to the two parties (figures 6-2 and 6-3) reveals many important differences between the two campaigns. Areas that were very important in the campaign for votes are often unimportant or relatively unimportant in the campaign for funds. Note in particular the differences between the electoral and contribution maps for the upper Midwest: the most hotly contested counties in the battleground states of Iowa, Minnesota, and Wisconsin were generally inconsequential for both parties' campaigns for funds. Although we also examined the relationship between competition and fundraising in a more rigorous statistical analysis, it is clear just

15. The maps were created with a geographic boundary file for counties using a GIS.

from visual inspection of these maps that electoral competition is not the key to understanding fundraising. Similarly, strong regional partisanship in voting does not predict the contribution maps. Many counties that are lopsidedly Republican (red) or lopsidedly Democrat (blue) are unimportant for fundraising. In particular, some of the most intensely Republican areas of the country—the Texas panhandle, the western Plains states—are almost wholly irrelevant to fundraising, showing up as pale swaths of low support on the map of Republican contributions. Meanwhile, areas that are solidly Democratic on the electoral map—Los Angeles, New York—are vital to Republican fundraising.

What is most remarkable about the geographic origins of contributions to the Republican and Democratic parties is their substantial similarity. In 2004 and in previous years, both Republicans and Democrats received large shares of their contributions from urban areas on three coasts, the Philadelphia-New York-Boston corridor, southern California, and the major Great Lakes cities of Chicago and Detroit. Both parties raise a great deal of money outside their electoral strongholds. Democrats found major fundraising pockets in Florida and Texas, as well as in Atlanta and its suburbs. Republicans gained large shares of their funds from the Bay Area, suburban Denver, and the Northeast. The most affluent donors flock together, regardless of their political party leanings.

Figure 6-4 depicts the top fifty contributor counties for each party in 2004, with Republican locations shown in red, Democratic in blue, and locations in the top fifty for both parties in purple. Most of the major fundraising counties are highly profitable for both parties, not just for one of them. Of the top fifty fundraising counties for each party, the two parties share thirty-five. Of the top twenty donor locations for each party, eleven were shared. In absolute terms, the two parties raised roughly similar amounts of money from their top fifty counties in 2004, Democrats reaping $390.5 million and Republicans garnering $367.8 million. Overall, Republican and Democratic contributions at the county level correlated with each other at $r = .80$ ($p \leq .001$).

Within the context of this broad geographic similarity, there are some notable differences in contributions to the two parties. A simple comparison of figures 6-2 and 6-3 indicates that Republicans did better than Democrats in suburban counties, in the border states, and in Florida and Texas; Democrats relied more heavily on counties on the East and West Coasts.

The national maps of campaign contributions also reveal that Democratic contributions are concentrated in fewer areas, while Republican contributions are more geographically dispersed. Contributions from Democrats' top fifty contributor counties alone accounted for 54 percent of the total FEC-reported contributions to the party, while contributions from Republicans' top fifty contributor counties accounted for 40 percent of reported contributions to the GOP. To get a better sense of the distribution of contributions, see figure 6-5. This figure underlines the extent of the Democratic Party's more concentrated contributor base. The distribution reveals that Democrats are remarkably dependent on their top three contributor counties: Los Angeles, New York, and Cook County, Illinois. Republicans also draw some of their largest contributions from these counties, but they raise less money in these places than do Democrats. Despite their relative disadvantage in the largest metro areas, Republicans raised more money overall than Democrats in 2004. The Republican edge does not stem from contributions from a few locations. Instead, the Republican advantage builds more gradually across a large number of dispersed locations. Cumulatively, the GOP more than counterbalances its second-place status in the largest urban areas with stronger fundraising returns in a wider range of locations.

As discussed earlier, the campaign for votes follows a different strategy and focuses on a different set of locations. Figure 6-6 helps to illuminate these differences. Here we display the counties within the leaning or battleground states of the 2004 election that were the focus of each party's campaign for votes. Counties are shaded if they contributed at least 1 percent of the party's statewide vote total in 2004, contributing substantially to the winning of that state's Electoral College votes. These were therefore the critical locations in these statewide winner-take-all electoral contests, the areas where the parties focused their advertising dollars and their get-out-the-vote efforts and where the campaign for votes was fiercest.

Three aspects of this map are noteworthy. First, there is little overlap between the campaign for votes and the campaign for funds for either party. The areas most important to the parties' campaign for funds are not among the counties most important to their electoral campaigns. Neither New York nor California was in play electorally in 2004; nevertheless the two states together contributed twenty-three cents of every dollar in FEC-filed contributions to the two major parties. Meanwhile, a mere fourteen of the 384 counties identified in figure 6-6 were ranked on both top-fifty contributor lists. Both Republicans and Democrats look for money in one set of locations and conduct their campaign for votes elsewhere.

Second, a large number of these counties are purple, meaning that both parties receive at least 1 percent of their statewide total from those locations. There are very few locations within battleground states that can be written off as contributing only to a Democratic win or to a Republican win. Within the battleground states, the campaign for votes is not a game of mobilizing geographically separate electorates. In seeking to accumulate votes to win a statewide majority, Republicans and Democrats contest many of the same areas and win substantial electoral support from the same locations.

Third, the campaign for votes occurs on a much bigger battlefield than the campaign for dollars. Compared with the top fifty fundraising locations shown in figure 6-4, this map reveals that a much larger number of locations are important for vote-getting than for fundraising. Even though some decry the small number of "battleground" states in presidential elections, the campaign for votes is a considerably more far-flung and inclusive operation than the campaign for money.

Methodological Issues in Spatial Regression Analysis

To systematically analyze the geographic distribution of campaign giving, we employ spatially weighted regression analysis of Republican and Democratic contributions from 1998 to 2004. Statistical estimation begins with the recognition that our observational units are counties, and county boundaries are arbitrary conventions. What this means is that the values of the dependent variable are not independently distributed across space, but are likely to be related to one another contingent upon geographic proximity.[16] Traditional regression approaches are aspatial, in that they assume that patterns on a map are randomly generated. Failure to reckon with spatial dependence in geographic data leads to standard errors and confidence intervals that are erroneously narrow.[17]

Fortunately, the spatial autoregressivity of geographic data can now be addressed using fully validated models and specialized software.[18] We do this by calculating a spatially lagged dependent variable, which is the weighted average of dependent variable values in those counties within a sixty-mile radius. This distance was determined on the basis of a straightforward practical calculation that few individuals will attend fundraising events if they are

---

16. See Fotheringham, Brunsdon, and Charlton (2000, pp. 164–66) and Anselin (1988). Tests of our dependent variables, with the *test* statistic Moran's *I* indicated moderate degrees of positive spatial autocorrelation, reported in appendix table 6B-1.

17. Anselin (2002); Cho (2003).

18. All statistical models were estimated in MLE, using *GeoDA*, following the computation of spatially lagged dependent variables. *GeoDA* is free, open-source software developed by Luc Anselin at the University of Illinois, Urbana-Champaign. As of March 2006, it can be downloaded from: www.geoda.uiuc.edu/default.php.

required to travel farther than this. The assumption, then, is that spatial auto-correlation diminishes with distance or that proximity matters to fundraising, as it does to many other forms of political participation.[19] A more complete description of the approach and methodological issues is provided in appendix table 6B-1.

To facilitate estimation, we standardized the dependent variable dollars reported by county, converting these amounts into z-scores. The coefficients from this model are reported in appendix table 6A-1 and can be interpreted as standard deviations of change in Y resulting from a one-unit change in X. For ease of interpretation, we calculated for each statistically significant coefficient the effect in fundraising dollars of a one-unit change in the independent variable and report these amounts in table 6-1.

Results: Explaining Geographic Contribution Patterns

Table 6-1 displays the results of the spatial regression models of Democratic and Republican Party contributions for each year between 1998 and 2004. The models account for much of the contribution patterns we observe on the national contribution maps shown in figures 6-1 and 6-2. As expected, contributions are strongly affected by the geographic distribution of resources, particularly high income and population density, and by some other demographic factors. But more important, the findings reveal the extent of the disjuncture between the campaign for funds and the campaign for votes at all levels. After controlling for a wide range of demographic influences on campaign giving, we find that electoral competition rarely sparks higher levels of campaign contributions. Furthermore, the local political tilt of an area bears little relationship to a party's ability to effectively raise funds there.

We find that party competition in local races does not predict a party's fundraising success. Parties may be heavily engaged in organizing to win votes in these areas, but they either do not try or do not succeed in extracting extra funds from residents there. Competitive House and Senate races, in fact, have no statistically significant positive effect on fundraising for either party in any campaign year. Presidential battleground status failed to consistently stimulate campaign contributions: in 2000 and 2002 it had a small positive effect on Republican fundraising, but it had no statistically significant effect for Democrats in any year. Previous county-level party competition—measured as 100 − |(average Democratic vote − average Republican vote)| in the

---

19. Anselin (1988, p. 23), Cho and Rudolph (2006).

Table 6-1. Sources of Campaign Contributions to the Republican and Democratic Parties in Election Years 1998–2004[a]

Effect on dollars raised

Factor	Republican				Democratic			
	1998	2000	2002	2004	1998	2000	2002	2004
Constant	0	0	0	0	0	0	0	0
Political factors								
Competitive Senate contest	0	0	0	0	0	−59,727	0	0
Senate incumbent	0	0	−30,757	0	0	0	−27,359	0
Local House incumbent	0	0	0	−123,408	0	0	0	0
Local competitive House	0	0	0	0	0	0	0	0
County competitiveness	0	2,508	1,389	4,345	0	0	0	0
Percent Democratic (Republican)	−1,236	0	0	0	0	0	−2,501	−10,407
Battleground state	0	48,488	31,949	0	0	0	0	0
Resources								
Voting-age population density (1,000s)	39,138	124,736	59,577	188,406	113,214	258,472	140,757	585,534
Median household income (1,000s)	−6,637	−15,596	−10,353	−25,166	−6,007	−9,117	−8,096	−21,778
Percent of households earning more than $150,000	51,059	90,877	74,281	156,767	45,099	48,107	57,522	118,284
Percent of households earning more than $150,000 squared	0	4,980	0	0	3,353	7,166	2,763	7,521
Percent with college degree	4,157	0	7,979	23,419	0	−8,182	0	0
Other demographic factors								
Percent black	0	0	0	0	0	0	0	−4,711
Percent age 65 or over	0	0	0	0	0	0	0	0
Percent employed in agriculture	0	0	0	5,204	0	0	0	0
Percent employed in manufacturing	1,155	0	0	0	0	0	0	6,916
Percent professional	6,273	14,480	10,690	15,326	4,891	9,907	10,042	17,203
Percent self-employed	−4,524	−17,106	−12,260	−27,502	0	0	0	0
Cross-county networks								
Spatial lag of contributions	101,727	168,256	94,515	425,905	0	0	0	0

Source: Estimates derived from spatial regression analysis reported in appendix table 6A-1.

a. Cell entries represent the increase or decrease in contributions associated with a one-unit increase in each variable listed in the far left column, controlling for all other variables. Only estimates significant at the $p \leq 0.05$ level are reported, as all other effects are indistinguishable from 0.

Color Plates

Figure 6-1. Electorally Competitive and Noncompetitive Counties in the 2004 Presidential Election

Figure 6-2. Republican Contribution Amounts in the 2004 Election Cycle, by County

Figure 6-3. Democratic Contribution Amounts in the 2004 Election Cycle, by County

Figure 6-4. Top Fifty Contributing Locations for Republicans and Democrats, 2004

Figure 6-5. Contributions to the Two Major Parties from Their Top Fifty Contributor Counties, 2004

Figure 6-6. Locations within Battleground States That Contribute at Least 1 Percent of Total Statewide Vote for One Party or Both

Figure 6-1. Electorally Competitive and Noncompetitive Counties in the 2004 Presidential Election[a]

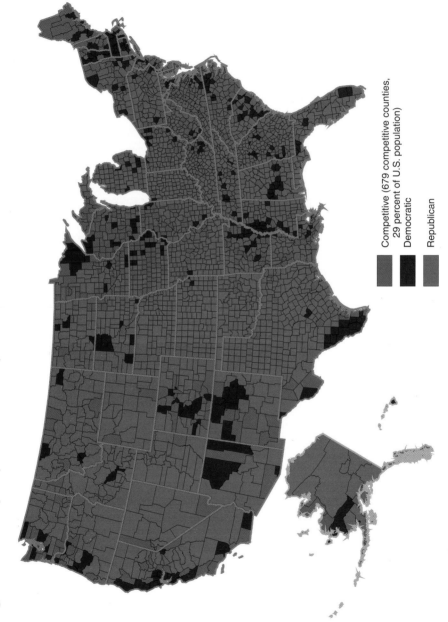

Competitive (679 competitive counties, 29 percent of U.S. population)

Democratic

Republican

a. In electorally competitive counties, the margin of victory was 10 percentage points or less.

Figure 6-2. Republican Contribution Amounts in the 2004 Election Cycle, by County

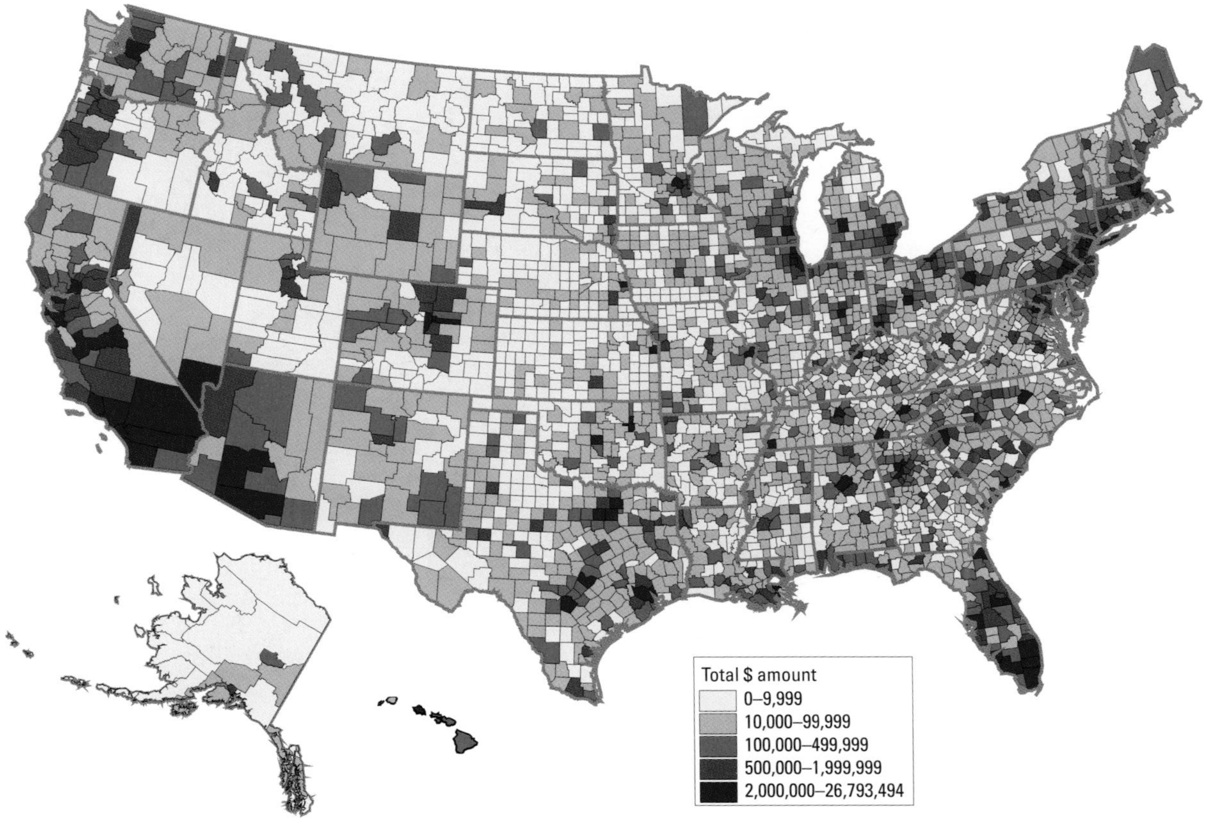

Total $ amount

- 0–9,999
- 10,000–99,999
- 100,000–499,999
- 500,000–1,999,999
- 2,000,000–26,793,494

Figure 6-3. Democratic Contribution Amounts in the 2004 Election Cycle, by County

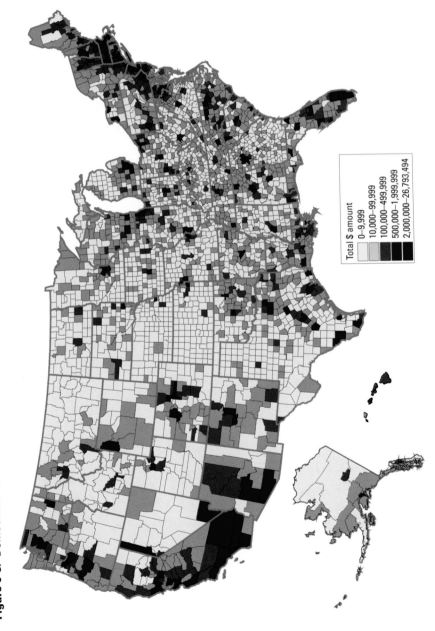

Total $ amount

0–9,999
10,000–99,999
100,000–499,999
500,000–1,999,999
2,000,000–26,793,494

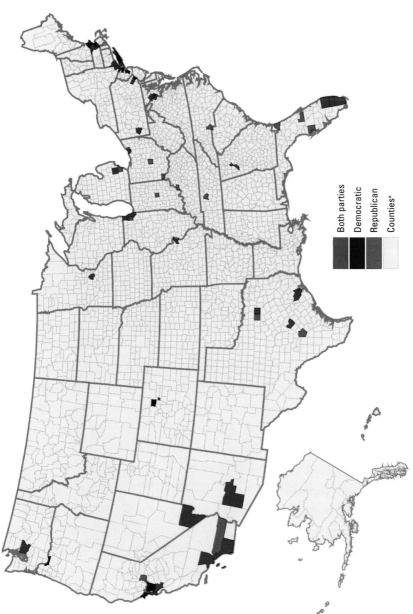

Both parties

Democratic

Republican

Counties[a]

a. The top fifty contributing counties for each party were the source of 54 percent of all Democratic contributions and 40 percent of all Republican contributions.

Figure 6-5. Contributions to the Two Major Parties from Their Top Fifty Contributor Counties, 2004[a]

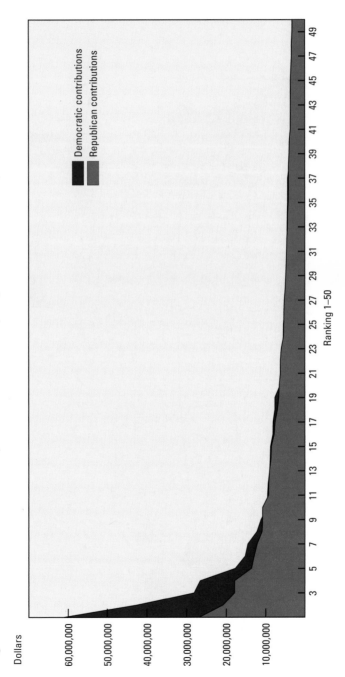

Dollars

a. Republican total = $367.8 million (54 percent of national total); Democratic total = $390.5 million (40 percent national total).

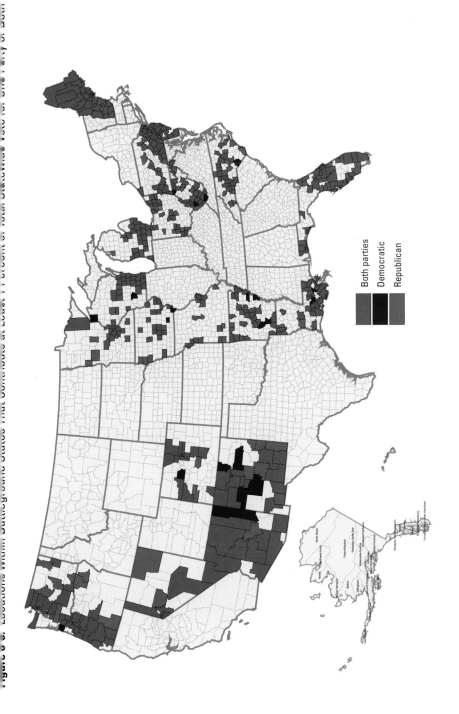

Both parties

Democratic

Republican

prior presidential election —was associated with modest increases in Republican contributions from 2000 to 2004, but never had any positive effect on Democratic fundraising. The overriding impression gleaned from these results is that campaign giving is little affected by local political winds, and certainly not by House and Senate contests.

Like local competition, House and Senate incumbency has little effect on overall party fundraising. Given that the presence of House and Senate incumbents tends to depress local electoral competition, areas represented by congressional incumbents running for reelection might be expected to yield lower contributions. On the other hand, if officeholders cultivate networks of local donors, then the presence of incumbents could have a positive effect on fundraising. Regardless of expectations, the data do not show any consistent effect one way or another. The presence of House and Senate incumbents has no statistically significant effect in either direction for most years for either party. When there is an effect—as in 2002 for Senate Republican incumbents, in 2000 for House Republican incumbents, and in 2002 for Senate Democratic incumbents—the presence of incumbents is associated with small reductions in their party's fundraising.

The partisan bias of the county has some effect on fundraising for Democrats, but none for Republicans. Our estimates show that strong Republican currents modestly depress Democratic contributions. When the effect is at its greatest (in 2004), a ten-point increase in the Republican bias of a county reduced contributions to the Democrats by about $104,000. In other years, the effect of local partisanship on Democratic fundraising was either substantially smaller or nonexistent. Republican fundraising, however, was neither helped nor hurt by a locale's party leaning in any year. As the maps reveal, affluent people capable of making campaign donations live in central cities (heavily Democratic areas in electoral terms), but these citizens contribute to both parties.

The most remarkable finding from these models is the relative weakness of political variables in explaining fundraising. Local party competition, the county's partisan tilt, and the presence of incumbents have either no effect or an inconsistent effect on fundraising. Instead, fundraising success for both parties is tied to local resources, primarily population density and wealth. Although the results are not identical for the two parties, both parties clearly contest the same turf when it comes to the campaign for cash. For example, population density (in 1,000s) greatly enhances both Republican and Democratic donations, though the effect is stronger for Democrats. A one-unit increase in density was associated with an increase in contributions of $188,400 to Republicans and $585,500 to Democrats in the 2004 cycle.

Republicans and Democrats both raise funds in the elite urban areas where wealth is most highly concentrated. A single percentage point increase in the percentage of high-income households is associated with a $157,000 increase in Republican contributions and a $118,000 increase for Democrats. Still, Democrats do better than Republicans in the areas where wealth soars to its highest levels. The squared value of high income indicates that Democrats reap an additional $7,521 for every doubling of the percentage of residents earning over $150,000, whereas the Republicans earn nothing extra. Republicans do well in locations with greater shares of college graduates, whereas Democrats do not. Taken together, the findings suggest that Republicans raise funds more successfully than Democrats in suburban and exurban areas with more evenly distributed riches. Democrats garner the most funds in city centers, where wealth rises to its peak levels of concentration.

As for occupational characteristics, both parties excel where there are hefty percentages of professionals and executives, those with the earnings and the social and business networks so useful to the fundraising enterprise. In 2004, both parties did well in locations with large percentages employed in manufacturing, though this effect is not consistent across elections. Locations with high levels of self-employment gave significantly less to Republicans in all four election cycles, while having no appreciable impact on Democrats. Although previous studies have shown that particular occupations such as farming and manufacturing have been associated with giving, we find that heavily agricultural or farming counties do not contribute more to either party.[20]

Finally, the spatially lagged dependent variable exhibits a positive and statistically significant coefficient for Republicans, but not for Democrats. This indicates that GOP contributions in neighboring counties are strongly and positively associated with Republican contributions in the typical county. Even after we control for other obvious predictors of contributing, geography still exercises an additional important effect on a locality's giving to Republicans. Specifically, in 2004, a one standard deviation increase in contributions from neighboring locations is associated with a $425,905 increase in the average county, a substantially larger effect than we observe in other years. Although the source of this spatial pattern is unknown, it is consistent with the inference that GOP contributor networks are more spread out geographically than Democratic networks.[21] By comparison, the absence of a statisti-

20. Earlier work reporting occupational effects on fundraising include Aguilar, Fordham, and Lynch (1997); Verba, Schlozman, Brady, and Nie (1993); Day and Hadley (2002); Miller and Sifry (2000).
21. Cho (2003).

cally significant coefficient on the spatial lag in the Democratic model suggests that Democratic fundraising networks lie well within counties, rather than routinely extending across county boundaries. As figure 6-4 illustrates, Democrats rely heavily on a few exceptionally large metro counties for a considerable share of their campaign funds, and unlike Republicans, they draw less on outlying suburban locations.

Discussion

In this essay, we have compared the political geographies of campaigning for votes and campaigning for funds. The two campaigns are governed by different strategic logics and are waged on different terrain. In our system of geographic representation and winner-take-all rules, the campaign for votes focuses on competitive jurisdictions where shifts in modest numbers of votes can decide election outcomes. The campaign for funds, by contrast, is a national effort in which both parties target those areas best positioned to give. These findings suggest interesting implications for both party competition and party polarization in contemporary U.S. politics.

First, attention to the geography of fundraising highlights an often overlooked facet of party competition in the United States. Areas of the country overlooked in electoral campaigns are vital to the campaign for dollars. Maps of "red" versus "blue" may be very important for understanding the two parties' electoral strategies, but they are of only limited use as parties make strategic choices about where to target their campaigns for financial capital. Campaign activity, party organizing, and partisan events are not confined to those few areas of the country that host competitive elections in any given year. Regardless of its partisan tilt in electoral terms, neither party has any incentive to write off the top fundraising locations.

Local electoral politics has little relevance to either party's ability to successfully raise funds in a locale. The competitiveness of House, Senate, and presidential contests is strikingly unimportant to the strategic logic of fundraising. Donors may be motivated by the threat of competition, but local competition is not the consideration that appears to loosen the purse strings. New Yorkers and Californians willingly and generously contribute even if their states are not in play at any level. For parties and contributors alike, fundraising is a national, not a local, contest.

Despite its national scope, party competition for funds nevertheless occurs on a small battlefield. Few voters contribute anything to the two major parties, and those who do tend to come from the nation's most densely populated, high-income counties. Both major parties need the nation's wealthy elite to fund their campaigns. As a result, they largely turn to the same areas of the country to fund their operations. The top fundraising counties for Republicans also tend to be the top fundraising counties for Democrats.

Our analysis indicated that over half of Democratic contributions and about 40 percent of Republican contributions come from just fifty counties. As these data reveal, the Republican fundraising base is more geographically dispersed than Democrats, requiring the GOP to go to more locations to equal the amount raised by Democrats. Democrats, by comparison, depend on a smaller set of super-donors (see figure 6-4, and high-income squared coefficient in table 6-1). This concentration may create greater efficiencies for Democratic fundraising than for Republicans, who may need to plow more resources back into their fundraising operations to pay for travel and event planning. But for both parties, the battle for funds is even more geographically focused than their electoral campaigns.

Second, these findings suggest some limits on partisan polarization. If large donors to the parties can be considered "party elites," then there is little question that the two parties rely on a very similar set of elites for their funds. Contributions to both parties originate from many of the same settings. Indeed, correlating zip-code-level contributions to Democrats and Republicans yields a coefficient of .67 ($p < .0001$) for 2004 and .71 ($p < .0001$) for 2002. This high level of correlation shows that the two parties are to a great extent drawing on the same neighborhoods within counties. However different donors to the two parties may be in other respects, one has to believe that this commonality plays a moderating role, bringing the parties closer together rather than contributing to greater polarization.

That the parties' financial bases intersect geographically also means that both major parties build and preserve ties to the foremost cultural and commercial centers throughout the country. The Democratic Party maintains lines of communication with economic interests and wealthy individuals in North Carolina, Georgia, and along the Gulf Coast from Houston to Florida's panhandle, areas that the party might neglect if electoral prospects alone dictated party strategy and organizational efforts. Similarly, the Republican Party nurtures fundraising networks in the San Francisco Bay Area, the Twin Cities, Detroit, and Chicago. Regardless of shifting electoral strategies as states' "battleground status" changes, both parties maintain these ties for fundraising purposes. Year after year, election after election, parties and candidates return to the same communities, and many of the same donors, to raise money.

Do donors have a greater voice in steering party policy than voters? Some think so and often denounce the undemocratic effects of money in politics. Without minimizing these normative concerns, the fact that the campaign for funds leads both major political parties to cultivate connections and supporters in all the population centers of the country may have some desirable side effects. The campaign for funds gives parties and candidates reason to devote time and resources to cultivating and maintaining organizations and networks in areas that may not be important to winning votes. To the extent that donors do carry weight beyond their numbers, the fact that the parties share such geographically and demographically similar donor bases may serve as a check on party polarization.

Appendix 6A. Variables and Variable Definitions

Population density: voting-age population of county/land area (expressed in 1,000s)

Percent earning $150,000 or more: percent of households earning $150,000 or more annually in county

Median household income: median household income of county (expressed in $1,000s)

Percent over age 65: percent of county population over age 65

Percent with a four-year college degree: percent of county population with a four-year college degree

Percent in farming: percent of working-age population of county employed in farming

Percent in manufacturing: percent of working-age population of county employed in manufacturing

Percent professional and executive: percent of working-age population of county employed as executives or professionals

Percent self-employed: percent of working-age population of county that is self-employed

Percent black: percent of county population of African American ancestry

Competitive Senate: 1,0 dummy evaluation of competitiveness of the county's Senate seat from *Congressional Quarterly Weekly* report

Presence of Senate incumbent: 1,0 dummy indicating open-seat contest, or Senate incumbent running for reelection

Presence of House incumbent(s): Proportion variable indicating open-seat contest (0), or House incumbent running for reelection (1). In cases where there was more than one House seat representing a county, we

Table 6A-1. Predictors of Republican and Democratic Campaign Contributions, 1998–2004[a]

Variable	Republican				Democratic			
	1998 MLEb[b]	2000 MLEb	2002 MLEb	2004 MLEb	1998 MLEb	2000 MLEb	2002 MLEb	2004 MLEb
Constant	-0.527 (0.218)	-0.301 (0.204)	-0.434 (0.190)	-0.200 (0.191)	0.170 (0.187)	0.022 (0.181)	0.240 (0.186)	0.390 (0.174)
Political factors								
Competitive Senate contest	0.073* (0.035)	-0.046 (0.037)	-0.039 (0.032)	-0.001 (0.036)	0.046 (0.033)	-0.083 (0.035)	-0.035 (0.031)	0.044 (0.035)
Senate incumbent	-0.015 (0.031)	-0.009 (0.029)	-0.078* (0.031)	0.024 (0.030)	0.023 (0.030)	-0.019 (0.028)	-0.059 (0.030)	0.032 (0.029)
Local House incumbent	-0.029 (0.067)	-0.046 (0.065)	-0.076 (0.042)	-0.107 (0.056)	-0.023 (0.064)	-0.009 (0.061)	-0.058 (0.041)	-0.028 (0.053)
Local competitive House	0.072 (0.049)	0.014 (0.045)	0.013 (0.042)	-0.048 (0.046)	0.077 (0.047)	0.008 (0.043)	-0.004 (0.041)	-0.024 (0.044)
County competitiveness	0.002* (0.001)	0.004* (0.001)	0.004* (0.001)	0.004* (0.001)	-0.0002 (0.0013)	0.0009 (0.0013)	0.0003 (0.0012)	0.0000 (0.0011)
Percent Democratic (Republican)	0.001 (0.002)	-0.001 (0.002)	0.000 (0.002)	0.001 (0.002)	-0.004 (0.001)	-0.003 (0.002)	-0.005 (0.002)	-0.006 (0.001)
Battleground state	-0.013 (0.021)	0.073* (0.020)	0.082* (0.019)	0.034 (0.022)	-0.016 (0.020)	0.034 (0.018)	0.023 (0.019)	-0.015 (0.021)
Resources								
Voting-age population density (1,000s)	0.159* (0.010)	0.187* (0.010)	0.152* (0.010)	0.163* (0.010)	0.359 (0.010)	0.360 (0.010)	0.301 (0.010)	0.335 (0.010)
Median household income (1,000s)	-0.027* (0.004)	-0.023* (0.003)	-0.026* (0.003)	-0.022* (0.003)	-0.019 (0.004)	-0.013 (0.003)	-0.017 (0.003)	-0.012 (0.003)
Percent of households earning more than $150,000	0.207* (0.036)	0.136* (0.026)	0.190* (0.026)	0.136* (0.020)	0.143 (0.035)	0.067 (0.024)	0.123 (0.026)	0.068 (0.019)
Percent of households earning more than $150,000 squared	0.003 (0.003)	0.007* (0.002)	0.002 (0.002)	0.001 (0.001)	0.011 (0.003)	0.010 (0.001)	0.006 (0.002)	0.004 (0.001)
Percent with college degree	0.017* (0.007)	0.009 (0.006)	0.020* (0.006)	0.020* (0.006)	-0.006 (0.007)	-0.011 (0.006)	-0.007 (0.006)	-0.003 (0.005)

Other demographic factors

Percent black	0.000 (0.001)	0.001 (0.001)	0.003* (0.001)	0.000 (0.001)	-0.001 (0.001)	-0.001 (0.001)	-0.001 (0.001)	-0.003 (0.001)
Percent of county population over age 65	0.004 (0.005)	0.002 (0.005)	0.001 (0.005)	0.001 (0.004)	-0.003 (0.004)	0.000 (0.004)	-0.003 (0.004)	0.000 (0.004)
Percent employed in agriculture	0.003 (0.004)	0.001 (0.004)	0.001 (0.004)	0.001 (0.003)	-0.002 (0.004)	-0.001 (0.003)	0.000 (0.004)	0.001 (0.003)
Percent employed in manufacturing	0.005* (0.002)	0.004* (0.002)	0.004 (0.002)	0.005* (0.002)	0.001 (0.002)	0.002 (0.002)	0.004 (0.002)	0.004 (0.002)
Percent professional	0.025* (0.006)	0.022* (0.005)	0.027* (0.005)	0.013* (0.004)	0.016 (0.006)	0.014 (0.004)	0.021 (0.005)	0.010 (0.003)
Percent self-employed	-0.018* (0.007)	-0.026* (0.006)	-0.031* (0.006)	-0.024* (0.006)	-0.001 (0.006)	-0.004 (0.006)	-0.009 (0.006)	-0.004 (0.005)
Cross-county networks								
Spatial lag of contributions	0.413* 0.025	0.252* 0.028	0.241* 0.028	0.368* 0.026	-0.058 0.032	-0.045 0.031	-0.055 0.032	-0.006 0.031
N	3,140	3,140	3,140	3,140	3,140	3,140	3,140	3,140
Standard error of estimate	0.78	0.78	0.79	0.79	0.75	0.74	0.77	0.75
Log-likelihood	-3720.1	-3693.5	-3729.7	-3750.3	-3563.5	-3637.0	-3493.6	-3546.1
R^2	0.39	0.39	0.37	0.37	0.44	0.46	0.41	0.43
AIC[c]	7480.1	7426.9	7499.3	7540.5	7132.2	7029.0	7314.1	7175.6
Moran's I	-0.014	0.011	-0.01	-0.044	0.01	0.02	0.01	0.03

Source: U.S. FEC-reported contributions to major parties and campaigns, aggregated to the U.S. county level for each year.

a. Cell entries are ML coefficients (standard errors); for full definitions of the variables listed here, see appendix 6A.

b. Maximum likelihood estimation with spatial lag.

c. Akaike Information Criterion.

*$p \leq 0.05$, two-tailed.

counted the share of all House seats contained within or intersecting the county boundaries in which an incumbent was running for reelection

Competitive House: 1,0 proportion variable for the county's House seat competitiveness from *Congressional Quarterly Weekly* report. In cases where there was more than one House seat representing a county, we counted the share of all House seats contained within or intersecting the county boundaries that were considered competitive

Previous Democratic vote (county): average Democratic vote for the previous presidential election

Previous Republican vote (county): average Republican vote for the previous presidential election

Party competitiveness of the county: $100 - |$ (average Democratic vote – average Republican vote)| for the previous presidential election

Battleground state: 0,1,2 indicating the classification of the state as safe (0), leaning for one party or the other (1), or battleground for both parties (2)

Contributions of neighboring areas: Weighted average of the contribution amount for the counties within sixty miles

Appendix 6B: Spatial Regression

The likely relationship between adjacent and proximate counties poses special challenges from a statistical standpoint because we must be cognizant of spatial structure. Therefore we perform appropriate diagnostic tests to determine the degree of spatial autocorrelation. Then we include an appropriate spatially lagged dependent variable to control for it.

Testing for Spatial Structure

Following recommended procedures, we first estimated a standard ordinary least squares regression model and tested for violation of the assumption of no spatial dependency in the resulting error term. Moran's I is a means of measuring the extent of spatial dependence (Griffith 1987; Anselin 1988). Moran's I is formulated to discriminate between different arrangements of x values on a planar surface. High positive values of Moran's I indicate positive spatial autocorrelation, showing that neighboring values are very similar. High negative values exhibit negative spatial autocorrelation, meaning neighboring values are dissimilar, following a checkerboard pattern. Values approaching zero indicate no significant spatial structure.[1]

1. Cho (2003); Goodchild (1986).

Moran's I assesses the degree of linear association between a set of observations and a weighted average of the values of the neighbors of those observations. A formal statement of Moran's I is as follows:

$$I = [N/S].\{[e'We]/e'e\},$$

where e is a vector of residuals, W is a spatial weights matrix, expressing the pattern of spatial dependency among units of analysis (zip codes), N is the number of observations, and S is a standardization factor equal to the sum of all the elements in the weight matrix. Since N/S is only a scaling term, it can be omitted from the test statistic, yielding the expression:

$$I = [e'We]/e'e$$

The weights matrix itself specifies how the individual units of observation are related to one another. Taking each county as a distinct unit, we calculated a sixty-mile distance band for all observations using the statistical software *GeoDa*™. This produced an $N \times N$ matrix specifying the spatial relationship between each observation to all observations whose centroids were within sixty miles, and to all other counties in the nation. We then converted the distance matrix to a binary contiguity matrix $(1,0)$. This conversion results in an $N \times N$ matrix, W, of 1s and 0s, with 1s indicating linkages to those observations within sixty miles, 0 indicating no such linkage. The spatial weights matrix, once constructed, is then standardized such that the row elements sum to one.

Moran's I is normally distributed and can be evaluated for statistical significance using a z-score test.[2] The results from least squares estimation revealed positive and statistically significant spatial autocorrelation in the models for the Republicans, but much lower for the Democrats (see appendix table 6B-1). Given the large sample size, all calculated Moran's I tests on residuals were statistically significant, regardless of magnitude.

Accounting for Spatial Structure

To account for spatial structure, we calculate a spatially lagged dependent variable, W, which is the weighted average of dependent variable values in those counties within a sixty-mile radius. W then is the spatial distance matrix for all counties, with the rows rescaled to sum to one. Adding the spatial distance matrix to the standard regression model leads to the estimation:

2. Anselin (1988, pp. 101–03).

$$y = \rho W y + X\beta + \epsilon,$$

where y is an $N \times 1$ vector of observations on the dependent variable, Wy is an $N \times 1$ vector of spatial lags for the dependent variable, ρ is the spatial autoregressive coefficient, X is an $N \times K$ matrix of observations on the explanatory variables, along with $K \times 1$ vectors of regression coefficients β, and ϵ is an $N \times 1$ vector of normally distributed random error terms, with mean 0, and homoskedastic error variance σ^2. The model is estimated via maximum likelihood because ρ is usually unknown. It can be shown that the valid range for ρ must be ≤ 1.[3] The estimated value of ρ tells us how the neighboring values of y are related to the values at y itself. Inclusion of this spatial lag reduced the level of spatial autocorrelation and brings the model into line with standard regression assumptions.

In addition to the sixty-mile distance matrix, we undertook several other specifications of the weights, including forty-mile and thirty-mile distance bands, as well as first- and higher-order contiguity weights. These specifications also reduced spatial dependency as tested by Moran's I as effectively as the specification we report in this paper. These results are available from the authors upon request.

Table 6B-1 displays Moran's I values for the dependent variable alone, for models after including the independent variables but no spatial lag, and full models with a spatial lag. The inclusion of the spatial lag reduces the level of spatial autocorrelation dramatically for Republicans over the OLS specification alone. The OLS specification succeeds in reducing spatial autocorrelation for Democrats, with the spatial lag producing coefficients that were statistically insignificant and substantively unimportant. Though unnecessary in the final estimation, we include the spatial lag for Democratic contributions to enhance comparability with the Republican contribution model.

Goodness of Fit

The standard R^2 measure of fit is not applicable in the spatial lag model, and in its place we report a simple ratio of the variance of the predicted values over the variance of the observed values for the dependent variable.[4] We also report the value of the maximized log-likelihood, and the Akaike Information Criterion (AIC).[5]

---

3. Griffith (1988); Fotheringham, Brunsdon, and Charlton (2000).
4. Anselin (1995).
5. Models with higher log-likelihoods or lower AICs are considered superior.

Table 6B-1. Values of Moran's *I* for Republican and Democratic Contribution Amounts Using Sixty-Mile Distance Matrix, 1998–2004

Year	Moran's I dependent variable		Moran's I OLS		Moran's I with spatial lag	
	Republican	Democrat	Republican	Democrat	Republican	Democrat
1998	.28	.12	.22	.01	−.04	.04
2000	.23	.14	.13	−.01	−.01	.01
2002	.20	.13	.12	.004	.01	.02
2004	.25	.14	.19	.02	−.01	.01

References

Aguilar, Edwin Eloy, Benjamin O. Fordham, and G. Patrick Lynch. 1997. "The Foreign Policy Beliefs of Political Campaign Contributors." *International Studies Quarterly* 41: 355–366.

Alexander, Herbert E. 1992. *Financing Politics: Money, Elections, and Political Reform.* Washington: CQ Press.

Amy, Douglas J. 2002. *Real Choices/New Voices.* 2nd ed. Columbia University Press.

Anselin, Luc. 1988. *Spatial Econometrics: Methods and Models.* Boston: Kluwer.

———. 2002. "Under the Hood: Issues in the Specification and Interpretation of Spatial Regression Models." *Agricultural Economics* 24 (7): 247–67.

Brady, Henry E., Kay Lehman Schlozman, and Sidney Verba. 1999. "Prospecting for Participants: Rational Expectations and the Recruitment of Political Activists." *American Political Science Review* 93 (1): 153–68.

Brown, Clifford W., Jr., Roman B. Hedges, and Lynda W. Powell. 1980. "Modes of Elite Political Participation: Contributors to the 1972 Presidential Candidates." *American Journal of Political Science* 24: 259–90.

Brown, Clifford W., Jr., Lynda W. Powell, and Clyde Wilcox. 1995. *Serious Money: Fundraising and Contributing in Presidential Nomination Campaigns.* Cambridge University Press.

Campbell, James E. 1996. *Cheap Seats: The Democratic Party's Advantage in U.S. House Elections.* Ohio State University Press.

Cho, Wendy K. Tam. 2003. "Contagion Effects and Ethnic Contribution Networks." *American Journal of Political Science* 47, 2 (April): 368–387.

Cho, Wendy K. Tam, and Thomas J. Rudolph. Forthcoming. "Emanating Political Participation: Untangling the Spatial Structure behind Participation." *British Journal of Political Science.*

Day, Christine L., and Charles D. Hadley. 2002. "Who Contributes? Similarities and Differences between Contributors to Emily's List and WISH List." *Women and Politics* 24 (2): 53–67.

Fotheringham, A. Stewart, Chris Brunsdon, and Martin Charlton. 2000. *Quantitative Geography: Perspectives on Spatial Data Analysis.* London: Sage.

Francia, Peter L., Paul S. Herrnson, John C. Green, Lynda W. Powell, and Clyde Wilcox. 2003. *The Financiers of Congressional Elections: Investors, Ideologues, and Intimates.* Columbia University Press.

Gimpel, James G., and Wendy Tam Cho. 2006. "Prospecting for Campaign Gold." Paper presented at the annual meeting of the Midwest Political Science Association, Chicago, April 21–23.

Gimpel, James G., and Jason E. Schuknecht. 2002. "Reconsidering Political Regionalism in the American States." *State Politics and Policy Quarterly* 2 (4): 325–52.

———. 2003. *Patchwork Nation: Sectionalism and Political Change in American Politics.* University of Michigan Press.

Gimpel, James G., Frances E. Lee, and Joshua Kaminski. Forthcoming 2006. "The Political Geography of Campaign Contributions in American Politics." *Journal of Politics.*

Griffith, Daniel A. 1988. *Advanced Spatial Statistics.* Dordrecht: Kluwer Academic.

Herrnson, Paul S. 2003. *Congressional Elections: Campaigning at Home and in Washington.* Washington: CQ Press.

Hinckley, Katherine A., and John C. Green. 1996. "Fundraising in Presidential Nomination Campaigns: The Primary Lessons of 1988." *Political Research Quarterly* 49 (4): 693–718.

Miller, Ellen S., and Micah L. Sifry. 2000. "Who Gives? Surveys of Political Contributors." *American Prospect* 11 (22): 10–11.

Mutz, Diana C. 1995. "Effects of Horse-Race Coverage on Campaign Coffers: Strategic Contributing in Presidential Primaries." *Journal of Politics* 57: 1015–42.

Pitney, John J., Jr. 2000. *The Art of Political Warfare.* University of Oklahoma Press.

Pew Research Center for the People and the Press. 2005. "The American Public: Opinions and Values in a 51–48 Nation." In *Trends 2005.* Washington: Pew Research Center.

Shaw, Daron R. 1999. "The Effect of TV Ads and Candidate Appearances on Statewide Presidential Votes, 1988–96." *American Political Science Review* 93 (2): 345–62.

Verba, Sidney, Kay Lehman Schlozman, Henry E. Brady, and Norman H. Nie. 1993. "Citizen Activity: Who Participates? What Do They Say?" *American Political Science Review* 87: 303–18.

Verba, Sidney, Kay Lehman Schlozman, and Henry E. Brady. 1995. *Voice and Equality: Civic Voluntarism in American Politics.* Harvard University Press.

PART TWO

Reform Mechanisms

7 Direct Democracy and Electoral Reform

John G. Matsusaka

Direct democracy is emerging as one of the central institutions of modern democracy.[1] Roughly half of all American states and cities now allow citizens to propose and directly approve laws using initiatives, and over 70 percent of the population lives in either a city or state that allows initiatives.[2] Since California's famous tax-cutting Proposition 13 in 1978, initiative use has exploded across the country, and in some states appears to be eclipsing legislatures as the primary agenda-setting institution. The number of state-level initiatives going before the voters over the decade 1996–2005—more than 360—exceeded the record of the previous decade, which exceeded the record of the decade before that. The number of local measures is unknown but, as an example, there were more than 800 in four Southern

I thank Melissa Cully Anderson and Thomas Stratmann for aid in assembling the data and Michael McDonald and Brad Smith for helpful comments.

1. "Direct democracy" includes a variety of practices ranging from town meetings to different kinds of ballot propositions. To define terms, an "initiative" is a statute or constitutional amendment that is proposed by a citizen, placed on the ballot by petition, and becomes law if adopted by voters in an election. A "referendum" is a popular vote on a law proposed or adopted by the legislature.

2. These numbers and other information not otherwise attributed are taken from Matsusaka (2004, 2005a).

California counties for the period 1991–2000, for which we do have data. In Europe, where referendums are becoming the accepted way of deciding issues related to national sovereignty, ten nations provide for initiatives in their constitutions, including at least six successor states to the Soviet Union, and the draft Constitution for the European Union allows both initiatives and referendums. Direct democracy is also gaining a foothold in Asia. In 2003, Taiwan adopted a law providing for national initiatives and referendums, and local initiatives are being used in Japan, South Korea, and Taiwan.

The growing popularity of direct democracy seems related to long-term changes in demographics and communications technology. Education levels have risen dramatically across the globe during the past fifty years, and satellites, the Internet, and a host of digital technologies have given ordinary citizens access to an unprecedented amount of information. A century ago, democracies had little alternative to appointing a group of "wise men," sending them to the capitals, and letting them settle the public policy issues of the day. However, ordinary citizens are now capable of grappling with important policy decisions themselves, and are increasingly unwilling to turn those decisions over to elected officials and to bear the associated agency costs. Opinion surveys reveal that 70 percent or more of Americans approve of direct democracy at the state level (with majorities in every state), and a majority of Americans are in favor of federal initiatives. The numbers are comparable in Europe.[3]

Perhaps the main justification for initiatives and referendums is to give the people an option to override government officials when those officials fail to pursue the public interest. The early twentieth-century Progressives who brought the initiative and referendum to the United States were concerned that government might be captured by powerful special interests. If public officials willfully ignore the many to serve the few, the initiative and referendum give voters tools to take matters into their own hands. Even if elected officials are not beholden to special interests, in an increasingly complex and dynamic world government officials might make poor policy decisions simply out of ignorance, what might be called "honest mistakes." A well-meaning representative might find it challenging to determine public opinion on a particular issue because voters elect candidates on bundles of issues and have no way of signaling their preferences on individual issues.

---

3. For polling information, see the websites of the Initiative and Referendum Institute at USC: www.iandrinstitute.org; and IRI-Europe: www.iri-europe.org. For additional discussion of trends, see Matsusaka (2005b).

Initiatives and referendums allow voters to correct policy "mistakes" without having to replace their representatives.[4]

One area in which the decisions of elected officials may be out of sync with voter preferences is on matters concerning political accountability and competition. For such electoral issues, incumbents may have a personal interest in limiting accountability and competition, an interest at odds with the preferences of their constituents. It is on these issues that allowing voters to make policy directly may matter the most.[5]

The first part of this essay describes and summarizes the ballot propositions concerning electoral reform in the American states over the period 1904–2005. More than 300 state-level initiatives relating to political accountability and competition have been decided since the first use of the initiative in Oregon in 1904. The most popular issues have been term limits, redistricting, and campaign finance, in that order. The main issues have changed over time, with women's suffrage, direct elections, and legislative structure (the number of seats in the legislature and how they are apportioned) important in the early twentieth century, and term limits and campaign finance more important recently.

The second part of the essay attempts to assess the extent to which direct democracy has been important in bringing about reform of electoral institutions. There are two challenges to such an assessment. The first is the ambiguity about which laws promote competition and which entrench incumbents. For example, public funding of campaigns is touted by some reformers as a way to increase competition by leveling the financial playing field for candidates with limited resources, while others have argued that the spending limits tied to public funding can work to the advantage of incumbents who are already well known.[6] Rather than making a subjective assignment, I cast a wide net over fourteen laws that have attracted reformers and for which state-by-state information was available for 2005, and investigate whether the initiative has promoted adoption of the laws.

But ballot propositions alone do not determine the impact of direct democracy. In a state with initiatives, the state legislature might adopt a law it would not have otherwise voted to enact in order to avoid having an initiative on the issue on the ballot; in such an instance the initiative matters but

---

4. Besley and Coate (2003) and Matsusaka (2005c) explore the idea that initiatives can improve democratic policymaking in a multidimensional world by "unbundling" specific issues.

5. Garrett (2005).

6. Samples (2005).

will not leave a trace in the record of ballot propositions (what has been called the "indirect effect"). We also need a benchmark: initiatives might lead to adoption of a particular reform in initiative states, but the same reform might be adopted by legislatures in states where initiatives are unavailable. In light of these issues, scholars typically test for the effect of direct democracy by comparing policy choices in states with and without initiatives, controlling for other factors that determine policy. The idea is that however the initiative affects policy—directly or indirectly—it will show up in the final outcome.

The main finding of the second part of the essay is that the initiative does not appear to have had much effect on the adoption of laws affecting political competition and accountability, controlling for a variety of demographic and political factors. The notable exception is term limits, where availability of the initiative has been essential. This evidence confirms the general finding of Persily and Anderson, based on a study of ten separate laws, that initiative and noninitiative states have fairly similar election rules,[7] and extends their analysis by showing that the similarities run fairly deep, remaining even after controlling for region, demographics, and ideology. The evidence also supports the idea that initiatives are critical for adoption of term limits, but it reaches a different conclusion on commission-based redistricting by showing that differences between initiative and noninitiative states are due to factors other than the initiative.

The essay concludes by discussing why direct democracy has been largely a sideshow in electoral reform. It seems that even though initiatives give voters a tool to introduce more competition into elections, a majority of voters do not want more competition because the current officials are chosen by the majority.

Electoral Reform Initiatives

The most comprehensive listing of state-level initiatives is the Initiative and Referendum Institute's Initiatives Database. The database lists 2,151 initiatives that have come before the voters since 1904, when the first measure appeared in Oregon, to 2005, a virtually complete list with just a few exceptions from early in the twentieth century. I extracted from the database the 302 initiatives pertaining to electoral reform and grouped them into several categories. Table 7-1 lists the categories and gives examples of the issues included in each. Each category could contain measures that promoted or repealed the institution in

---

7. Persily and Anderson (2005).

Table 7-1. Initiatives Concerning Political Competition and Accountability

Category	Laws (examples)
Ballot access	Petition requirements for candidates; party registration deadlines
Ballot design	English-only ballots; nonpartisan ballots; party column vs. office arrangements
Campaign finance	Regulations on contributions and expenditure, disclosure, and public financing; restrictions on unions and corporations
Direct election	Direct elections for U.S. senators; party nominations by direct vote
Election administration	Bipartisan election boards, ethics commission
Initiatives and referendums	Petition requirements; amendment by legislature
Legislative structure	Number of seats; bicameral vs. unicameral; multimember versus single-member districts
Primaries	Open versus closed; instant runoff
Recall	Allowing officeholders to be recalled
Redistricting	Redistricting by commission; timing of redistricting
Term length	Shortening or lengthening terms
Term limits	Limits on the number of terms a person can hold an office
Voter eligibility	Women's suffrage; poll tax; property requirement to vote in bond elections
Voter registration	Election day registration; registration while applying for driver's license; registration by mail
Voting procedures	Absentee ballots; voting machines

Source: Compiled by author.

question, so there is a mix of progressive, conservative, and sometimes just unusual measures. For example, the term-limits category includes both measures to adopt term limits and measures to relax them.

Figure 7-1 shows the number of initiatives by state, and the number approved by voters. California and Oregon are the leaders, with thirty-seven electoral reform initiatives each. These states are the leading users of initiatives overall as well. Other states with more than twenty reform initiatives are Colorado, Arkansas, and North Dakota. One reason these particular states had so many initiatives is that signature requirements to qualify a measure for the ballot are fairly low.[8]

Figure 7-2 shows the number of measures of each type and the fraction that were approved by voters. The most popular subject was term limits, with fifty-seven measures, most of which imposed or tightened the limits. The next most popular subject was campaign finance, with forty measures, followed closely by redistricting, with thirty-six measures. Of the three, voters approved a majority of the measures concerning term limits and campaign finance, but only a little more than a third of the redistricting measures. The popularity of term-limits measures suggests that legislatures do a particularly poor job of

8. Matsusaka (2004, appendix A1.1).

Figure 7-1. Electoral Reform Initiative by State, 1904–2005[a]

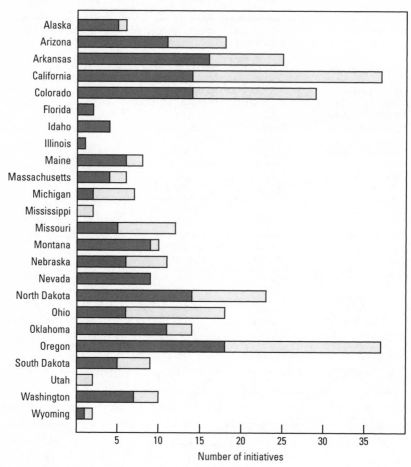

Number of initiatives

Source: Initiative and Referendum Institute, University of Southern California.
a. The figure shows the total number of electoral reform initiatives during the period 1904–2005. The dark segments indicate the number approved by the voters.

responding to constituent interests on this issue, forcing citizens to fall back on initiatives to bring about the changes they want.

Figure 7-3 shows the number of issues by decade going back to 1904.[9] This figure compresses the subjects into four categories: campaign finance,

9. The first "decade" is actually twelve years, incorporating the extra two years of the 102-year sample.

Figure 7-2. Subjects of Initiatives in the United States, 1904–2005[a]

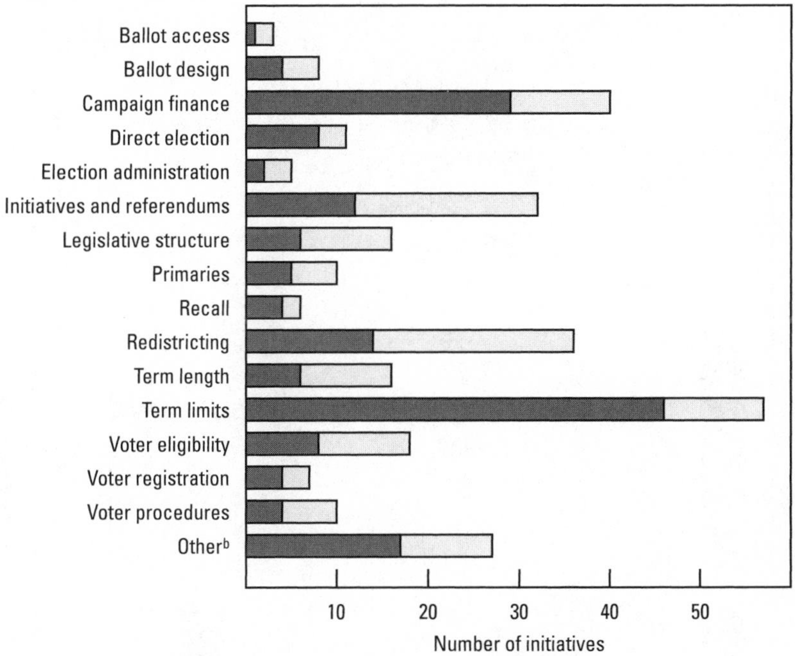

Source: Initiative and Referendum Institute, University of Southern California.

a. The figure shows the total number of electoral reform initiatives during the period 1904–2005. The dark segments indicate the number approved by the voters.

b. Includes measures such as requiring election of the commissioner of education and sheriffs, setting compensation and privileges of legislators, establishing eligibility requirements for serving in the legislature, prohibiting the use of government funds for political purposes, and allocating presidential electoral votes proportionally instead of on a winner-take-all basis.

redistricting, terms (length and limits), and elections and voting. As can be seen, there was a burst of activity in the first period, 1904–15. Even adjusting for the two extra years of this period, the total number of initiatives did not reach the 1904–15 level again until the late 1980s. The issues in the early twentieth century were somewhat different than what we saw in the most recent twenty-year period, from 1986 to 2005. Reformers were interested in elections (direct primaries), voting rights (poll taxes and women's suffrage), and legislative structure (districts based on population rather than geography). In contrast to recent experience, there was little interest in campaign finance and term limits in the first six decades of the initiative period (the early "terms" initiatives largely concerned term length, although there were some limits placed on the number of terms served by a governor). As I have

Figure 7-3. Initiative Subjects by Decade, 1904–2005

Percent

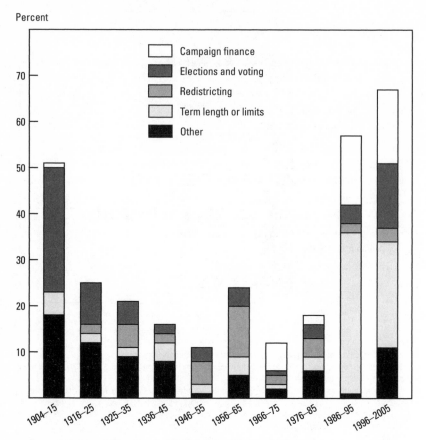

Source: Initiative and Referendum Institute, University of Southern California.

argued elsewhere,[10] much of the initiative activity in the early twentieth century was the result of malapportioned legislatures. In the days before the one-person one-vote principle was established, state legislatures tended to overweight rural interests. With the dramatic growth in cities around the turn of the nineteenth century, many states found themselves with new urban majorities but with legislatures dominated by rural interests. Reformers used the initiative to try to correct the situation by reapportioning legislatures on the basis of population and taking away the power of legislatures

10. See Matsusaka (2004, chap. 7).

to select U.S. senators. Initiatives in this period were also used to bring about substantive policies favored by the urban population, such as workers' compensation and old-age pensions.[11]

Reform activity was muted from 1916 to 1985, perhaps because much of the pent-up reform agenda had been adopted. A new surge in initiative activity began in the late 1970s following California's tax-cutting Proposition 13, and interest in electoral reform initiatives took off about a decade later. The character of recent activity is different than in previous decades, with an emphasis on campaign finance and term limits, both of which were largely ignored before the late 1960s. By far the most important were measures concerning terms, with a total of fifty-eight initiatives over the two decades 1986–2005.

Overall, figure 7-3 shows that reformers have embraced the initiative as a tool to advance their agendas. Whether all of this citizen lawmaking adds up to significantly different electoral institutions is the subject of the next section.

Are Electoral Laws Different in Initiative States?

To estimate the impact of the initiative on the adoption of political institutions, it is not enough to study the propositions that were approved by voters because the threat of an initiative could influence policy choices without a measure appearing on the ballot. And even when a reform was approved by an initiative, the initiative might not have been essential. It is possible the reform would have been approved by the legislature if the initiative had not appeared. Measuring the impact of direct democracy requires tracing the effect back to *availability* of the initiative by comparing the policies of states that have direct democracy with those that do not have it. Any differences that remain after controlling for other factors, such as the ideology of state electorates, can be attributed to the availability of direct democracy.

There is a healthy literature that estimates the effect of the initiative on policy using this strategy. More than ten studies have found that initiative states spent and taxed less than noninitiative states beginning around the mid-1970s, all else equal.[12] My research indicates that initiative states shifted spending from state to local governments, and shifted financing from broad-based taxes to user fees and charges for services, requiring those who use

11. Matsusaka (2000).
12. These studies are listed in Matsusaka (2004, appendix 4).

government services to pay for them.[13] Gerber found that initiative states were more likely than noninitiative states to allow the death penalty and to require parental notification before a minor could get an abortion.[14]

There is also some evidence on how the initiative affects political institutions. Initiative states pay their top officials (governor, secretary of state, attorney general, lieutenant governor, treasurer) lower salaries, controlling for population, wealth, and region of the state.[15] Research has also found that campaign finance regulations were stricter in initiative states than in noninitiative states;[16] that initiative states were more likely to adopt legislative term limits;[17] and that initiative states were more likely to adopt gubernatorial term limits.[18] In a study of ten different policies that did not control for other factors, Persily and Anderson found only three meaningful differences between initiative and noninitiative states: initiative states were more likely to adopt legislative term limits and commission-based redistricting, and less likely to adopt direct primaries (before 1915).[19]

My approach here is to identify laws associated with electoral reform and explore whether availability of the initiative influenced adoption of those laws. I was able to collect information on fourteen separate laws that often appear as part of a reform agenda. The fourteen laws are listed in table 7-2, and the fraction of initiative and noninitiative states with each law is reported. To bring some structure to the blizzard of information, I grouped the laws into four categories: campaign finance, elections and voting, redistricting, and terms, and constructed group indexes by summing the values for the individual laws. For example, if a state provided public funding for executive races and public funding for legislative races, and had an independent election board, then its index score was 3; if it had only two of these three laws, its score was 2, and so on. The table does not tell us if the initiative was responsible for different electoral laws because it does not isolate the effect of the initiative from other factors that influence policy choices, such as region, population, and so on. The table also does not tell us which states have more political accountability and competition because whether these laws actually

13. See Matsusaka (1995; 2004, chap. 3). These fiscal patterns—lower spending, decentralization from state to local government, and revenue shifts from taxes to fees—hold for Swiss cantons as well (Feld and Matsusaka, 2003; Schaltegger and Feld, 2001).

14. Gerber (1999).

15. Matsusaka (2005c).

16. Pippen, Bowler, and Donovan (2003).

17. Tolbert (1998).

18. Matsusaka (2005c).

19. Persily and Anderson (2005).

Table 7-2. Fraction of States with Laws Relating to Political Competition and Accountability[a]

Law	Initiative states	Noninitiative states	p value: means are different
Campaign finance			
Public funding, executive	0.26	0.33	.586
Public funding, legislature	0.13	0.11	.838
Oversight board for elections	0.65	0.52	.350
Campaign finance index (0–3)	1.04	0.96	.751
Elections and voting			
Absentee ballots allowed	0.74	0.33	.004
Ballot access fee less than $100	0.70	0.63	.632
Ballot accessible without signatures	0.70	0.56	.319
Fusion ballots allowed	0.22	0.19	.782
Open primaries	0.70	0.59	.460
Elections and voting index (0–5)	2.65	2.19	.165
Redistricting by commission	0.39	0.15	.052
Terms			
Term limits, executive	0.70	0.67	.831
Term limits, legislature	0.61	0.04	<.001
Two-year terms, lower house	0.91	0.89	.782
Two-year terms, upper house	0.26	0.26	.990
Recall of executive officials allowed	0.48	0.26	.112
Terms index (0–5)	2.96	2.11	.003
Index of all	5.74	5.41	.005

Source: Public funding data come from Common Cause's "Public Financing in the States" (www. commoncause.org [April 2005]). "Oversight boards" mean the state has an agency with statewide jurisdiction over campaign finance and ethics, taken from Council of State Governments (2005). Absentee ballot and redistricting information is from the National Conference on State Legislatures (www.ncsl.org). Ballot access fees and signature requirements were provided by Thomas Stratmann. I follow Stratmann (2004) in using $100 as the critical cutoff level for the ballot access fee. An open primary is anything but a strictly closed primary. Information on fusion ballots is from the New Majority Education Fund (www.nmef.org). Information on primary elections is from the National Voter Registration Application guide. Term-limits information is from U.S. Term Limits (www.ustermlimits.org). Term-length and recall information is from *Book of the States* (2004).

a. The table shows the fraction of states that had adopted a given law as of 2005. Initiative states are those that allow either statutory or constitutional amendment initiatives, except Illinois, which is classified as a noninitiative state. Policies are coded 1 if the policy has been adopted, and zero otherwise. Index values are calculated by summing the individual laws within a category. Data sources are given in the text.

help is still a matter of debate in many cases. For example, public financing of campaigns is advocated by some in the belief that it will level the financial playing field, while others argue that the spending limits attached to public funding protect incumbents from unknown challengers.

Perhaps the main conclusion that can be drawn from table 7-2 is that electoral laws in initiative and noninitiative states are not that different. Only three statistically or quantitatively significant differences appear: initiative states are 57 percent more likely to have legislative term limits (61 percent versus 4 percent), 24 percent more likely to redistrict by commission (39 percent versus 15 percent), and 41 percent more likely to allow absentee ballots (74 percent versus 33 percent).[20] The terms index is significantly higher in initiative states than in noninitiative states, as is the elections and voting index, but the latter difference is not within the bounds of statistical significance.

The next question is: Were the electoral law differences between initiative and noninitiative states caused by availability of the initiative, or are initiative states different in some other dimension that is causing them to adopt different election laws? In order to provide an answer, it is necessary to separate the effect of the initiative from other factors that differ across states. I consider a variety of possible confounding explanatory factors or "control variables." The first two control variables are whether the state is in the South or in the West. A state's region may capture aspects of political culture that are left out of other variables. Thirteen percent of initiative states and 30 percent of noninitiative states are in the South; in comparison, 43 percent of initiative states and 7 percent of noninitiative states are in the West.[21]

The third control variable is the number of years since the state entered the union, as of 2005, or "years since admission" for short. To the extent that institutions and laws are sticky, older and younger states might have different laws for historical reasons. A state's age could also capture differences in political culture. Initiative states are younger on average than noninitiative states, 140 years versus 187 years. Since the purpose of including this variable is to capture sources of variation associated with a state's age that are unrelated to the initiative, it is not necessary to establish exactly what the variable represents, only to capture the variation. As will be seen, the variable seems to be capturing something important in explaining the prevalence of many electoral laws.[22]

The fourth and fifth controls are demographic variables, population and income per capita. Large states may face different problems than small states (for example, it may be more difficult for voters to monitor and control their

20. The patterns for term limits and redistricting are consistent with Persily and Anderson (2005).

21. The Southern states are Alabama, Arkansas, Florida, Georgia, Louisiana, Mississippi, North Carolina, South Carolina, Tennessee, Texas, and Virginia. The Western states are Alaska, California, Colorado, Hawaii, Idaho, Montana, Nevada, New Mexico, Oregon, Utah, Washington, and Wyoming.

22. It may be worth noting that none of the main results are materially different if the years-since-admission variable is omitted.

representatives in large states than in small states), leading them to adopt different laws. The fact that large cities are more likely to allow initiatives than small cities suggests that representative government is more difficult with a large population.[23] Similarly, wealthy states may face different problems than poor states. The average population of initiative states is 5.5 million and 6.0 million for noninitiative states. The average per capita income is $26,577 in initiative states and $28,100 in noninitiative states.

The final control is a measure of state ideology developed by William Berry and his colleagues.[24] They calculated the ideological position of each incumbent U.S. representative using ADA (Americans for Democratic Action) and AFL-CIO ratings, and imputed ideology ratings for challenger candidates by taking the average rating of members of the same party in the state. The incumbent and challenger scores were then averaged based on election vote shares and aggregated across districts to yield a state measure. The final variable takes on values between 0 and 100, with 100 being the most liberal. I downloaded the most recent information from Berry's website and averaged the numbers from 1990 to 1999 to construct a measure of state ideology. The mean for initiative states is 41.7 and 54.7 for noninitiative states, suggesting that candidates are more conservative in initiative states than in noninitiative states.

Table 7-3 reports the effects of the initiative and other control variables on the different electoral law indexes. For each law, a state was coded 1 if the law was in place as of 2005, and 0 otherwise. A value of 1 corresponds to the legal position usually favored by reformers. The statistical tool that allows the different effects to be isolated is the cross-sectional multivariate regression, which can be thought of as calculating average differences controlling for other factors. Thus the top left entry under "Initiative" indicates that the campaign index was 0.06 higher in initiative states than in noninitiative states, controlling for region, years since admission, population, income, and ideology. Since the campaign index takes on values from 0 to 3, a difference of 0.06 is negligible. The measured effect is also not statistically significant, meaning that the difference cannot be distinguished from purely random variation. Table 7-4 reports the initiative's effect on individual policies.[25]

23. Matsusaka (2003).

24. Berry and others (1998).

25. Because the dependent variables in table 7-4 are binary, the ordinary least squares regressions reported in the table are not econometrically appropriate. All regressions were also estimated using a logistic regression, and the findings are essentially the same. I report the linear probability coefficients because they are simple to interpret.

Table 7-3. Factors That Influence Electoral Law Indexes[a]

Variable	Initiative	South	West	Years since admission	Population	Income per capita	Ideology	Intercept	R^2
Campaign index (0–3)	0.06 (0.26)	-0.03 (0.35)	-1.18*** (0.35)	-0.015*** (0.004)	0.13 (0.13)	0.01 (0.04)	0.02** (0.01)	0.83 (1.76)	.343
Elections and voting index (0–5)	0.30 (0.29)	0.36 (0.39)	0.47 (0.39)	-0.001 (0.004)	-0.45*** (0.14)	-0.01 (0.04)	-0.01 (0.01)	9.86*** (1.97)	.420
Redistricting (0–1)	0.11 (0.15)	-0.12 (0.20)	0.12 (0.20)	-0.002 (0.002)	0.06 (0.07)	0.00 (0.02)	0.000 (0.003)	-0.43 (1.00)	.159
Term index (0–5)	0.95*** (0.34)	-0.26 (0.45)	-0.31 (0.46)	-0.001 (0.005)	0.08 (0.17)	-0.02 (0.05)	0.004 (0.008)	1.26 (2.30)	.190
Overall index (0–14)	1.42*** (0.53)	-0.05 (0.70)	-0.91 (0.70)	-0.02** (0.01)	-0.17 (0.26)	-0.01 (0.07)	0.01 (0.01)	11.52*** (3.53)	.416
Overall index without term limits (0–12)	0.64 (0.50)	-0.03 (0.66)	-0.45 (0.67)	-0.02** (0.01)	-0.33 (0.24)	0.05 (0.07)	0.00 (0.01)	11.65*** (3.35)	.367

Source: Author's calculations.

a. Each row is an ordinary least squares regression with fifty observations, one for each state. The main entries are coefficient estimates, with standard errors beneath in parentheses. "Initiative" is equal to 1 if the state allows initiatives and 0 otherwise. Illinois is counted as a noninitiative state. "South" and "West" are equal to 1 if the state is in the South or West, respectively, and 0 otherwise. "Years since admission" is 2005 minus the year the state entered the Union. Population is expressed as a logarithm. Ideology is the Berry and others (1998) measure of "citizen ideology."

* Significant at the 10 percent level.

** Significant at the 5 percent level.

*** Significant at the 1 percent level.

Table 7-4. Effect of Constitutional versus Statutory Initiatives in Initiative States[a]

Law	Initiatives allowed for constitutional amendments and statutes		Initiatives allowed for constitutional amendments only	
	Initiative effect (percent)	Standard error	Initiative effect (percent)	Standard error
Campaign finance				
Public funding, executive	3.4	1.4	1.4	13.4
Public funding, legislature	−2.9	1.0	−7.0	9.6
Oversight board	6.0	15.3	−1.6	14.3
Elections and voting				
Absentee ballots allowed	6.2	12.1	2.9	11.3
Ballot access fees less than $100	−0.1	14.9	2.2	13.9
Ballot accessible without signatures	17.6	17.0	16.4	15.8
Fusion ballots allowed	9.2	13.5	3.2	12.7
Primaries, open	−2.6	16.5	−6.9	15.3
Redistricting by commission	11.2	15.0	6.2	14.0
Terms				
Term limits, executive	12.5	15.6	24.6*	14.1
Term limits, legislature	66.1***	12.1	66.5***	10.6
Two-year terms, lower house	−3.9	10.3	−6.0	9.6
Two-year terms, upper house	16.4	14.3	6.0	13.5
Recall for executive officials	3.4	16.1	9.3	15.0

Source: Author's calculations.

a. Each row reports the number from two regressions that differ in how an initiative state is defined. The main entry can be interpreted as the difference in the probability that an initiative state and a noninitiative state will have the law in question. The dependent variable is a dummy equal to 1 if the state adopted the indicated policy. All regressions included South and West region dummies, years since admission, log of population, income per capita, and a measure of ideology, but the coefficients on those variables are not reported.

* Significant at the 10 percent level.

** Significant at the 5 percent level.

*** Significant at the 1 percent level.

The first cluster of policies concerns campaign finance: public funding for statewide officials, public funding for legislatures, and independent election administration or ethics boards. As mentioned, the tables show that initiative states are more likely to have each policy in place, but the differences are tiny and none of them are distinguishable from noise for either individual laws or the index. Whether a state adopts these campaign finance regulations seems to depend mainly on region, years since admission, and ideology. States are more likely to adopt if they are relatively young states outside the West with relatively liberal voters.

The second cluster of laws concerns elections and voting: availability of absentee ballots, ballot access fees of less than $100 for candidates, absence of signature requirements for candidate ballot access, use of open primaries, and allowing fusion ballots. The index value is 0.30 higher in initiative states than noninitiative states, indicating that election and voting reform laws are more prevalent in initiative states. However, a difference of 0.30 is quite small given that the index runs from 0 to 5, and the effect is not different from zero at conventional levels of statistical significance. Table 7-4 shows that initiative states, controlling for other factors, are more likely to allow fusion ballots and ballot access without signature requirements, but less likely to allow absentee ballots, allow ballot access with a fee below $100, and use open primaries. However, in none of the cases are the differences statistically different from zero. The most significant factor for election and voting reform laws is population; small states are more likely to adopt them than large states.

The third category is redistricting. Recall that initiative states are more likely to employ commission-based redistricting than noninitiative states. This result does survive inclusion of controls: after taking into account that initiative states are more likely to be in the West, less likely to be in the South, and so on, we see that initiative states are only 11 percent more likely to use redistricting commissions, and this difference is not statistically significant. Unfortunately, neither table paints a clear picture of what actually causes the differences because none of the control variables are measured precisely enough to distinguish them from zero. In short, even though initiative states are more likely than noninitiative states to employ commission-based redistricting, that difference cannot be attributed to availability of the initiative.

The fourth category is terms. Here we see, for the first and only time, significant initiative effects. There are three types of laws concerning terms: term limits, term length, and recall. Backers argue that term limits remove entrenched incumbents, that short terms will make elected officials more accountable, and that recall will improve accountability by allowing voters to remove unsatisfactory officeholders. The term index is 0.95 higher in initiative states than in noninitiative states, a nontrivial difference given the range of 0 to 5, and the difference is statistically different from zero at better than the 1 percent level. We can see from the individual policies in table 7-4, however, that this effect is almost entirely driven by the effect of the initiative on term limits for legislators. Initiative states are 66.1 percent more likely to have term limits for legislators than noninitiative states, controlling for the usual factors. The initiative makes a state much more likely to adopt legislative term limits, but does not have a significant effect on adoption of other term-related policies.

The initiative's effect on the overall index that sums the fourteen laws is positive (1.42) and different from zero at better than the 1 percent level. Initiative states appear to adopt more of these laws than noninitiative states, all else equal. However, the difference is almost entirely the result of term limits. If the overall index is constructed without the term-limits variables, as shown in the last row, the coefficient falls to 0.64 and is no longer different from zero at conventional levels of significance.

Some electoral reform policies cannot be implemented by statute and require amending the state constitution, for example, term lengths in some cases. Alaska, Idaho, Utah, Wyoming, and Washington allow voters to use initiatives only for statutes. The initiative process in these statute-only states may be too limited to bring about policy change. To check for this possibility, table 7-4 compares the effect of the initiative in states that allow initiatives to amend the constitution with all other states, controlling for the same other explanatory variables as before. This allows for the possibility that constitutional initiatives are different from statutory initiatives. As can be seen, the estimated effects are fairly similar when we consider only constitutional initiatives, and as before only significant for the term-limits variables. The only noteworthy change in the pattern is that term limits on executive officials are now also significantly more likely in initiative states. States that allow constitutional initiatives are 24.6 percent more likely to limit executive terms than states that do not allow constitutional initiatives.[26]

The main message of this section is that the initiative does not appear to have played much of a role in the adoption of laws related to political competition and accountability. This may not be particularly surprising. The majority that rules in initiative elections might also be able to dominate the legislature, and thus be content with a lack of competition. For example, voters in a heavily Democratic state may prefer to have redistricting performed

26. By controlling for the obvious sources of policy variation across states, these regressions go part of the way toward isolating the causal effect of the initiative on policy. They do not address what is known as the problem of endogeneity, however: an unobserved factor may have caused certain states to adopt the initiative and also be driving their policy decisions. While a serious issue, concern is ameliorated by the fact that twenty of the twenty-three initiative states adopted the process during the period 1900–20, long before 2005. Unless the hypothesized factor is of very long duration, it would not lead to a spurious correlation. As a robustness check, I also estimated the initiative effect after including an interaction term between availability of the initiative and ideology. The main story was unchanged.

on a partisan basis by a Democratic-controlled legislature than by a nonpartisan commission. Consistent with this, voters in Democratic-controlled California and Republican-controlled Ohio strongly rejected initiatives in 2005 that would have established nonpartisan redistricting commissions. The only policy where the initiative has clearly been decisive is term limits. Using the same logic, one might expect a majority of voters to prefer to keep their own incumbents secure. Why voters are willing to upset the status quo and adopt term limits but not redistricting or other competition measures is an open question.

Concluding Comments

The evidence reported in this essay reveals that although reformers often have used ballot propositions to advance their agendas, initiatives on balance have not led to significant institutional changes in democratic rules. There is one notable exception—term limits for legislators—that has been brought about almost entirely through initiatives. The initiative's modest role in electoral reform could be because the majority of voters are not interested in competition per se. The majority of voters may be perfectly happy with limited competition if it secures and extends their grip on the government. Thus reforms such as redistricting by nonpartisan commissions that tip the balance of power away from the dominant party are not likely to find any more favor with the voters than with their representatives. The only exception is reforms that allow the majority to better control their representatives. The broad implication is that if reformers are looking to direct democracy as the magic bullet for electoral reform, they are likely to be disappointed. The electorate at large is not any more inclined than legislatures to adopt laws enhancing political competition. The only obvious benefit of direct democracy is in adopting anti-incumbent rules, such as term limits.

Although the initiative does not appear to be an important factor driving adoption of electoral reforms, the initiative may increase political competition and accountability in other ways. As I have argued at length elsewhere, when the initiative is unavailable, competition over laws takes place between political professionals who run for office.[27] They state their policy goals and compete for votes in order to take office and push their policies through. With the initiative, policies can be formulated and proposed by individuals who are not political professionals and do not wish to hold office. A growing

27. See Matsusaka (2004, chap. 9).

body of theory and evidence suggests that the initiative does in fact make policy more responsive to voter interests.[28] Whether a closer correspondence between policy and public opinion is a good or bad thing is far from clear—there are reasons to fear majority rule as well as to favor it—but increasing responsiveness is one of the underlying goals of electoral reform. The initiative may play a limited role in bringing about electoral reform, but it does seem to serve the goals of reformers when it comes to policy responsiveness.

References

Berry, William D., Evan J. Ringquist, Richard C. Fording, and Russell L. Hanson. 1998. "Measuring Citizen and Government Ideology in the American States, 1960–1993." *American Journal of Political Science* 42 (1): 327–48.

Besley, Timothy, and Stephen Coate. 2003. "Issue Unbundling via Citizens' Initiative." Working Paper, London School of Economics and Cornell University.

Council of State Governments. 2004. *Book of the States 2004*. Lexington, Ky.

———. 2005. *Book of the States 2005*. Lexington, Ky.

Feld, Lars P., and John G. Matsusaka. 2003. "Budget Referendums and Government Spending: Evidence from Swiss Cantons." *Journal of Public Economics* 87 (3): 2703–24.

Garrett, Elizabeth. 2005. "Who Chooses the Rules?" *Election Law Journal* 4 (2): 139–46.

Gerber, Elisabeth R. 1999. *The Populist Paradox: Interest Group Influence and the Promise of Direct Legislation*. Princeton University Press.

Gerber, Elisabeth R., and Arthur Lupia. 1995. "Campaign Competition and Policy Responsiveness in Direct Legislation Elections." *Political Behavior* 17: 287–306.

Lupia, Arthur, and John G. Matsusaka. 2004. "Direct Democracy: New Approaches to Old Questions." *Annual Review of Political Science* 7: 463–82.

Matsusaka, John G. 1995. "Fiscal Effects of the Voter Initiative: Evidence from the Last 30 Years." *Journal of Political Economy* 103 (June): 587–623.

———. 2000. "Fiscal Effects of the Voter Initiative in the First Half of the 20th Century." *Journal of Law and Economics* 43 (October): 619–48.

———. 2003. "I&R in American Cities: Basic Patterns." In *Initiative and Referendum Almanac*, edited by M. Dane Waters. Durham, N.C.: Carolina Academic Press.

———. 2004. *For the Many or the Few: The Initiative, Public Policy, and American Democracy*. University of Chicago Press.

———. 2005a. "Direct Democracy Works." *Journal of Economic Perspectives* 19 (2): 185–206.

———. 2005b. "The Eclipse of Legislatures: Direct Democracy in the 21st Century." *Public Choice* 124 (1): 157–77.

———. 2005c. "Direct Democracy and the Executive." Working Paper. University of Southern California.

28. See, for example, Gerber and Lupia (1995); Gerber (1999); Matsusaka and McCarty (2001); Matsusaka (2004); Lupia and Matsusaka (2004).

Matsusaka, John G., and Nolan M. McCarty. 2001. "Political Resource Allocation: Benefits and Costs of Voter Initiatives." *Journal of Law, Economics, and Organization* 17: 413–48.

Persily, Nathaniel, and Melissa Cully Anderson. 2005. "Regulating Democracy through Democracy: The Use of Direct Legislation in Election Law Reform." *Southern California Law Review* 78 (4): 997–1034.

Pippen, John, Shaun Bowler, and Todd Donovan. 2002. "Election Reform and Direct Democracy: Campaign Finance Regulations in the American States." *American Politics Research* 30 (6): 559–82.

Samples, John, ed. 2005. *Welfare for Politicians? Taxpayer Financing of Campaigns.* Washington: Cato Institute.

Schaltegger, Christoph A., and Lars P. Feld. 2001. "On Government Centralization and Budget Referendums: Evidence from Switzerland." Working Paper. University of St. Gallen.

Stratmann, Thomas. 2004. "Ballot Access Restrictions and Candidate Entry in Elections." *European Journal of Political Economy* 21 (1): 59–71.

Tolbert, Caroline J. 1998. "Changing Rules for State Legislatures: Direct Democracy and Governance Policies." In *Citizens and Legislators: Direct Democracy in the United States,* edited by S. Bowler, T. Donovan, and C. J. Tolbert. Ohio State University Press.

8 The Place of Competition in American Election Law

Nathaniel Persily

In recent years it has become fashionable for legal academics to conceive of problems in American election law as ones concerning regulation of the political marketplace as opposed to infringements on constitutionally guaranteed individual or associational rights.[1] This shift in scholarly attention derives from several sources. First, although new challenges such as increased disfranchisement of felons and restrictive voter identification provisions have emerged, most of the classic barriers to participation have been replaced with complicated and subtle strategies dedicated to maintaining incumbent parties and officeholders in their current positions of power. Second, while often phrased in the language of individual rights derived from earlier cases, the alleged harm these new strategies cause is broadly shared and systemic (a harm to the "polity"), as opposed to discrete and targeted. The constitutional material used to redress government infringements of individual political rights, the argument goes, is ill-suited to the task of regulating political

Thanks are owed to Dana Powers, Javier Serrano, David Spiegel, Erika Wayne, and Richard Winger for assistance with this chapter.

1. See, for example, Garrett (1999, 2004); Hasen (1998); Issacharoff (2000, 2001, 2002, 2004); Issacharoff and Pildes (1998); Karlan (1999); Levinson (2000); Lowenstein (2000); Persily (2001a, 2001b, 2002); Persily and Cain (2000); Pildes (1999, 2004, 2006).

171

monopolies or duopolies or of checking self-serving moves by incumbents. Finally, unprecedented parity in membership of the national political parties, ideological polarization among officeholders, and remarkable rates of incumbent reelection have given rise to fears that self-serving election laws have made the electoral system unresponsive and unrepresentative of the underlying electorate. Or, even if the law is not responsible, both statutes and judge-made constitutional law might help correct these problems.

The task of this chapter is to identify the problem of diminished political competition, describe the relevant legal analogies concerning regulation of economic competition, and explain how the law shapes the competitive environment for elections. I also detail how Supreme Court justices have sometimes tried to incorporate competitiveness concerns into their election law decisions in cases concerning ballot access, redistricting, campaign finance, party reform, and term limits. For the most part, constitutional law proves to be both a blunt and a coarse instrument for addressing excesses of partisan greed or self-interest, but justices of varying ideological leanings have invoked such concerns to highlight why one or another election law violates the Constitution.

The Definition, Purpose, and Trade-offs of Electoral Competition

Although the other chapters in this volume do a good job of assessing the level of competition in American elections, it is worth spending a few paragraphs here identifying the legally relevant measures of competition. The specific concerns of political scientists may differ considerably from those of lawyers and judges, though, and the law may be able to shape the competitive environment in some respects, but not others. Furthermore, if judges are to create or administer a legal regime with promoting competition as a guidepost, we need to know how better to define such a goal.

Leaving aside for the moment the normative question as to whether competition is an inherent good, and the empirical questions as to whether elections today are, in fact, uniquely uncompetitive and what the causes of the lack of competitiveness might be, we can easily identify the features of an uncompetitive electoral system. The following constitutes a nonexhaustive list:

—Rates of contestation: How many races go uncontested and how many parties and candidates tend to appear on the primary and general election ballot?

—Incumbent reelection rates: How often do incumbents get reelected? How much of an electoral advantage do incumbents have over challengers?

—Actual or expected margins of victory: Do winners usually win by a lot? What is the expected vote share of the candidates competing in a given election?

—Rates of turnover and length of time in office: How often do open seats materialize? How stable is the membership in the legislature from one election to the next? What is the average length of tenure in office?

—Changes in control of government: How likely or frequently is there a change in which party controls the legislature or government?

Different election laws will have different competition-related effects, and maximizing competitiveness along one dimension might diminish it on another. Partisan gerrymanders may decrease competition for control of legislative chambers, for example, but they may increase the competitiveness of many individual districts where the majority party has spread its supporters too thin. Term limits, almost by definition, will lead to greater turnover in government, but may lead to less contestation and higher margins of victory in the years when incumbents run for reelection because challengers will bide their time until the seat opens up.

Not only should we be aware of the different dimensions of political competition in our assessment of legal strategies to increase them, but we should acknowledge that political competition is primarily a means to other ends: namely, greater accountability, responsiveness, representation, and participation in government. Competition fosters greater accountability, the argument goes, by keeping legislators honest with the omnipresent threat that they might lose their jobs. It also makes elections meaningful (responsive) by translating shifts in voter preferences into shifts in the partisan composition of the legislature. Moreover, others argue that competitive districts lead to less bias or polarization in the legislature: they maintain that if districts are more balanced politically then their representatives will be more moderate than if the districts are heavily skewed toward one or the other party.[2] Likewise, in such districts perhaps turnout will increase as parties and candidates put greater effort into mobilizing voters, who also might feel their vote has more value than in a district where the victor is all but assured.

Whether electoral competition produces the alleged benefits of responsiveness, accountability, representation, and participation is a matter of empirical debate, as are the alleged trade-offs from a pro-competition election

2. Issacharoff (2004); Eilperin (2006).

law regime. Critics point to the fact that a singular focus on increasing competitiveness could lead to a very unrepresentative legislature, if, for example, small shifts in voter preferences in many evenly split districts led to heavy overrepresentation of the dominant party in the legislature.[3] Just as a redistricting plan filled with noncompetitive districts could be biased in favor of the political extremes, so too competitive districts could be biased in favor of the moderate median voter. Finally, although foreordained, noncompetitive elections, in theory, might alienate voters who think their vote does not matter, the same could be true with respect to competitive election campaigns with their higher costs and acrimony and with their guarantee that close to half of the electorate will have voted for the loser.

Importing Competition from Corporate Law into Election Law

The above description of the concept, benefits, and trade-offs of competition is useful in assessing the constitutional importance (if any) of political competition. On the one hand, the Constitution is silent on the topic of electoral competition, as it presupposes that elections and the franchise can be largely regulated by state legislatures and Congress.[4] On the other hand, article 4, section 4 of the Constitution provides that "the United States shall guarantee to every State in this Union a Republican Form of Government," and the notion that totally uncompetitive elections might suggest something less than republicanism does not constitute a radical idea. Although the courts have not enforced that constitutional command, they have found other avenues—principally in the First Amendment and the Equal Protection Clause of the Fourteenth Amendment—to derive a right to vote and to delineate permissible and impermissible forms of political regulation. Both of those provisions, as discussed further in the cases in the next section, establish norms against unreasonable treatment in favor of one group, association, or set of ideas to the detriment of another. Those who would work within the current constitutional doctrine to further judicial innovations in the direction of greater

3. Persily (2002).

4. Article I, section 4 of the Constitution provides: "The Times, Places and Manner of holding Elections for Senators and Representatives, shall be prescribed in each State by the Legislature thereof; but the Congress may at any time by Law make or alter such Regulations." Some have recently latched onto this phrase to suggest that this power to regulate federal elections does not include the power to remove from them any competitive content. Pildes (2006); Brief of Samuel Issacharoff, Burt Neuborne, and Richard H. Pildes as Amici Curiae in Support of Appellants at 1, *League of United Latin Am. Citizens* v. *Perry*, Nos. 05-204, 05-254, 05-276, 05-439 (U.S. Aug. 11, 2005).

political competition view self-serving election laws as equal to any others that reinforce the position of the already powerful or limit the permissible scope of debate.[5]

Rather than obsessing over the textual constitutional hook for a political markets theory of election law, the new generation of scholarship advocating this view focuses on analogies to corporate law. In particular, Samuel Issacharoff and Richard Pildes's seminal article that redirected the focus of the legal academy toward barriers to electoral competition attempted to find analogies in antitrust law and the law governing the market for corporate control.[6] In the economic sphere, these two bodies of law serve to check actions by firms to diminish competition for consumers and actions by managers to insulate themselves from replacement. In both contexts the bad behavior that judicial action restrains concerns an abuse of economic power to the detriment of some group (consumers, shareholders, competitors) for whom vigorous competition otherwise would be expected to provide benefits (lower-priced, high-quality products or shares of greater value).

The analogy to antitrust is straightforward: just as a firm can strategize to become an economic monopolist or a set of firms can behave like a cartel, so can one or two parties behave in ways to diminish political competition. Whereas in the economic sphere competition keeps firms honest by forcing them to strive toward lower prices and better quality in order to win over consumers, in the political realm competition could force parties and officeholders to be honest—that is, not to stray too far from the median voter or not to deliver a low-quality "product" (for example, unresponsive legislators or poor constituent service). Political monopolies or duopolies, under this view, lead to unrepresentative and unresponsive government as reflected in politicians who are "out of touch" and legislatures that ignore shifts in voter preferences.

The analogy to the market for corporate control comes from the identification of a similar problem: incumbents' use of their lawmaking or rule-writing power to insulate themselves from competition that might result in their losing their jobs. In the case of a typical "poison pill," directors seeking to prevent a takeover will bind a corporation into agreements that then make the corporation less attractive to outsiders who may be bidding for control. As a result, the shareholders lose the potential benefit in an increased share price that would inure to them if competition for control of the corporation were unfettered.

5. Ely (1980).
6. Issacharoff and Pildes (1998).

So too with politics, the argument goes. Incumbent politicians can write election laws to diminish the chance that viable competitors will emerge and to ensure that they do not lose their jobs. For those who urge it, judicial action in both spheres prevents some breach of a duty of loyalty to shareholders or constituents when the managers or incumbents place their personal interest over the firm's or public's interest. Judicial oversight can check abuses of power by those in charge by removing conflicts of interest, and by ensuring that fidelity to one's faction or firm does not lead to monopoly politics or political market breakdown.

This thumbnail sketch of the relevant corporate law analogies is necessarily a caricature of what are complicated and developing concepts in a vast area of law. An active theoretical and empirical debate exists over what constitutes a competitive market or whether "poison pills" actually harm shareholders in the short or long run. Moreover, the analogy to politics fits uncomfortably: we do not have a metric akin to price with which to measure the relative desirability of government policy to constituents. We also do not have many market analogies that produce natural duopolies similar to those produced by single-member election districts operating under plurality-based rules. Even so, conceptualizing election law problems as problems of competition, as opposed to group or individual rights, might lead to different judicial policymaking, or at least to a redefinition of the nature of the problem litigation in this arena is designed to remedy.

How the Law Shapes the Competitive Environment

Incumbent parties and officeholders can use election law in any number of ways to hobble the competitive position of outsiders. They can raise the barriers to entry, skew or divide up the relevant market, or sabotage competitors' efforts to win over voters. Judges are in the best position to regulate anticompetitive behavior, it is thought, because lawmakers will be unwilling to rewrite the rules in ways that threaten their own positions of power. Just as they can best protect powerless political minorities who have no chance of gaining control of government, judges are also institutionally situated to prevent the political foxes from guarding the henhouse and to clear the "channels of political change."[7] Despite the ominous predictions of dissenters, our experience with the one-person, one-vote cases demonstrates that the courts, on occasion, can break political strangleholds and do so without losing credibility or inviting backlash.

7. Ely (1980); *United States v. Carolene Products Co.*, 304 U.S. 144 (1938).

As difficult as it might be for judges to assess competitive economic markets, though, regulating or promoting political competition presents greater challenges given the few articulable constitutional standards available. As mentioned, there is no agreed upon indicator for political market breakdown or any obvious way to prevent it. In many, if not most, election law contexts a court adopting the political markets approach can do no better than declare that those in charge simply went too far, were too greedy, or were too hostile to their opponents. In the case law concerning ballot access, redistricting, campaign finance, term limits, and regulation of party primaries, the Supreme Court has not identified incumbent protection—whether of individual office-holders or dominant parties—as an impermissible motivation. Indeed, in several contexts it has specifically given its blessing to anticompetitive state action in the election law arena.

Whether courts intend it or not, judicial decisions shape the environment for electoral competition. Even if they do not reference competitiveness concerns explicitly, the courts' decisions whether and how to be involved in a domain of election law affect the strategies of the actors seeking to immunize themselves from competition. Involvement by the judiciary, whether justified under the First and Fourteenth Amendment or otherwise, constrains the available options for parties and politicians seeking to entrench themselves or hobble their competitors. Moreover, litigation over election laws has become part of the competition for office and power itself, as lawyers fight out the ground rules for how and when votes will matter.

What follows in the remainder of this chapter is a cataloguing of the case law that bears on the topic of electoral competition, even though majority opinions rarely analyze an issue from a political markets perspective. With that said, one can see flickers of the competitiveness rationale in the debates among the justices in these cases, even if the argument rarely wins over a majority. For each topic, I also try to sketch out the proposals often made to judges and legislatures to increase electoral competition.

Ballot Access

Through regulation of the number of parties or candidates appearing on the ballot, those with the power to write electoral rules can raise the barriers to entry for new participants in the electoral system. Competition in this realm focuses on levels of (or at least the potential for) contestation. A true antitrust approach to politics would seek to ensure that enough parties and candidates appear on the ballot, such that elections actually reflect voter demand instead of being the product of the artificial constraints imposed by the dominant parties crafting the law. Perhaps because it provides the best analogy to antitrust, ballot access law has been the principal arena of election law where the Supreme Court has explicitly analyzed the problem from the standpoint of its anticompetitive effects. However, because it has clung to available doctrine emphasizing competition in the marketplace of ideas as opposed to competition for office per se, the marketlike language the Court employs supports a metaphor more than it pushes a theory of democracy.

Restrictions on ballot access endanger First Amendment freedoms of speech and association when they curtail a voter's ability to express his preference on the ballot and associate with the candidate of his choosing. Moreover, the ballot access rules can chill the participation of parties and candidates in campaigns, thereby narrowing the scope of political debate, and as such the Court has borrowed liberally from First Amendment precedent emphasizing the importance of a marketplace of ideas. Of course, ballots are not public forums, and the First Amendment does not require that the number of "speakers" allowed access to the ballot be comparable to that allowed on the Boston Common. Therefore, the Court is always confronted with the task of balancing between the state's interests in preserving order and preventing confusion and the party, voter, and candidate's rights to express themselves in the campaign and on the ballot.

It is worth excerpting at length the few cases that place the market metaphor front and center. *Williams* v. *Rhodes*, which struck down a 15 percent signature requirement for minor parties attempting to get on the Ohio presidential ballot, clarified that ballot regulations favoring the Democratic and Republican parties, in particular, raise serious constitutional questions: "There is, of course, no reason why two parties should retain a permanent monopoly on the right to have people vote for or against them. Competition in ideas and governmental policies is at the core of our electoral process and of the First Amendment freedoms."[8] *Anderson* v. *Celebrezze,* which struck down early filing deadlines that prevented independent presidential candidate John Anderson from getting on the Ohio ballot in 1980, sounded a similar theme:

By limiting the opportunities of independent-minded voters to associate in the electoral arena to enhance their political effectiveness as a group, such restrictions threaten to reduce diversity and competition in

8. *Williams* v. *Rhodes*, 393 U.S. 23, 32 (1968).

the marketplace of ideas. . . . In short, the primary values protected by the First Amendment—"a profound national commitment to the principle that debate on public issues should be uninhibited, robust, and wide-open,"—are served when election campaigns are not monopolized by the existing political parties.[9]

For all the flowery talk about competition among candidates, parties, and ideas, however, these early signals of an aggressive judicial role in eliminating barriers to entry have not carried the analogy too far. In fact, while *Williams v. Rhodes* may stand for the proposition that ballot regulations cannot advantage the Democratic and Republican parties, in particular, *Timmons* v. *Twin Cities Area New Party* makes clear that such laws can be biased in favor of a two-party system.[10] Upholding Minnesota's ban on fusion candidacies, which prohibited a candidate from being the nominee of more than one political party, the Court explained: "[T]he States' interest [in political stability] permits them to enact reasonable election regulations that may, in practice, favor the traditional two-party system, and that temper the destabilizing effects of party-splintering and excessive factionalism. The Constitution permits the Minnesota Legislature to decide that political stability is best served through a healthy two-party system." In other words, just as the single-member district system should not raise judicial eyebrows because of its bias in favor of two parties, so too regulations of the ballot can naturally be biased in favor of a duopoly. Of course, the practical effect of such a rule is to bias the system both in favor of two parties in the abstract and in favor of the current two parties in control.

While paying lip service to the notion that the barriers to political market entry should not be too high, the Supreme Court has stressed that there is no "litmus-paper test" that can separate valid from invalid ballot access restrictions.[11] Indeed, one cannot avoid a rule of decision in these cases that sidesteps a totality-of-the-circumstances type of analysis. The actual "test," if one can call it that, applied in such cases is the following:

When deciding whether a state election law violates First and Fourteenth Amendment associational rights, we weigh the "character and

---

9. *Anderson* v. *Celebrezze*, 460 U.S. 780, 794 (1983) (internal citations omitted).
10. *Timmons* v. *Twin Cities Area New Party*, 520 U.S. 351, 382 (1997).
11. *Storer* v. *Brown*, 415 U.S. 724, 730 (1974).

magnitude" of the burden the State's rule imposes on those rights against the interests the State contends justify that burden, and consider the extent to which the State's concerns make the burden necessary. Regulations imposing severe burdens on plaintiffs' rights must be narrowly tailored and advance a compelling state interest. Lesser burdens, however, trigger less exacting review, and a State's "important regulatory interests" will usually be enough to justify "reasonable, nondiscriminatory restrictions."[12]

All of the work in this analysis is done at the front end with the decision concerning whether the burdens imposed are severe. Rarely, if ever, will a court determine a severe burden to be constitutional or a nonsevere burden to be unconstitutional. The severity of the burden, though, is on rights of expression and association, not on the competitive position of minor parties. A ballot access regime that protects minor parties' ability to get their message out will usually be upheld, despite the fact that it ensures they will not compete effectively against the two major parties. This is true even when the context is a complete ban on write-in voting, which dissenters viewed as entrenching a single party in office.[13]

For the most part, a similar type of analysis is at work whenever courts consider barriers to entry by minor parties or independent candidates: for example, in the context of candidate debates or receipt of public funding.[14] Administrative necessities, scarce resources (whether ballot positions, time in a debate, or the amount of money to be distributed), and a desire to draw the line somewhere lead inevitably to context-specific decisions about how burdensome or necessary the regulations are. In general, when it presents itself, the competition argument is not so much about electoral competition as it is about promoting the marketplace of ideas, with marginal candidates and parties tolerated but removed as threats to the two parties' hegemony.

It is also somewhat unclear how a political antitrust approach would differ from the one currently in place. A presidential system with single-member

12. *Timmons*, 520 U.S., 358 (internal citations omitted).
13. *Burdick v. Takushi*, 504 U.S. 428, 444 (1992) (Kennedy, J., dissenting). Justice Kennedy viewed Hawaii's ban on write-in votes as impermissibly advantaging the dominant Democratic Party: "The majority's approval of Hawaii's ban is ironic at a time when the new democracies in foreign countries strive to emerge from an era of sham elections in which the name of the ruling party candidate was the only one on the ballot. Hawaii does not impose as severe a restriction on the right to vote, but it imposes a restriction that has a haunting similarity in its tendency to exact severe penalties for one who does anything but vote the dominant party ballot."
14. *Arkansas Educational Television Comm'n v. Forbes*, 5235 U.S. 666 (1998).

districts and plurality voting rules is biased in favor of two parties. In such a system, minor parties and independent candidates pose little threat of replacement and have claimed only sporadic and localized electoral successes. Their *competition* with the major-party candidates manifests itself in their offering ideas that influence the campaigns and incumbents' policies (as already recognized in the jurisprudence) and in the threat they pose from spoiling the election (à la Nader in the 2000 election). At most, a jurisprudence focused on the value of contestation would look askance at those states (such as Florida, Georgia, Arkansas, and West Virginia) that had fewer than two candidates, on average, appearing on ballots for the 2004 elections to the House of Representatives.[15] In the end, though, adopting such an approach would do little more than establish a rule that ballot access requirements cannot be so high as to make contestation unlikely.

Redistricting

The Texas redistricting controversy, as well as failed redistricting reform initiatives in Ohio and California, has placed redistricting at the top of the reform agenda.[16] The grab bag of problems that proposed reforms (either judicial or legislative) target are some subset of those described above—low turnover, few high-quality challengers, high victory margins, low responsiveness, heavy bias, and increasing polarization. The spate of gerrymandering in the 2000 round, followed as it was by uncompetitive elections in many House districts and biased delegations in several states, has caused many to blame redistricting for one or another democratic malady or at least to look to redistricting reform as a potential cure.[17]

Despite the urgings of plaintiffs and academics, thus far the political markets approach has not won over a majority of the Court in the gerrymandering cases. Indeed, while some dissenting justices may mention "competition," for the most part, the Court has been preoccupied with issues of representation and bias. Such is the case when the Court has considered either partisan gerrymanders, which give one party an advantage across the districting plan as a whole, or bipartisan gerrymanders, which attempt to make each district noncompetitive for the nominee of one or the other party. The injury is such cases, to the extent that the Court recognizes one, is conceived as underrepresentation of voters, not prevention of competition between parties and candidates.

15. Richard Winger, "How to Compare U.S. House Ballot Access," *Ballot Access News*, May 5, 2005 (www.ballot-access.org/2005/0505.html).

16. Reform Institute (2005).

17. Pildes (2006); Mann and Cain (2005).

Bipartisan and Incumbent-Protecting Gerrymanders. Although complaints against gerrymandering take many forms, those who worry about intra-district competition focus on districting plans that divide the state into safe Republican and Democratic enclaves or otherwise protect incumbents from effective challengers.[18] As noted above, this critique usually dovetails with a concern about polarization, since it is presumed that politically homogeneous districts will produce representatives farther away from the median voter in the given state. Not only has the Supreme Court failed to entertain this critique; it has all but blessed incumbent protection as a legitimate state interest and bipartisan gerrymanders as furthering a rational policy of proportional representation.

With respect to bipartisan gerrymanders, the only case directly on point is *Gaffney v. Cummings.*[19] There the Court upheld a plan that divided the state into safe Democratic and Republican strongholds in an effort to create a legislature that mirrored the partisan balance in the state. Doing so was not only constitutionally permissible but arguably desirable. The Court explained that "judicial interest should be at its lowest ebb when a State purports fairly to allocate political power to the parties in accordance with their voting strength and, within quite tolerable limits, succeeds in doing so."[20] Because it assessed the potential constitutional injury solely in terms of representation in the legislature rather than competition within the district, the Court found no problem with bipartisan gerrymandering.

In other contexts, the Court has even gone so far as to declare incumbent protection to be a legitimate (and traditional) districting principle.[21] In fact,

---

18. See Issacharoff (2002, p. 594); Persily (2002, p. 649).

19. *Gaffney v. Cummings,* 412 U.S. 735 (1973).

20. *Gaffney v. Cummings,* 753.

21. *Burns v. Richardson,* 384 U.S. 73, 89 n. 16 (1966) ("The fact that district boundaries may have been drawn in a way that minimizes the number of contests between present incumbents does not in and of itself establish invidiousness."); *White v. Weiser,* 412 U.S., 797. See also *Johnson v. Miller,* 922 F. Supp., 1565 (finding that the protection of incumbents was a legitimate consideration for a court-drawn plan); *Colleton County Council v. McConnell,* 201 F. Supp. 2d 618, 647 (D.S.C. 2002) (finding incumbent protection to be a traditional state interest in South Carolina); *Arizonans for Fair Representation v. Symington,* 828 F. Supp. 684, 688–89 (D. Ariz. 1992) (three-judge court) ("The court [plan] also should avoid unnecessary or invidious outdistricting of incumbents. . . . The voting population within a particular district is able to maintain its relationship with its particular representative and avoids accusations of political gerrymandering" [citation omitted]); *Prosser v. Elections Bd.,* 793 F. Supp. 859, 871 (W.D. Wis. 1992) (discussing the court plan's lack of incumbent pairings and the correlative avoidance of "perturbation in the political balance of the state").

protection of incumbents[22] or the creation of a safe district for a party[23] can be a defense to an otherwise unconstitutional racial gerrymander. In other words, one way for a jurisdiction to defend a district that might raise concerns because it used race predominantly would be to argue that it was drawn to be a safe Democratic district or one that avoids the pairing of two incumbents. Far from suggesting constitutional liability because of its anticompetitive effect, incumbent protection could be the legal saving grace of a district.

Partisan Gerrymanders. A political markets approach would consider partisan gerrymanders to be a means through which the party in control of the legislature undercuts the competitive position of the party out of power, which otherwise might be better able to win a greater number of seats and perhaps control of the legislature. In practice, dominant parties tamper with the market for legislative control by packing their opponents into a few safe districts (packing), spreading their supporters efficiently (cracking), and pairing incumbents so as to favor the party in power (kidnapping). Some partisan gerrymanders do not look characteristically different from bipartisan gerrymanders, since shoring up the partisan balance of the status quo may be the most efficient strategy for insulating the dominant party from challenge. Although partisan gerrymanders remain potentially unconstitutional, the Supreme Court has not yet struck one down, nor has a majority of justices settled on a standard for what constitutes excessive partisanship in redistricting.

In cases arising from Pennsylvania and Texas, the Court has recently confronted the issue of partisan gerrymandering and blinked in both instances. Although most of the justices have assumed that "the excessive injection of politics is unlawful,"[24] even while finding an administrable standard elusive, only dissenters appear preoccupied with the anticompetitive effects of gerrymandering.[25] As Justice David Souter's dissent in the Pennsylvania case, *Vieth v. Jubelirer*, explained: "the Court's job must be to identify clues, as objective

---

22. *Bush* v. *Vera*, 517 U.S. 952, 964 (1996) ("We have recognized incumbency protection, at least in the form of avoiding contests between incumbents, as a legitimate state goal.").

23. See *Easley* v. *Cromartie*, 532 U.S. 234 (2001).

24. *Vieth* v. *Jubelirer*, 541 U.S. 267, 293 (2004) (plurality opinion).

25. *Vieth* v. *Jubelirer*, 318 (Stevens, J., dissenting) ("In my view, when partisanship is the legislature's sole motivation—when any pretense of neutrality is forsaken unabashedly and all traditional districting criteria are subverted for partisan advantage—the governing body cannot be said to have acted impartially"); *League of United Latin American Citizens* v. *Perry*, 548 U.S. __ (2006), slip op. at 26 (Stevens, J., dissenting) (decrying safe seats as "harming the democratic process" by leading to representatives unresponsive to political minorities, low voter turnout, and polarization in the legislature).

as we can make them, indicating that partisan competition has reached an extremity of unfairness."[26] While all those who would provide a judicial check on gerrymandering worry about the bias such gerrymanders produce, Justice Stephen Breyer has focused on the possibility that through gerrymandering a party might be able to entrench itself such that any change in the partisan preferences of the electorate would not translate into electoral risk.[27] Drawing on the concerns that motivated the Court to enter the political thicket with the one-person, one-vote rule, Breyer warned of the "unjustified use of political factors to entrench a minority in power." Just as representatives from rural districts maintained their power by leaving century-old district lines in place, parties that redraw lines to insulate themselves from challenges to their hegemony should violate the Equal Protection Clause. Dissenters in these cases usually propose criteria for excessive partisan gerrymandering that focus on the irregularities of the redistricting process, intentions of the line-drawers, strangeness of the districts, or the disproportionality of results. In the recent Texas case, the Court rejected such a standard proposed by a group of political scientists who urged the Court to adopt a rule of "partisan symmetry," which would require redistricting plans to treat each party equally with respect to the propensity of shifts in voter preferences to be reflected in shifts in legislative composition.[28]

Because the Court has failed to develop a rule that would constrain partisan gerrymanders, litigants attempt to upend such redistricting plans by appealing to other legal theories, such as the one-person, one-vote rule or constitutional and statutory prohibitions on race discrimination. In 2004 the Court summarily affirmed a district court ruling that held a Democratic gerrymander of Georgia state legislative districts unconstitutional because it overpopulated Republican districts and underpopulated Democratic districts.[29] Moreover, in the notorious recent case where it considered the mid-decade re-redistricting of Texas congressional districts, the Court struck down part of the Republican gerrymander because it discriminated against Hispanics in violation of the Voting Rights Act.[30] By preventing the dilution of the vote of racial minorities in the drawing of district lines, the Voting

26. *Vieth* v. *Jubelirer*, 344 (Souter, J., dissenting).
27. *Vieth* v. *Jubelirer*, 361 (Breyer, J., dissenting) ("political gerrymandering that so entrenches a minority party in power violates basic democratic norms and lacks countervailing justification"). *League of United Latin American Citizens* v. *Perry*, 548 U.S. __ (2006), slip op. at 2 (Breyer, J., dissenting) (applying the rationale to the Texas gerrymander).
28. Grofman and King (2006).
29. *Cox* v. *Larios*, 542 U.S. 947 (2004).
30. *League of United Latin American Citizens* v. *Perry*, 548 U.S. __ (2006), slip op. at 17.

Rights Act limits the ability of those in control of the redistricting process in multiracial jurisdictions to overconcentrate their opponents and spread their supporters most efficiently.

Reformers have proposed a variety of legislative and judicial remedies for the anticompetitive effects of gerrymandering. The most extreme may be to mandate—either by statute or judicial decree—a requirement that districts be drawn with the goal of increasing competition. Arizona does so in its constitution. In theory, judges could interpret such a requirement in the U.S. Constitution, striking down districting plans unless a certain share of districts have a partisan balance that suggests the election will be competitive. (Again, of course, the questions are what constitutes a competitive district, how many districts need to be competitive, what lengths one should go to contort a state so that districts can be competitive, and so forth.) Somewhat less drastic would be a requirement akin to that governing the redistricting process in Iowa, which forbids partisanship or incumbency to be taken into account in the redistricting process. Ignoring such factors (or requiring that only considerations such as compactness and respect for political subdivision lines influence redistricting) does not necessarily lead to greater competition, especially in the many states with stark political segregation. However, such requirements, if followed and enforced, at least prevent the use of political criteria in the furtherance of a noncompetitive districting plan.

In addition to these substantive proposals, procedural requirements enforced by judges or inserted into statutes could mute the anticompetitive tendencies of politicians drawing their own districts. One option that Samuel Issacharoff has advocated is for judges to enforce a prophylactic rule deeming any redistricting conducted by self-interested officials to be unconstitutional.[31] Many states indeed conduct redistricting through commissions, although such institutions vary considerably in their degree of insulation from political pressures. The proposed but ultimately defeated initiatives in Ohio and California would have had retired judges appoint redistricting officials or draw the lines themselves. Others would urge redistricting by a commission made up of ordinary citizens selected through some aspirational nonpartisan process.

Campaign Finance Regulations

Regulation of campaign finance presents an interesting problem for advocates of a market approach to election law regulation. Antitrust- or antientrenchment-style arguments concerning the effect of the campaign finance

---

31. Issacharoff (2002).

regime on incumbents and challengers are thrown about by both reformers and their opponents. On the one hand, reformers argue that incumbents have a disproportionate advantage when it comes to fundraising, so restrictions on contributions or expenditures are necessary to allow challengers to mount effective campaigns. Like a firm with bountiful marketing resources available to drown out an upstart competitor's advertisements, incumbents have such a natural advantage in fundraising that legal restrictions are necessary to "level the playing field." The Court has generally rejected this state interest and reasoned that it is impermissible to favor one person's speech over that of another.[32] Thus, preventing corruption or its appearance, but not promoting competition by leveling the electoral playing field, is a permissible interest for regulating campaign contributions.

For critics of reform, the political markets approach rears its head in a critique of the incumbent-protecting effects of campaign finance reform. Because incumbents, given their name recognition and access to the perks of office, naturally have an electoral edge, restricting the flow of money into and out of campaigns places challengers at a distinct disadvantage in getting their message out.[33] In other words, the only way challengers can close the gap between themselves and incumbents is to raise and spend enormous sums to achieve name recognition and mobilize their electorate. As Justice Scalia put it in his dissent from the Court's decision upholding the Bipartisan Campaign Reform Act, "[A]s everyone knows, this is an area in which evenhandedness is not fairness. If all electioneering were evenhandedly prohibited, incumbents would have an enormous advantage. Likewise, if incumbents and challengers are limited to the same quantity of electioneering, incumbents are favored. In other words, any restriction upon a type of campaign speech that is equally available to challengers and incumbents tends to favor incumbents."[34]

---

32. *Buckley* v. *Valeo*, 424 U.S. 1, 25–27 (1976).

33. See *U.S. Term Limits* v. *Thornton*, 514 U.S. 779, 921 (1995) (Thomas, J., dissenting) ("Congress imposes spending and contribution limits in campaigns that 'can prevent challengers from spending more . . . to overcome their disadvantage and name recognition.' . . . Many observers believe that the campaign finance laws also give incumbents an 'enormous fund-raising edge' over their challengers by giving a large financing role to entities with incentives to curry favor with incumbents") (internal citations omitted).

34. *McConnell* v. *Federal Election Com'n*, 540 U.S. 93, 249–50 (2003) (Scalia, J., dissenting) (internal citations omitted); see also *Colorado Republican Federal Campaign Committee* v. *Federal Election Com'n*, 518 U.S. 604, 644 n. 9 (1996) (Thomas, J., dissenting) ("There is good reason to think that campaign reform is an especially inappropriate area for judicial deference to legislative judgment. What the argument for deference fails to acknowledge is the potential for

This argument appears to have recently won over a majority of the Court, at least in the narrow context of excessively low contribution limits. In *Randall* v. *Sorrell*,[35] Justice Breyer's controlling opinion for the Court struck down Vermont's limits on contributions and expenditures, in part, because of the perceived benefits that such limits heaped upon incumbents. For some time the Court had been asking in its campaign finance cases whether a contribution limit, justified as an anticorruption measure, nevertheless prevented a candidate from "amassing the resources necessary for effective advocacy"[36] or would "drive the sound of the candidate's voice below the level of notice."[37] In striking down a contribution limit for the first time, Justice Breyer's opinion in *Randall* was explicit that the constitutional inquiry requires the Court to ask whether such limits "magnify the advantages of incumbency to the point where they put challengers to a significant disadvantage," because "contribution limits that are too low can also harm the electoral process by preventing challengers from mounting effective campaigns against incumbent officeholders, thereby reducing democratic accountability."[38] "The critical question concerns," he wrote, "the ability of a candidate running against an incumbent officeholder to mount an effective *challenge*."[39]

Prior to *Randall*, the Court had shown great deference to legislatures in the exercise of their "expertise" concerning the conduct of campaigns. Far from suggesting skepticism of politicians' motives, the Court's holdings and reasoning evinced a level of trust sometimes even exceeding that brought to bear outside the election law context. With the exception of *Randall*, the Court has upheld every individual contribution limit it confronted, while striking down regulations of individual expenditures as violating core speech guarantees protected by the First Amendment.

Despite the emphatic pronouncements of the justices in these cases, those who study the relationship between campaign finance reforms and levels of electoral competition have not arrived at any firm conclusions as to the reforms' effects. Although the Court has assumed what seems to be an intuitive

---

legislators to set the rules of the electoral game so as to keep themselves in power and to keep potential challengers out of it. Indeed, history demonstrates that the most significant effect of election reform has been not to purify public service, but to protect incumbents and increase the influence of special interest groups.") (citations omitted).

35. *Randall* v. *Sorrell*, 548 U.S. __ (2006).

36. *Buckley* v. *Valeo*, 21.

37. *Nixon* v. *Shrink Missouri Gov't PAC*, 528 U.S. 377, 397 (2000).

38. *Randall* v. *Sorrell*, slip op. at 13-14.

39. *Randall* v. *Sorrell*, slip op. at 21 (emphasis in original).

pro-incumbent bias of campaign contribution limits, the actual support for that relationship is mixed, at best, with most studies finding no effect and some concluding that limits enhance competition.[40] While the litigation has focused on campaign contribution and expenditure limits, many reformers, recognizing that such regulations of the supply of money do not affect politicians' demand, have turned to public financing to enhance electoral competition. The most recent empirical study of the effect of public financing argues: "There is no question that public funding programs have increased the pool of candidates willing and able to run for state legislative office. This effect is most pronounced for challengers, who were far more likely than incumbents to accept public funding.... Public funding appears to have increased the likelihood that an incumbent will have a competitive race."[41]

However, for both contribution limits and public funding programs the variations between states make definitive conclusions as to their impact on competitiveness difficult. Contribution limits vary considerably as to both their severity and the type of actors in the campaign finance system whose contributions are regulated. Any effect of contribution limits on incumbent reelection rates and margins of victory probably depends on the severity of those limits and how well the campaign finance regime closes off other avenues of campaign spending. Similarly, public funding programs differ in the process by which they are funded, the incentives they provide for participation, the amounts they make available to candidates, and the restrictions they impose as a tradeoff for participation. They extend from inadequate programs with low participation to generous schemes with greater compliance. If public financing does in fact make elections more competitive, we should expect to see an effect only when such programs are well enough funded to engender widespread participation.

Regulation of the Primary Electorate

The political markets approach can be expanded beyond general elections to the regulation of party primary voters and candidates.[42] In such cases, the Court confronts state regulations that seek to tell a party who can and cannot vote in its primary. Although the Court usually considers these laws from the

---

40. Stratmann and Aparicio-Castillo (2006); Gross and Goidel (2003); Gross and Goidel (2001).

41. Mayer, Werner, and Williams (2005).

42. I do not deal here with the context of primary ballot access because the analysis with respect to competition is the same as in the general election context. For a lengthy analysis of the relevant issues, see Persily (2001a).

standpoint of the party's associational rights and the right to choose its standard-bearer, in the background is always the question whether, through regulation of the primary, one party is attempting to hobble the competitive position of its opponent.

As with campaign finance, the political markets approach to primary election regulation often cuts in opposing directions. On the one hand, just as one firm ought not be able to dictate the way its competitor can choose its CEO, so too a party that crafts the nomination rules ought not to be able to structure them in a way that gives it an advantage. On the other hand, party leaders can capture the nomination process and structure it in a way that hinders competition in both the primary and general elections. In effect, party leaders may have a conflict of interest when it comes to regulating their membership; thus the Court ought to allow for the party's membership (for example, through a ballot initiative) to check party leaders' pro-management selection policies.

Concerns about incumbent entrenchment usually present themselves when the state (that is, the party controlling the lawmaking process) prevents a party from opening itself to nonmembers. For example, in the case of *Tashijian v. Republican Party of Connecticut*, the Republican Party wanted to broaden its base of support by allowing independents to vote in its primary.[43] Doing so would presumably lead the party to nominate more moderate nominees (that is, nominees closer to the median voter) who would have a greater chance of winning general elections. State law, justified on the grounds of protecting the party from nominating candidates who did not share its message, prevented them from doing so. The Court found that the law abridged the party's right of expressive association, in part because it distrusted the "views of the State, which to some extent represent the views of one political party transiently enjoying majority power."[44]

The same concerns animated several opinions in a recent and similar case involving a challenge by the Libertarian Party to Oklahoma's law that prevented parties from allowing members of other parties to vote in their primary.[45] Although the majority opinion distinguished *Tashijian* and upheld the law, five justices signed on to opinions reflecting some concern about the potentially anticompetitive effect of this regulation or similar ones in the future. Justice Sandra Day O'Connor's concurrence (joined by Justice Breyer) explained:

43. *Tashijian v. Republican Party of Connecticut*, 479 U.S. 208 (1986).
44. *Tashijian v. Republican Party of Connecticut*, 224.
45. *Clingman v. Beaver*, 544 U.S. 581 (2005).

Although the State has a legitimate—and indeed critical—role to play in regulating elections, it must be recognized that it is not a wholly independent or neutral arbiter. Rather, the State is itself controlled by the political party or parties in power, which presumably have an incentive to shape the rules of the electoral game to their own benefit. . . . As such restrictions become more severe, however, and particularly where they have discriminatory effects, there is increasing cause for concern that those in power may be using electoral rules to erect barriers to electoral competition. In such cases, applying heightened scrutiny helps to ensure that such limitations are truly justified and that the State's asserted interests are not merely a pretext for exclusionary or anticompetitive restrictions.[46]

Justice Stevens's dissent (joined by Justices Souter and Ginsburg) was more adamant:

It is the [Libertarian Party's] belief that attracting a more diverse group of voters in its primary would enable it to select a more mainstream candidate who would be more viable in the general election. Like the Republicans in *Tashijian*, the [Libertarian Party] is cognizant of the fact that in order to enjoy success at the voting booth it must have support from voters who identify themselves as independents, Republicans, or Democrats.[47]

While focusing in general on the expressive associational right of a party to define the contours of its organization, critics of compelled open primaries also lodge a complaint founded on a political markets theory: namely, that forcing the party to accept outsiders could also hurt the chances of its nominee in the general election. In particular, advocates of closed primaries suggest that forcing a party to open its primary could subject it to raiding: that is, the strategic voting of nonmembers in an opposition party's primary so as to nominate a weaker opponent for the general election.[48] In theory, forcing a party to open itself up to a takeover could harm its ability to compete in elections. However, the empirical support for widespread raiding when primaries are opened up is quite thin.[49]

---

46. *Clingman v. Beaver*, 603 (O'Connor, J., concurring).
47. *Clingman v. Beaver*, 614 (Stevens, J., dissenting).
48. *Rosario v. Rockefeller*, 410 U.S. 752 (1973).
49. Cain and Gerber (2002).

Outside the context of race discrimination, the Court has been uniformly protective of parties' ability to exclude voters the "state" wants to force into its primaries.[50] For the most part, the opinions in such cases reflect general concerns about parties' First Amendment right to select their standard-bearer and to be free from the primary regulations that adulterate the message of the party membership. When it comes to the parties' right to include outsiders, the case law is more mixed. The party has a constitutional right to include unaffiliated voters but not voters that have registered with another party.[51]

The effect of primary voter rules on levels of general election competition is not well understood; thus the character of a reform agenda founded on enhancing competition is unclear. I think it is fair to say that most reformers with such intentions prefer open systems to closed systems on the assumption that more opportunities for voter participation make the emergence of a quality challenger at some stage more likely, or may provide some incremental potential for accountability through the primary in districts where the general election is skewed in favor of one party. In addition, political marketeers are naturally suspicious of party leaders whose incentives to keep the primary "pure" sometimes run contrary to those of a party membership who might welcome greater choice and access.

Term Limits

The nuclear weapon when it comes to enhancing competition is limiting the number of terms an individual can serve in office. If one's measure of the competitiveness of an electoral system depends on turnover, length of time in office, or the number of open seats, term limits would appear to be about the most procompetitive measure a state could adopt. For state offices, state constitutional law governs, and voters acting through direct democracy have successfully limited the number of terms one can serve in the state legislature, as governor, or in any other office.[52] For Congress, however, the Court has struck down term limits as unconstitutional, and quite ironically, it has done so in the service of preventing incumbent manipulation of qualifications for office.

In *U.S. Term Limits* v. *Thornton*, the Court ruled unconstitutional a provision of the Arkansas constitution that prevented an incumbent member of Congress from appearing on the ballot if he or she had served a specified

---

50. *California Democratic Party* v. *Jones,* 530 U.S. 567 (2000); *Democratic Party of the United States* v. *LaFollette,* 450 U.S. 107 (1981).

51. *Tashijian* v. *Republican Party of Connecticut; Clingman* v. *Beaver.*

52. Persily and Anderson (2005).

number of terms (two terms for U.S. senators and three terms for members of the House).[53] The Court held that the provisions of the U.S. Constitution setting forth the qualifications for those offices prevented either Congress or states from adding qualifications, such as the requirement that one would be disqualified to serve after a certain time spent in office. Moreover, in a later case, the Court went even further and struck down a state constitutional provision that did not limit the number of terms per se, but rather added a ballot notation indicating whether that candidate had supported term limits.[54]

In both of these cases the Court noted the intent of the Framers of the Qualifications Clause that neither state legislatures, nor Congress itself, ought to be able to limit the types of people who could serve in the federal legislature. Echoing Madison, the Court explained that "reposing the power to adopt qualifications in Congress would lead to a self-perpetuating body to the detriment of the Republic,"[55] and citing Hamilton it described the state's power to regulate elections as merely a "grant of authority to issue procedural regulations, and not as a source of power to dictate electoral outcomes, [or] to favor or disfavor a class of candidates."[56] In other words, the fear that incumbents might manipulate the qualifications for office to entrench themselves or to serve their own interests prevents voters from adopting term limits grounded on the exact same motivation.

This irony was not lost on Justice Thomas, who would have allowed states to adopt term limits. Pointing to incumbents' "astonishingly high reelection rates" due to name recognition, campaign-related perks of office, and benefits with respect to campaign financing, Thomas warned that "current federal law (enacted, of course, by congressional incumbents) confers numerous advantages on incumbents, and these advantages are widely thought to make it significantly more difficult for challengers to defeat them."[57] Installation of term limits or even the more conservative measure that forces incumbents to run as write-in candidates after serving a certain number of terms could counterbalance "the thumb on the . . . scale" that the law otherwise provides in favor of incumbent reelection. At the very least, argued Thomas, the Qualifications Clause does not force voters to accept as inevitable the possibility that the incumbency advantage could be so strong as to make elections an

---

53. *U.S. Term Limits* v. *Thornton* (1995).
54. *Cook* v. *Gralike*, 531 U.S. 510 (2001).
55. *U.S. Term Limits* v. *Thornton*, 794, n. 10.
56. *U.S. Term Limits* v. *Thornton*, 833–34; *Cook* v. *Gralike*, 525 (noting the potential for ballot notations to "handicap candidates" by placing "their targets at a political disadvantage").
57. *U.S. Term Limits* v. *Thornton*, 921 (Thomas, J., dissenting).

ineffective check on the other legal maneuvers politicians engage in to make themselves irremovable.

As Cain, Hanley, and Kousser's contribution to this volume explains, the effect of term limits on competition has not exactly turned out as advertised. Quality challengers who previously may have taken a shot at an incumbent now often bide their time until a seat becomes open. As a result, elections throughout an incumbent's allotted terms may be less competitive, even though competition in open seats is more frequent and fierce.

Conclusion

As the media and reform groups have focused on the problem of safe districts and uncompetitive elections, so have legal scholars (and to a lesser extent judges) begun to think about how the Constitution might be viewed as regulating self-serving moves by incumbents. The solutions—to be found either in policy or in constitutional law—are not simple. We have become quite accustomed to thinking about election law controversies as battles between state interests and individual, associational, or group rights. Shifting focus toward the background conditions of the political market requires a reconceptualization of the judicial role as political trustbuster with the available decision-rule in contexts, such as partisan gerrymandering and ballot access, being no better than declaring that incumbents or the party or parties in power have gone "too far." In other arenas the judicial role would be geared more toward looking into the minds of the drafters of an election law to see if incumbent or party entrenchment constituted the true motivation of the law. As difficult as it may be to come up with administrable election law standards to promote competition, reformers will continue to view the courts as the most promising agents for "clear[ing] the channels of political change."[58] The alternative—hoping that those in charge of the crafting of election laws will become amenable to rules that make their jobs less secure—has never shown much promise.

References

Cain, Bruce E., and Elisabeth R. Gerber, eds. 2002. *Voting at the Political Fault Line: California's Experiment with the Blanket Primary.* University of California Press.

Eilperin, Juliet. 2006. *Fight Club Politics: How Partisanship Is Poisoning the U.S. House of Representatives.* Lanham, Md.: Rowman and Littlefield.

58. Ely (1980, p. 105).

Ely, John Hart. 1980. *Democracy and Distrust: A Theory of Judicial Review*. Harvard University Press.

Garrett, Elizabeth. 1999. "The Law and Economics of 'Informed Voter' Ballot Notations." *Virginia Law Review* 85: 1533–87.

———. 2004. "New Issues in the Law of Democracy: Democracy in the Wake of the California Recall." *University of Pennsylvania Law Review* 153: 239–84.

Grofman, Bernard, and Gary King. Forthcoming 2006. "Partisan Gerrymandering Claims after *Vieth* v. *Jubilerer*: A Social Science Perspective on Conceptualization and Measurement." *Election Law Journal*.

Gross, Donald A., and Robert K. Goidel. 2001. "The Impact of State Campaign Finance Laws." *State Politics and Policy Quarterly* 1: 180–95.

———. 2003. *The States of Campaign Finance Reform*. Ohio State University Press.

Hasen, Richard L. 1998. "The 'Political Market' Metaphor and Election Law: A Comment on Issacharoff and Pildes." *Stanford Law Review* 50: 719–30.

Issacharoff, Samuel. 2000. "Oversight of Regulated Political Markets." *Harvard Journal of Law and Public Policy* 24: 91–100.

———. 2001. "Private Parties with Public Purposes: Political Parties, Associational Freedoms, and Partisan Competition." *Columbia Law Review* 101: 274–313.

———. 2002. "Gerrymandering and Political Cartels." *Harvard Law Review* 116: 594–648.

———. 2004. "Collateral Damage: The Endangered Center in American Politics." *William and Mary Law Review* 46: 415–37.

Issacharoff, Samuel, and Richard H. Pildes. 1998. "Politics as Markets: Partisan Lockups of the Democratic Process." *Stanford Law Review* 50: 643–717.

Karlan, Pamela S. 1999. "Politics by Other Means." *Virginia Law Review* 85: 1697–1724.

Levinson, Daryl J. 1999. "Market Failures and Failures of Markets." *Virginia Law Review* 85: 1745–59.

Lowenstein, Daniel H. 2000. "The Supreme Court Has No Theory of Politics—And Be Thankful for Small Favors." In *The U.S. Supreme Court and the Electoral Process*, edited by David K. Ryden. Georgetown University Press.

Mann, Thomas E., and Bruce E. Cain, eds. 2005. *Party Lines: Competition, Partisanship, and Congressional Redistricting*. Brookings.

Mayer, Kenneth R., Timothy Werner, and Amanda Williams. 2005. "Do Public Funding Programs Enhance Electoral Competition?" Paper presented at the Fourth Annual Conference on State Politics and Policy Laboratories of Democracy: Public Policy in the American States, Kent State University. (www.campfin.polisci.wisc.edu/Wisc%20Camp%20Fin%20Proj%20%20Public%20Funding%20and%20Competition.pdf.)

Persily, Nathaniel. 2001a. "Candidates v. Parties: The Constitutional Constraints on Primary Ballot Access Laws." *Georgetown Law Journal* 89: 2181–2225.

———. 2001b. "Toward a Functional Defense of Political Party Autonomy." *NYU Law Review* 76: 750–824.

———. 2002. "In Defense of Foxes Guarding Henhouses: The Case for Judicial Acquiescence to Incumbent-Protecting Gerrymanders." *Harvard Law Review* 116: 649–81.

Persily, Nathaniel, and Melissa Cully Anderson. 2005. "Regulating Democracy through Democracy: The Use of Direct Legislation in Election Law Reform." *Southern California Law Review* 78: 997–1034.

Persily, Nathaniel, and Bruce E. Cain. 2000. "The Legal Status of Political Parties: A Reassessment of Competing Paradigms." *Columbia Law Review* 100: 775–812.

Pildes, Richard H. 1999. "The Theory of Political Competition." *Virginia Law Review* 85: 1605–26.

———. 2004. "Foreword: The Constitutionalization of Democratic Politics." *Harvard Law Review* 118: 28–154.

———. 2006. "The Constitution and Political Competition." *Nova Law Review* 30: 269.

Reform Institute. 2005. *Beyond Party Lines: Principles for Redistricting Reform.* Washington.

Stratmann, Thomas, and Francisco J. Aparicio-Castillo. 2006. "Competition Policy for Elections: Do Campaign Contribution Limits Matter?" *Public Choice* 127: 177–206.

PART THREE

Reforms and Competition

9 | Term Limits: A Recipe for More Competition?

Bruce Cain, John Hanley, and Thad Kousser

One of the promises term-limits proponents made was that restrictions on time in office would foster greater electoral competition. A ballot argument for California's Proposition 140, for instance, stated: "Limiting terms will create more competitive elections, so good legislators will always have the opportunity to move up the ladder. Term limitations will end the in-grown, political nature of both houses—to the benefit of every man, woman and child in California." Amidst widespread concern that the incumbency advantage at all levels of government had increased measurably and that the political system was insulated from changing electoral swings, twenty-one states adopted state legislative term limits by 2000 (twelve of them between 1990 and 1992 alone). Six states subsequently repealed or had their term limits invalidated by the courts, leaving fifteen states to carry through their imposed limits on legislative tenure. Even though most of these laws were passed before 1996, over half of the term-limited state legislatures did not fully experience the first effects on any house until 2000. But now that all but two lower houses and three upper houses have fully implemented one cycle of term limits, we can try to shed some light on the proposition that term limits enhance political competition.

Why would people believe that term limits foster political competition? Limiting an incumbent's term of service to a specified number of years guarantees a minimum level of legislator turnover, in effect compensating for inadequate levels of electoral competition by creating more "open seats" (that is, seats without incumbents) than the electoral process would otherwise do. In an ideal electoral model, competitive elections produce regular turnover of both incumbents (descriptive turnover) and parties (party turnover). Theoretically, this should increase electoral responsiveness (the rate at which electoral shifts result in seat changes) and possibly reduce systemic partisan bias (a party holding a higher share of seats than the other party would if it had the same electoral share).

In practice, incumbency advantages of various sorts mute the value of competition by reducing both descriptive and party turnover, thereby weakening electoral responsiveness and increasing systemic bias. Campaign finance and redistricting reforms have tried to lessen incumbent advantages, but to little or no effect. Hence, the reasoning goes, if incumbency effects cannot be lessened, they can at least be eliminated periodically through formal limits. Actual turnover might exceed the minimum if there is a higher rate of anticipatory or office-jumping retirements, but the rate can never drop below the legal minimum. Whether that minimum is constraining depends upon the length and permanence of the term limitation. A limit of six years is guaranteed to produce more descriptive turnover than a limit of twelve years. A lifetime ban from a given office will prevent recidivism completely whereas a temporary ban only makes returning to office more difficult.

The guaranteed effect of legislative term limits is regularized descriptive turnover, but what about the competitive effects? Does the imposition of term limits increase the overall proportion of open seats, creating a new mixture of contests that is a recipe for more competition? If so, does the higher number of open-seat races lead only to more descriptive turnover or does it increase party turnover as well? Do term limits increase the share of contested races, on average? Do they make races closer, on average? In short, how well do term limits compensate for the failure of normal electoral processes to produce competition?

In this chapter we will first review what the political science literature, largely produced since the mid-1990s, says about the competitive effects of term limits. Then we look at data across a broad range of states to see whether the indicators of competitive state legislative elections increased or decreased as the term limits were implemented. Next we examine the unique natural experiment of Oregon, where term limits operated briefly before being abandoned. To explore the theoretical basis of some of our findings, we then compare data on the strategic entry of candidates with prior elective office experience into California legislative contests before and after the implementation of term limits. Finally, we analyze levels of primary election competitiveness in California and Colorado.

In general, our analyses reveal that the effects of term limits on competition are mild to nonexistent. Descriptive turnover has increased, but party turnover and the margins of victory in races have shown little or no change. The reasons for this, we believe, are the other trends in the electoral environment and the strategic behavior of incumbents. As to the first, term limits might have worked if other factors, such as redistricting and rising electoral polarization, had not occurred at the same time. In addition, since the odds of defeating an incumbent are long, serious challengers wait for open-seat opportunities. Competition is lessened in incumbent seats and concentrated in the open ones. While term limits opened up more seats, the overall pattern of competition reflects the common strategic assessment that it is usually better to wait for a member to "term out" before running for a seat.

The Existing Literature on Term Limits and Electoral Competition

One of the most important predictions made in the debate over the modern adoption of legislative term limits was that they would boost electoral competition.[1] This anticipated effect often formed a primary basis for the theoretical arguments in their favor. Term limits would, according to Cromwell, bring an end to what Everett Carll Ladd had earlier called "a conspiracy of circumstances that has, de facto, robbed the electorate of a meaningful say in who does and does not belong in office."[2] The seriousness and certainty of these declarations can perhaps be explained by the fact that term limits promised an automatic increase in turnover, creating the open seats that scholars and political practitioners have long recognized usually produce closer contests than races featuring an incumbent. Term limits would change the balance between open seats and districts filled by incumbents, and the new weighted average would lead to higher overall levels of competition. The

---

1. See Fund (1991); Petracca (1991); Barcellona and Grose (1994).
2. Cromwell (1991, p. 90).

effects of the reform could occur purely by electoral math, bringing an axiomatic effect that did not depend on the decisions of politicians or the complexities of the legislative process.

Recent research confirms that the implementation of term limits has indeed led to more descriptive turnover (that is, to a new person in the office) and more open seats. Research by the Joint Project on Term Limits (JPTL) conducted under the direction of the National Conference of State Legislatures (NCSL) reveals that, on average, term limits led to an increase in descriptive turnover of about 14 percent.[3] However, that average hides a great deal of variation over time and across states. Descriptive turnover was much higher in the years the term limits kicked in than in the years before and after. For instance, in the Ohio House descriptive turnover had averaged about 20 percent for each two-year election cycle, but this jumped to 50 percent when a large group of incumbents reached the term limit, falling back to 30 percent thereafter. There was also considerable variation by state. States like Colorado that had high turnover to begin with (as high as 30 percent) experienced only a very small increase (to 35 percent). And states that had shorter cycles, such as California, had higher average turnover per year than states with a longer limit, such as Nevada (which has a twelve-year limit).

By shifting the mixture of open and incumbent-held seats, did the new recipe of the term-limits era cook up closer races? The first empirical investigation of the link between term limits and competition appeared to confirm this expectation fully. Daniel and Lott examined California Senate and Assembly races from 1976 to 1994, elections held before and after the state's enactment of its term-limits law (but notably before its implementation actually removed legislators from office).[4] They found that term limits increased the number of major-party candidates, shrank margins of victory, made incumbents more likely to lose, and brought the added bonus of reducing campaign costs. This unequivocal good news for electoral competition, though, deserves a closer look. The estimated term-limits effect comes from only two elections, both held before term limits removed legislators from office and one of which—the 1994 Republican landslide—presents an atypical case. And California itself is certainly an atypical case, with the nation's most professional legislature[5] and the nation's most expensive campaigns.[6] Studies conducted after the implementation of term limits and those looking

---

3. Moncrief, Niemi, and Powell (2004).
4. Daniel and Lott (1997).
5. Squire (1992); Council of State Governments (2004).
6. Thompson and Moncrief (1998).

at states other than California suggest two important caveats to the prediction that term limits automatically increase competition.

The first caveat is that even though term limits create more open seats, both open-seat races and races that feature an incumbent may be less competitive than these types of contests are in the absence of term limits. Term limits may make races with incumbents less competitive through the logic outlined by Fowler: serious candidates will hold off on challenging incumbents, biding their time until the incumbents are "termed out" and thus giving officehold-ers a free ride until the limits kick in.[7] The story for open seats is more com-plex. In the absence of term limits, open seats are more competitive than races with an incumbent because of both treatment and selection effects. The treat-ment is the lack of an incumbent and the electoral advantage that incumbency brings. The selection process is that, in the absence of term limits, seats often become open owing to forces that may also create tighter electoral competi-tion. Perhaps a scandal leads to the resignation of a sitting legislator, or the incumbent strategically retires because he or she anticipates a strong chal-lenger or a difficult reelection campaign.[8] In each of these cases, the open-seat race will likely be close precisely because of the forces that led it to be open.

Term limits remove incumbents without regard to electability, creating open seats in a less systematic way. As Masket and Lewis demonstrate, limits move many formerly safe districts with extremely liberal or conservative elec-torates into the open column.[9] The treatment effect (the lack of an incum-bent) is still present for open seats after term limits, but the selection effect, which made them so competitive before term limits, has largely disappeared. Unsurprisingly, Masket and Lewis find that open-seat contests held after term limits for the California Assembly are less competitive (with margins of vic-tory 5.3 percent larger on average) than open-seat races before term limits. Comparisons of Michigan elections before term limits and with term limits in place find the same effect.[10] Of course, it is crucial to note that these stud-ies also found that term limits did indeed increase the number of open seats. In Michigan, where the initial impact of term limits in the lower house was especially sharp, open seats went from constituting 10 percent of races before term limits to 57 percent of races afterward.

The two effects that term limits seem to bring—more open seats, but fewer competitive races—counterbalance each other. While it is entirely possible

7. See Fowler (1992, p. 184).
8. Jacobson and Kernell (1983).
9. Masket and Lewis (forthcoming 2006).
10. See Allebaugh and Pinney (2003) and Pinney, Serra, and Sprick (2004).

that term limits will, once all of the districts in a state are averaged, lead to closer elections, the countervailing effects are likely to dampen the impact of term limits.

The second caveat is that although term limits *may* make elections more competitive, that does not mean that they *will be* competitive in any meaningful sense. Even the positive effects of term limits reported by Daniel and Lott are tempered by a close look at the scale of their findings. Term limits shrink margins of victory by an estimated 4.3 percentage points, but these margins still averaged 69.6 percentage points in California during the time of their study.[11] Masket and Lewis find that term limits bring a 1.8 percentage point reduction in the margin of victory for contested seats, but that this margin averaged 38 points before term limits.[12] In Michigan, Allebaugh and Pinney find that the imposition of term limits attracts more candidates to party primaries, but does not make them more competitive.[13] Term limits may bring marginal and statistically significant increases in competitiveness, but still not deliver meaningful competition. This suggests that scholars need to look not only at the number of candidates entering races and margins of victory, but also at whether term limits lead to more seats changing hands.

Cross-State Analysis

Our analysis of state legislative election results uses general election data produced under the direction of James Snyder (MIT), Richard Niemi (University of Rochester), and Thomas Carsey and William Berry (Florida State University). Our data set of primary elections was compiled by research assistants at the University of California, Berkeley. Because of the preliminary nature of some of the data, not all states could be used. Maine, a term-limits state, was removed from our analysis for this reason. In addition, we removed from our analysis states in which one or both houses of the state legislature had multi-member districts over some portion of our study window. This restriction eliminated three term-limits states, Arizona, North Dakota, and South Dakota.

Aggregating candidate general election returns up to the district level for each state in the years 1991–2003 produced one case for every district up for election in a given year. These were then coded for whether the general elec-

11. See Daniel and Lott (1997, pp. 173, 181).
12. Masket and Lewis (forthcoming 2006).
13. Allebaugh and Pinney (2003).

tion featured candidates from both the Republican and Democratic parties, and also whether an incumbent was ineligible for reelection due to term limits.[14] We also coded district elections based on whether or not they were held in a term-limits environment, a concept that is critical to our analysis. The phrase "term-limits environment" means that some portion of a chamber's membership was ineligible for reelection in a given year. To take an example, while the lower houses of the legislatures in Michigan and Arkansas became term-limits environments in 1998, their senates did not become term-limits environments for our purposes until later (2000 in Arkansas, 2002 in Michigan). States that never enacted term limits, such as New York and Massachusetts, are categorized as no-term-limits environments throughout our period of study. This means that the term-limits effects that we observe are generated both by variation across states (comparing states with and without term limits) and across time (comparing states before and after their term-limits laws were implemented).[15] Other scholars have constructed this category more broadly, considering a term-limits environment to exist from the moment that term limits are legally enacted. Our purpose in adhering to a stricter conceptualization is to capture more purely the effects that term limits had on the election outcomes by focusing on the results after term limits were implemented rather than before.

We then computed mean rates of two-party competition for term-limits and no-term-limits environments for open seats and seats with incumbents running for reelection. Using our data on which incumbents were termed out, we further broke down the open-seat category for term-limits states in order to separate districts in which an incumbent chose not to run from those in which he or she was *ineligible* to run. For the districts where two-party

14. We received lists of term-limited legislators via personal communication from Jennie Bowser at the National Conference of State Legislatures, and these data were entered by a research assistant at the University of California, San Diego.

15. In the appendix to this chapter, we conduct a similar analysis of the same data in order to evaluate the effects of these two types of variation separately. In table 9A-1, we look only at the states that enacted term limits, and compare measures of competition from before the implementation of term limits with those afterward. In table 9A-2, we look only at the states that have not enacted term limits, and compare our measures from early in the 1990s (before term limits were implemented in other states) with the late 1990s and early 2000s. This clean research design reveals two facts. First, the states that enacted term limits happened to have slightly more competitive contests even before term limits came into effect. Second, in all of the states, and according to all three of our measures, elections grew less competitive in the late 1990s and early 2000s. The fact that the magnitude of this trend is about as large in states with term limits as in states without limits increases our confidence that the overall effects of term limits on political competition are negligible.

Table 9-1. Term Limits and Electoral Competition, 1991–2002

Environment	Number of seats	Percent contested (Republican vs. Democrat)	Number of contested seats	Average margin of victory for contested seats (percent)
Term-limits environment				
Open seat, due to term limits	698	82.09**	573	24.58**
Open seat, not due to term limits	435	79.54**	346	23.81**
Incumbent	1,399	68.98**	964	29.20
All seats, term-limits environment	2,532	74.41**	1,883	26.80
No-term-limits environment				
Open seat	4,754	74.25**	3,528	22.51**
Incumbent	17,131	55.54**	9,485	28.45
All seats, no-term-limits environment	21,885	59.60**	13,013	26.84

Sources: Authors' calculations using data provided by Snyder, Niemi, Carsey, and Berry, and by the National Conference of State Legislatures.

** The difference between competition levels in the term-limits and no-term-limits environments is statistically significant at the 99 percent confidence level in a two-sample *t* test.

competition existed, we calculated the mean margin of victory for open seats and seats featuring an incumbent, in both the term-limits and no-term-limits environments, again distinguishing further between open seats where the incumbent was ineligible for reelection and those where the incumbent was eligible but did not run. Last, we computed the rate at which state legislative seats changed party over the period 1993–2000.

Our analysis, presented in tables 9-1 and 9-2, shows a number of statistically significant effects. First, the rates of two-party contestation of legislative seats are higher in term-limits environments than in no-term-limits environments. This result holds for both open seats and seats with incumbents. Under term limits, incumbents are challenged in the general election by the opposite major party in almost 70 percent of cases; where term limits have not been enacted, or have been enacted but not yet begun to bar individuals from seeking reelection, only 55 percent of incumbents were challenged. Looking exclusively at open seats, we see again that rates of two-party contestation were higher in term-limits environments, though this difference is approximately half of that observed where incumbents were present. Eighty-one percent of all open seat races in term-limits environments featured head-to-head competition between a Democrat and a Republican, while only 74 percent of open seat races outside of term limits were a contest between

Table 9-2. Term Limits and Turnover, 1993–2000

Environment	Number of seats	Party turnover rate (percent)
Term-limits environment		
Open seat, due to term limits	484	11.77**
Open seat, not due to term limits	211	18.48**
Incumbent	916	2.84**
All seats, term-limits environment	1,611	7.57
No-term-limits environment		
Open seat	2,469	19.08**
Incumbent	11,504	5.3**
All seats, no-term-limits environment	13,973	7.74

Sources: Authors' calculations using data provided by Snyder, Niemi, Carsey, and Berry, and by the National Conference of State Legislatures.

** The difference between competition levels in the term-limits and no-term-limits environments is statistically significant at the 99 percent confidence level in a two-sample *t* test.

the major parties. Averaging across the two types of seats, the rate of major-party contestation is about 15 percentage points higher under term limits.

The news for competition is not so sunny, however, when we look at the average margin of victory in these contested seats. Comparing the average margin for all seats in a term-limits environment (26.80 percent) with all seats without term limits (26.84 percent) shows that limits have absolutely no aggregate effect. Yet underneath this overall stasis are some important changes of the type found in single-state studies in the existing literature. Term limits bring a larger percentage of open seats, our analysis shows. But for each type of seat, margins of victory are not as close under term limits as they are in a no-term-limits environment. In open seats with term limits, the spread between the two candidates is significantly *larger* than it is in the absence of term limits, meaning that contested seats become less competitive. Incumbent-held seats also feature slightly higher winning margins, though the effect is not statistically significant. These increases in the margin for each category of seat have almost perfectly counterbalanced the term-limits effect of creating more open seats.[16]

16. In an analysis presented in another chapter of this volume, Niemi and his coauthors find that there have been more competitive seats in the states with term limits since 1996 than in the states without term limits. There are two possible explanations of why their finding differs from ours, even though we use the same data set and reach the same findings about other term-limits effects and noneffects that they do. First, Niemi and colleagues employ a dichotomous measure of competitive seats (those in which the winning candidate receives less than

For similar reasons, our measure of turnover in party control of seats shows no overall difference between those districts that are in term-limits environments and those that are not. While total rates of party turnover are the same, incumbents do better in term-limits environments, losing only 2.8 percent of races, as opposed to 5.3 percent in no-term-limits environments. Parties looking to hold on to open term-limited seats also do better in term-limits environments, losing 13.8 percent of seats versus 19.1 percent in no-term-limits environments. Both of these results are statistically significant. That the overall rate of party turnover is nearly equal between the two environments is explained by a greater number of seats becoming open in term-limits environments.

Imagine two legislative chambers: one without term limits, and the other with a four-term, eight-year limit. Were we to pretend that in the term-limited legislature no members ever left before being termed out, and that in the limitless chamber members served an average of six terms, we would expect the limitless chamber to produce more party turnover than the term-limited chamber. Though our assumptions of this hypothetical are somewhat unrealistic, it illustrates that a sizable proportion of the gain in the absolute number of open seats under term limits is taken away by the lower rate at which seats opened by term limits change party control.

Our result is reinforced by another finding from the data, specifically that the margin of victory in open, contested seats is higher in the term-limits environments than in chambers without term limits. Higher margins of victory, of course, imply that the candidates are less evenly matched in term-limits environments than in traditional two-party races. What the data suggest, therefore, is that candidates in term-limits environments may be entering legislative contests in greater numbers, even though their chances of winning are smaller. Since legislative term limits are a relatively new innovation, it remains to be seen whether the higher rates of contestation present in term-limits environments result from the novelty of large numbers of open seats, or whether the new strategic environment truly encourages increased contestation.

---

60 percent of the vote) while we use a continuous one (the margin of victory). Second, it may be because Niemi and his colleagues compare term-limits states after they implement their limits with states without limits, in the same years. Since the analysis that we summarize in appendix tables 9A-1 and 9A-2 shows that the states that pass term limits have slightly higher levels of competition to begin with, this difference between states (rather than a true term-limits effect) may be driving some of the effect that Niemi and his coauthors report.

Oregon's Natural Experiment

To confirm the patterns that we observe in our comprehensive analysis, we take a closer look at a state which, owing to a court decision, conducted a "natural experiment" with term limits. Oregon voters adopted term limits in a 1992 initiative dubbed "LIMITS," for Let Incumbents Mosey Into The Sunset.[17] Many House members and several senators were forced to mosey after their terms expired in 1998 and 2000, but the sun set on LIMITS before the 2002 elections. A county judge's decision in July 2001, upheld by the Oregon Supreme Court in January 2002, threw out the initiative on the grounds that it violated the state's prohibition on addressing multiple subjects in one initiative, because it applied the limits to different categories of officeholders.[18] This technicality made Oregon the only state to overturn term limits after implementing them, providing a relatively clean way to gauge the impact of limits on electoral competition.

In this section, we track our multiple measures of competition in Oregon from the years before term limits to the 1998 and 2000 elections when they went into effect, and through the 2002 contests in which veterans were again eligible to run. This time-series analysis holds constant the peculiarities of a state's politics, isolating the effects of the implementation and disappearance of term limits. It is similar to the analyses of California and Michigan that other scholars have conducted, yet it broadens our range of knowledge about the context of term limits. Unlike the highly professional legislatures of California and Michigan, Oregon's General Assembly is closer to the "citizen" ideal for which many states still strive. The legislature meets only in odd-numbered years, and members receive annual salaries of just $15,396.[19] Over the course of our study, elections in Oregon's sixty-member lower-house districts have averaged about 20,000 voters, while contests for the thirty Senate seats typically turn out 40,000 voters. While there are some legislative bodies in the South, New England, and the Mountain West with even smaller districts and lower levels of professionalism, Oregon provides a very different context than California or Michigan in which to examine the effects of term limits.

17. Steve Law, "Initiator of Term Limits Casts Long Shadow," *Salem Statesman Journal,* February 13, 2001.

18. Peter Wong, "Term Limits Overturned in Court," *Salem Statesman Journal,* July 21, 2001; National Conference of State Legislatures, 2006; Summaries of Court Decisions (www. ncsl.org/programs/legman/about/terms.htm [February 2006]).

19. Council of State Governments (2004).

Figure 9-1. Competition before, during, and after Term Limits in Oregon, 1990–2002[a]

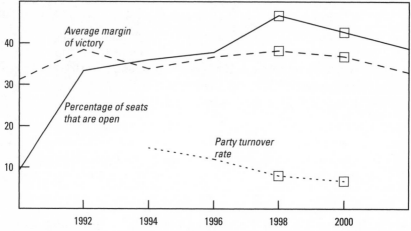

Sources: Authors' calculations using data provided by Snyder, Niemi, Carsey, and Berry, and by the National Conference of State Legislatures.

a. The empty icons indicate the years in which term limits were in effect in Oregon, 1998 and 2000. Data on switches in the party control of a district are missing from 1992 and 2002 because each election followed a redistricting; figures are missing for 1990 because we do not have data on party control in 1988.

As figure 9-1 and table 9-3 demonstrate, however, the story from Oregon parallels both the findings of previous studies and of our cross-state analysis. Term limits did create more open seats when they went into effect, but the counterbalancing trend of less competition for both open and incumbent seats eroded all of the gains in competition that term limits promised. Overall, races were no closer and party switches less frequent during the term-limits era in Oregon.

Figure 9-1 tracks the number of open seats and two of our competitiveness measures from the days before the passage of LIMITS through the two elections in which it was in effect and finally after it was overturned in court. It shows that the percentage of open seats in the Oregon House and Senate rose steeply in 1998, when term limits removed a large cohort of veteran legislators. The portion of seats that were open—and thus more likely to produce competitive elections—remained high in 2000 when another wave of members was termed out. But after the limits were overturned in 2002, the percentage of open seats returned to more typical levels, even though we would have expected redistricting to push the portion of open seats upward. The first con-

Table 9-3. Competition in Oregon by Type of Seat, 1990–2002

Percent

Environment	Percent contested (Republican vs. Democrat)	Average margin of victory for contested seats	Party turnover rate, 1993–2000
Term-limits environment			
Open seat, due to term limits	87.8	21.3	7.3
Open seat, not due to term limits	80.8	19.4	26.9
Incumbent	63.9	24.1	1.2
All seats, term-limits environment	73.3	22.3	7.3
No-term-limits environment			
Open seat	90.5	17.7	27.3
Incumbent	76.7	24.3	5.3
All seats, no-term-limits environment	81.0	22.0	13.4

Sources: Authors' calculations using data provided by Snyder, Niemi, Carsey, and Berry, and by the National Conference of State Legislatures.

dition necessary to create more electoral competition, an increase in the percentage of open seats, was present when term limits were in place in Oregon. Yet the other two time series in figure 9-1 show that term limits did not deliver on their potential to bring about closer races. Average margins of victory stayed about as wide as they ever were after LIMITS was implemented, and actually narrowed a bit after the initiative was overturned (though again, this may be a result of redistricting). The percentage of seats that changed party hands was lower in the two term-limits elections than it was during the prior two contests. Breaking down these aggregate competitiveness measures by type of district can help to explain why term limits did not create more competition as a result of opening up more seats. Table 9-3 presents the same breakdown that our cross-state analysis provided.[20]

While the mix of open versus incumbent races may have shifted when term limits were implemented in Oregon, declines in the level of competition for each type of seat counteracted this effect. The percentage of incumbent-held seats contested by the major parties was lower, at 63.9 percent compared to 76.7 percent, supporting Fowler's prediction that potential candidates bide their time until incumbents are forced out.[21] The rate of contestation in open

20. Districts with term-limited incumbents in the 2000 elections were identified using the materials provided in a personal communication from Jennie Bowser of the National Conference of State Legislatures, and districts in 1998 were identified using the list contained in Steve Law, "Lawmaking Talent Lost through Revolving Door," *Salem Statesman Journal*, February 13, 2001.

21. See Fowler (1992).

seats also declined, dropping from 87.8 percent in term-limited districts and 80.8 percent in other open seats during these years to 90.5 percent in the years without term limits. On balance, this led to an 8 percentage point decline in the proportion of contested races. The story is similar for margins of victory, with a widening of margins in open seats during the term-limits era leading to no net change in the average margin of victory. Finally, the overall rate of party turnover declined from 13.4 percent to 7.3 percent when term limits were in effect. This occurred because party switches were slightly rarer in open seats under term limits and because very few incumbents—only 1.2 percent of those running for reelection—were defeated when LIMITS was in place in 1998 and 2000.

The Strategic Entry Decisions of Potential Candidates

The fact that major-party candidates were less likely to challenge incumbents when term limits were in place in Oregon suggests that the strategic entry decisions of potential candidates deserve further investigation. Perhaps limits alter the behavior of possible candidates, especially those with elective office experience who could pose the most serious challenges to incumbents. Instead of taking on incumbents when political conditions appear most favorable, the pattern that Jacobson and Kernell observed for experienced congressional candidates,[22] perhaps politicians now synchronize their ambitions with the timing of term limits. It is possible that they will rarely challenge incumbents, since they know that these incumbents will soon be ineligible to run for reelection. Potential candidates who have held a previous local or state elective office are the ones most likely to be guided by this strategic entry calculus, and their decisions will have the most important consequences for electoral competition.

If "experienced" candidates who have held prior office do indeed follow this logic, we should see: (1) more of them running when seats become open than when an incumbent remains in office; and (2) more challenges of incumbents taking place before term limits are implemented than afterward, when potential candidates can simply wait for the seat to open up. If these patterns exist, they can help explain why term limits do not bring the aggregate increases in electoral competition that we might expect. For incumbents, the silver lining in the looming cloud of term limits may be that they are more likely to get a free ride by facing a weak challenger or no opposition in

---

22. Jacobson and Kernell (1983).

their remaining elections. In addition, if the term-limits calendar rather than the overall political climate is what drives the entry decisions of experienced candidates, it may be that fewer take advantage of an atmosphere that would give them a decent chance at defeating a current officeholder. These two dynamics may explain why only 1.2 percent of incumbents lost during Oregon's two election cycles held under term limits.

We test our predictions by using pre- and post-term-limits data from the California Assembly, because we have located elusive measures of candidate experience from only this state. Since most challengers lose, it is often difficult to track down records of their prior elected office experience. Fortunately, the wealth of information available about California politics allowed us to identify whether each major-party nominee had elective experience or whether the party was left to be represented by someone with fewer obvious qualifications (examples include a self-described "mediator/skydiver," a San Francisco MUNI bus driver, and an actor whose claim to fame was a minor role in *Anaconda 2: King Cobra*).[23] We compared the rates at which experienced candidates entered contests in two elections held before term limits were enacted in the state, 1982 and 1984, with two elections held well after they went into effect, 2002 and 2004. Each of these similar pairs of contests includes an election held after a redistricting, and both took place at times in which Democrats held a strong majority of seats in the Assembly.

The first prediction that table 9-4 confirms is that experienced candidates enter open races at higher rates. For each pair of elections, the percentage of major-party nominees who had previously held local or state office was two to three times as high in open-seat races as in races for incumbent-held seats. Experienced candidates, we are not surprised to see, do not like to tilt at windmills. More important for understanding the dynamics of term limits is that the data confirm our prediction that experienced candidates are less

---

23. For 2004 nominees, our biographical information came from *The California Target Book*, a district-by-district analysis prepared for the press and political consultants (Hoffenblum 2004). For each 2002 nominee, we compiled biographical information from the profiles posted at www.smartvoter.org and www.calvoter.org and from searches on www.google.com identifying nominees as Assembly candidates. Our lists of nominees came from Kevin Shelley, California Secretary of State, *Statement of Vote, 2002 Primary Election* (www.ss.ca.gov/elections/sov/2002_primary/contents.htm [April 2004]; and Kevin Shelley, *Statement of Vote, 2004 Presidential Primary Election* (www.ss.ca.gov/elections/sov/2004_primary/contents.htm [April 2004]). For the pre-term-limits era, we obtained candidate biographies from the primary election recaps reported in the *California Journal* (1982, 1984). Although we found biographies for both party nominees in all 160 Assembly elections in 2002 and 2004, we were able to find similar information for only eighty-eight races in 1982 and 1984 combined.

Table 9-4. Candidates with Prior Elective Experience in California, before Term Limits and with Term Limits in Effect

Percent

	Before term limits, 1982 and 1984	With term limits in effect, 2002 and 2004
Candidates for open seats	40.5	42.6
Challengers for incumbent-held seats	22.4	13.1

Sources: The figures were compiled from *California Journal* (1982, 1984); Hoffenblum (2004); from biographical profiles posted at www.smartvoter.org and www.calvoter.org; and from searches on www.google.com identifying nominees as Assembly candidates.

likely to challenge incumbents after the implementation of term limits. The rate of serious challenges to incumbents dropped from 22.4 percent to 13.1 percent, consistent with the prediction that experienced candidates bide their time until incumbents are termed out of office. The fact that experienced candidates still enter open-seat races at a very high rate after term limits also fits with this story. Overall, our findings on strategic entry help to explain why races for incumbent-held seats are often less competitive after term limits than they were before: the most serious challengers typically sit out until the end of an incumbent's term, giving him or her a free ride (and thus fewer incentives to be responsive to voters) until then.

Competition in Party Primaries

For our final look at the possible effects of term limits on electoral competition, we gathered data on primary elections in two states that were among the first to adopt term limits, California and Colorado. Though we have found no evidence so far that limits make general elections closer or more likely to result in party turnover, it may be that their real effects come in party primaries. When term limits create open seats, even though many of them may be safe seats that are unlikely to produce close races or party turnover in November, at least they will be up for grabs in the primary. With the incumbent termed out, primaries that were once a cakewalk become a free-for-all. Because term limits create more open seats, we expected to observe: (1) a higher overall rate of contested primaries with term limits in effect; (2) more candidates getting into these primaries, because their outcome is less certain and the party's nomination more likely to lead to a general election victory in an open seat; and (3) closer primaries on average because more of their fields are crowded.

We track each of these trends from before the implementation of term limits until after veteran members have been removed from office. We examine California, which has a highly professional legislature that pays its members six-figure salaries and features very expensive elections, and Colorado, a state in the middle of the professionalism scale that pays salaries of $30,000[24] and produces much less costly campaigns. In each state, we expected that all three of our measures of primary election competition would rise when term limits removed the first large cohort of legislators, and then fall slightly in successive elections as the limits affected fewer and fewer incumbents. We also expected the level of legislative professionalism to condition the effects of term limits, though we were not certain whether the impact of term limits would be stronger or weaker in the highly professional California legislature. On the one hand, serving in this high-paying body is such an attractive proposition that many potential candidates should take advantage of the open seats that term limits create. On the other hand, the cost of entering a California Senate or Assembly campaign is so high that the greater number of candidates and higher level of competition that we might expect from term limits could be muted.

Indeed, the effects of term limits appear to be different in the two states, as demonstrated by the time series for all three measures of competitiveness presented in figure 9-2 (Colorado) and figure 9-3 (California). In Colorado, where the price of political entry is low, we see slightly more contested primaries after term limits implementation and more candidates entering these primaries. While only 8.9 percent of district primaries were contested in the four Colorado elections held before term limits, 11.7 percent were contested after term limits were in place. The average number of candidates in these contested races edged upward from 2.0 to 2.2 entrants. But perhaps because these races attracted less formidable candidates, they were not as close as primaries before term limits. The average margin of victory grew from 17.2 percent before term limits to 20.4 percent with term limits in effect, indicating that primary voters in Colorado have had more candidates to choose from yet have not seen tighter contests.

In California, where entering campaigns is so expensive, the implementation of term limits has not led to any clear gains in primary election competition. The percentage of primaries that were contested declined from 36.0 percent before term limits to 31.5 percent afterward, leaving voters in fewer districts with a choice in the race for their party's nomination. The other two measures

24. Council of State Governments (2004).

Figure 9-2. Competition in Colorado Primaries, before and during Term Limits, 1990–2002[a]

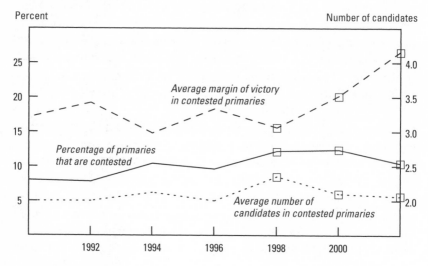

Source: Authors' calculations.
a. The empty icons indicate the years in which term limits were in effect in Colorado, 1998–2002.

of competitiveness that we examine remain stable from the pre-term-limits to term-limits era. The number of candidates running in contested primaries averaged 2.9 entrants in both eras, while primary margins of victory averaged 25.0 percent before 1996 and 25.7 percent afterward. Much to our surprise, the fact that term limits have opened up more seats in California's highly professional legislature has not led to more competition for party nominations.[25]

Conclusion

A fundamental premise of the term-limits movement turns out to be mostly untrue in several important senses. What is clearly true is that term limits increase descriptive turnover by about 14 percent on average. Even so, the level varies from state to state depending upon the length of the term limit.

25. It might be suggested that looking at primary and general elections together would show a more robust competitive environment after the institution of term limits—in other words, that some districts would have highly competitive primaries and others competitive general elections. We find limited evidence for this claim: where there is not two-party competition in the general election, Democratic primaries are slightly closer after the institution of term limits, but this result does not hold for Republicans. Also, only about 2 percent of seats are contested in the primary election but not the general.

Figure 9-3. Competition in California Primaries, before and during
Term Limits, 1990–2002[a]

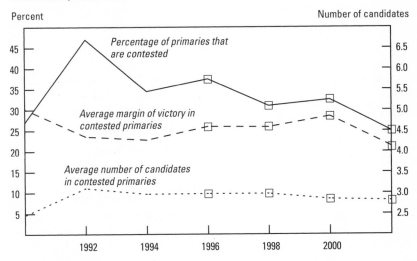

Percent   Number of candidates

Source: Authors' calculations.
a. The empty icons indicate the years in which term limits were in effect in California, 1996–2002.

Term limits also appear to increase the level of contestation in both open and incumbent seats. But term limits have not made races closer or led to more party turnover. What do we make of all this?

The increase in descriptive turnover cannot be dismissed out of hand. New faces count for something. The JPTL has documented that some term-limited states have seen dramatic increases in the number of Latino representatives, a trend that would have likely occurred eventually, but happened more quickly because of the higher level of churning caused by limiting incumbency.[26] Curiously, term limits do not seem to have increased the number of women in office relative to the number in non-term-limited legislatures.

Beyond gender and racial differences, new members have come in with different perspectives, and the legislatures they work in have been transformed in important ways. Committee seniority and experience have declined, and in many states this has put more power in the hands of party leaders and more action on the floor. There is less deference to committees in some states, and weaker leadership in the lower houses. Where the effects are

26. Moncrief, Powell, and Storey (forthcoming 2006).

most dramatic, legislative oversight has declined and executive control of the budget has increased.[27] In short, term-limited legislatures tend to be less powerful, and executives more so. To put it another way, more descriptive turnover has altered important institutional structures and the perspectives that representatives bring to lawmaking.

The lack of effect on party turnover rates is unfortunate. Ideally, by creating more open seats, term limits would have heightened legislative responsiveness and lessened bias. There is no sign that this has happened. It is certainly a good thing that the level of contestation has gone up. An incumbent who faces even a weak opponent is more accountable than one with no challenger, and may be forced to take up the issues championed by the challenger.[28] But the fact that party turnover rates are at best no better and possibly worse than in states without term limits is not encouraging. The margin of victory being no lower (and in some instances higher) suggests that capping incumbency does not matter: the main advantages of being an incumbent are apparently realized very quickly. In addition, primary contests have not become more competitive after the implementation of term limits either.

In hindsight, these findings make sense. Using term limits to tackle the problems of lower competition in America is a partial equilibrium solution to a general equilibrium problem. Yes, incumbency is part of the reason that legislative races have become less competitive, but short of eliminating incumbents every two years, the advantages of incumbency (name recognition, money, staff, projects, constituency service, and others) will still be there. Moreover, other factors such as redistricting, the incentives of primary systems, the influence of groups with money, and the general trend of voter polarization and social sorting are pushing in the opposite direction of safer seats. Opening up more seats could have led to more competition if everything else had stayed the same, but that was not the case. Indeed, it is possible that weakened incumbents might have let the underlying partisan forces matter more. In the 1980s, some Democratic incumbents held on to seats that were politically and demographically Republican by virtue of their incumbency and tailored moderation. But as they have been termed out, the underlying partisan makeup has become even more the controlling factor. Hence descriptive turnover has no effect on party turnover.

A serious attempt to increase party turnover in American legislative elections would require a multipronged attack on several causes at once. And

27. Cain and Kousser (2004); Kousser (2005).
28. Sulkin (2005).

even if this were politically and constitutionally possible (which it is not), there is the question raised by others in this volume of whether a system that is jiggered to create more close races and enhance party turnover is any better than the one we have. In the end, term-limits laws succeeded in bringing more descriptive turnover, but failed to create more competition either through closer races or increased party turnover.

Table 9A-1. Electoral Competition and Party Turnover in States with Term Limits[a]

Environment	Number of seats	Percent contested (Republican vs. Democrat)	Number of contested seats	Average margin of victory for contested seats (percent)
Term-limits environment				
Open seat, due to term limits	698	82.09	573	24.58
Open seat, not due to term limits	435	79.54	346	23.81
All open seats	1,133	81.11	919	24.29**
Incumbent	1,399	68.98**	964	29.20**
All seats, term-limits environment	2,532	74.41**	1,883	26.80**
Pre-term-limits environment				
Open seat	1,367	80.18	1,096	21.91**
Incumbent	3,654	64.37**	2,352	26.86**
All seats, pre-term-limits environment	5,021	68.67**	3,448	25.29**

Environment	Number of seats	Party turnover rate (percent)
Term-limits environment		
Open seat, due to term limits	484	11.77
Open seat, not due to term limits	211	18.48
All open seats	695	13.81**
Incumbent	916	2.84**
All seats, term-limits environment	1,611	7.57**
Pre-term-limits environment		
Open seat	741	21.32**
Incumbent	2,559	6.57**
All seats, pre-term-limits environment	3,300	9.88**

Sources: Authors' calculations using data provided by Snyder, Niemi, Carsey, and Berry, and by the National Conference of State Legislatures.

a. Electoral competition figures summarize elections held from 1991 to 2003; party turnover figures summarize elections held from 1993 to 2000.

** The difference between competition levels in the term-limits and pre-term-limits environments is statistically significant at the 99 percent confidence level in a two-sample *t* test.

Table 9A-2. Electoral Competition and Party Turnover in States
without Term Limits

	Number of seats	Percent contested (Republican vs. Democrat)	Number of contested seats	Average margin of victory for contested seats (percent)
1997–2003				
Open seat	1,459	68.88**	1,004	23.24
Incumbent	6,924	48.63**	3,365	29.95**
All seats, 1997–2003	8,383	51.15**	4,369	28.41**
1991–96				
Open seat	1,927	74.10**	1,427	22.45
Incumbent	6,553	57.50**	3,768	27.10**
All seats, 1991–96	8,480	61.27**	5,195	25.82**

	Number of seats	Party turnover rate (percent)
1997–2000		
Open seat	826	14.89**
Incumbent	4,658	3.67**
All seats, 1997–2000	5,484	5.36**
1993–96		
Open seat	910	20.99**
Incumbent	4,287	6.32**
All seats, 1993–96	5,197	10.78**

Sources: Authors' calculations using data provided by Snyder, Niemi, Carsey, and Berry, and by the National Conference of State Legislatures.

** The difference between competition levels in the earlier and later era is statistically significant at the 99 percent confidence level in a two-sample *t* test.

References

Allebaugh, Dalene, and Neil Pinney. 2003. "The Real Costs of Term Limits: Comparative Study of Competition and Electoral Costs." In *The Test of Time: Coping with Legislative Term Limits*, edited by Rick Farmer, John David Rausch, and John C. Green. Lanham, Md.: Lexington Books.

Barcellona, Miriam M., and Andrew P. Grose. 1994. *Term Limits: A Political Dilemma.* San Francisco: Council of State Governments.

Cain, Bruce E., and Thad Kousser. 2004. *Adapting to Term Limits: Recent Experiences and New Directions.* San Francisco: Public Policy Institute of California.

California Journal. 1982. "Assembly." *California Journal* (July). Sacramento: StateNet.

———. 1984. "The Assembly," *California Journal* (July). Sacramento: StateNet.

Council of State Governments. 2004. *The Book of the States, 2004 Edition*. Vol. 36. Lexington, Ky.: Council of State Governments.

Cromwell, Oliver, II. 1991. "Yes: A Reform Whose Time Has Come." *Annual Report of the Cosmos Club*: 89–90.

Daniel, Kermit, and John R. Lott Jr. 1997. "Term Limits and Electoral Competitiveness: Evidence from California's State Legislative Races." *Public Choice* 90: 165–84.

Fowler, Linda. 1992. "A Comment on Competition and Careers." In *Limiting Legislative Terms*, edited by Gerald Benjamin and Michael J. Malbin. Washington: CQ Press.

Fund, John. 1991. "Term Limitation: An Idea Whose Time Has Come." In *Limiting Legislative Terms*, edited by Gerald Benjamin and Michael J. Malbin. Washington: CQ Press.

Hoffenblum, Alan, ed. 2004. *The California Target Book, Volume 4, 2004 General Election Edition*. Los Angeles: Alan Hoffenblum and Associates.

Jacobson, Gary C., and Samuel Kernell. 1983. *Strategy and Choice in Congressional Elections*. 2nd ed. Yale University Press.

Kousser, Thad. 2005. *Term Limits and the Dismantling of State Legislative Professionalism*. Cambridge University Press.

Masket, Seth, and Jeffrey B. Lewis. Forthcoming 2006. "A Return to Normalcy? Revisiting the Effects of Term Limits on Competitiveness and Spending in California Assembly Elections." *State Politics and Policy Quarterly*.

Moncrief, Gary, Lynda Powell, and Tim Storey. Forthcoming. "Term Limits and the Composition of Legislatures." In *Institutional Change in American Politics: The Case of Term Limits*, edited by Karl Kurtz, Bruce Cain, and Richard Niemi. University of Michigan Press.

Petracca, Mark P. 1991. "The Poison of Professional Politics." Policy Analysis 151. Washington: Cato Institute.

Pinney, Neil, George Serra, and Dalene Sprick. 2004. "The Costs of Reform: Consequences of Limits Terms of Service." *Party Politics* 10: 69–84.

Squire, Peverill. 1992. "Legislative Professionalization and Membership Diversity in State Legislatures." *Legislative Studies Quarterly* 17: 69–79.

Sulkin, Tracy. 2005. *Issue Politics in Congress*. Cambridge University Press.

Thompson, Joel A., and Gary F. Moncrief. 1998. *Campaign Finance in State Legislative Elections*. Washington: CQ Press.

10 Redistricting and Competitive Districts

Michael P. McDonald

In the wake of the round of redistricting following the 2000 census, editorial pages across the political spectrum claimed that redistricting reduced the number of competitive elections by reducing the number of competitive districts.[1] The distinction between elections and districts is important: competitive elections are those with a close election outcome, while competitive districts are those with a near partisan balance between the two major political parties.[2] Competitive elections arise out of a number of factors, such as whether an incumbent is running for reelection, whether a quality challenger emerges to contest the incumbent, the issue positions the candidates take, the money candidates raise, and intangible factors such as scandals. The partisan composition of districts, too, directly and indirectly affects the competitiveness of elections.

Election handicappers can reliably predict over 90 percent of congressional election outcomes by knowing if the presidential vote within a district

1. See, for example, *Washington Post*, "The Partisan Fix," September 14, 2003, p. B06; *Wall Street Journal*, "No Contest," November 12, 2004; *Economist*, "Curb Your Enthusiasm," November 2, 2002.
2. See Niemi and Deegan (1978) for a theoretical treatment of competitive districts.

is sufficiently large and leans in the direction of the incumbent.[3] There are a number of reasons why homogeneous partisan districts reliably elect members of the same party while competitive districts are less likely to do so.[4] Of course, there is the direct link: within a highly partisan electorate, competitive districts are those where the median voter is more likely an independent and thus persuadable. Competitive districts are associated with the presence of strong, qualified challengers to incumbents.[5] Anticipated close races between quality candidates attract money.[6] Thus the partisan composition of a district has both direct and indirect effects on the overall competition of the election within it. District competition also affects other aspects of politics, such as the degree of political polarization in Congress, as "more competitive districts tend to produce more moderate candidates."[7]

In a recent exchange in the journal *PS: Political Science and Politics*, I debated whether redistricting is responsible for the recent decline in competitive districts.[8] Here, I elaborate on this debate. I provide evidence that redistricting has indeed depressed the number of competitive districts. I explain how current redistricting institutions around the country enable partisan and incumbent protection gerrymanders, neither of which favors drawing competitive districts. Finally, I examine reform efforts and ask the prospective question, can redistricting institutions be designed to produce a more competitive outcome?

The Decline of Competitive Districts

To assess the effect of redistricting on the competitiveness of congressional districts, I use a common measure in academic redistricting research: the "normalized" presidential vote of the presidential election that most recently

3. See, for example, statistics released by the Center for Voting and Democracy, Monopoly Politics series for 2000 and 2002, at www.fairvote.org.

4. See Jacobson (2001, p. 132) and Swain, Borrelli, and Reed (1998).

5. Maisel and Stone (1997).

6. For example, Grenzke (1988, p. 245) states that "researchers agree that . . . electoral competition is important to most PACs." The link between competitive districts and campaign contributions is often not explicitly tested. The measurement of competitive elections is often given as the closeness of the incumbent's vote in the previous election (see, for example, Box-Steffensmeier and Dow 1992, p. 617).

7. See Ansolabehere, Snyder, and Stewart (2001, p. 143) and Erikson and Wright (2001).

8. See Abramowitz, Alexander, and Gunning (2006a); Abramowitz, Alexander, and Gunning (2006b); McDonald (2006a); and McDonald (2006b).

preceded the redistricting. One group of scholars described this measure as an "excellent indicator of change in the partisan composition of a district."[9] This is not simply an academic exercise. Map drawers aggregate available demographic and political data into different district configurations to evaluate their political consequences.[10] Often, measures of district partisanship are most valid when analyzing down-ballot statewide races, such as those for secretary of state and attorney general, where candidate partisanship primarily guides voter decisions, and when averaging many such elections, which reduces local effects created by a particularly strong candidate. Presidential elections are the only elections common to all congressional districts, but fortunately the normalized presidential vote demonstrates similar patterns in the change of the number of competitive districts as more sophisticated measures.[11]

The change in the number of districts with a normalized presidential vote within two competitiveness ranges, 45–55 and 48–52 percent, are presented in figure 10-1 for four pairs of elections bracketing a national round of redistricting, 1970–72, 1980–82, 1990–92, and 2000–02. The wider 45–55 percent range is presented since it is commonly used to describe competitive congressional elections; however, my analysis of the relationship between competitive districts and competitive elections suggests that the tighter range is a more valid definition of a competitive district.[12]

9. See Glazer, Grofman, and Robbins (1987, p. 682). Normalized presidential vote within a district is calculated as the percentage of the "two-party" or Democratic presidential vote divided by the Democratic plus Republican vote. The value is "normalized" by subtracting the national two-party presidential vote from each district's value. For presentation, I add back 50 percent to conceptualize district competitiveness around 50 percent. I explain the validity of this measure in McDonald (2006a) and McDonald (2006b). Some examples of scholarly work using this measure include Gopoian and West (1984); Gelman and King (1994); and Swain, Borrelli, and Reed (1998).

10. To draw districts that adhere to equal population standards articulated by the United States Supreme Court in the 1960s, census population data are released at the census "block" level, which is roughly the size of a city block in an urban area. Some states correspond census blocks to political boundaries such as their current districts and what are known as "Voting Tabulation Districts," more familiarly known as voting precincts or wards. This in turn allows election data to be aggregated within proposed districts and analyzed during the course of redistricting.

11. The patterns of change in the number of competitive districts are similar using the normalized presidential vote and the more sophisticated method proposed by Gelman and King (1994). See McDonald (2006a).

12. McDonald (2006a). I found similar results in my analysis of competitive districts for the Arizona Independent Redistricting Commission.

Figure 10-1. Competitive Districts before and after Redistricting, 1970–2002

Number of districts[a]

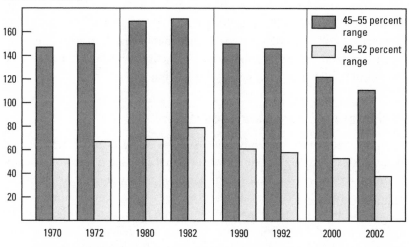

a. Number of congressional districts with a "normalized" two-party presidential vote within a competitive range before and after a redistricting.

Figure 10-1 locates the decline in the number of competitive districts in the last two rounds of redistricting. In 1970–72 and 1980–82, the number of competitive districts increased after redistricting. In 1990–92, there were four fewer districts in the 45–55 percent range and three fewer in the 48–52 percent range. In 2000–02, there were eleven fewer districts in the 45–55 percent range and fifteen fewer in the 48–52 percent range. There were also significant declines between 1992 and 2000, when there was a minimal amount of court-ordered redistricting: twenty-four districts in the 45–55 percent range and five in the 48–52 percent range. Thus, changes in the underlying distribution of partisans within districts between redistricting are also contributing to the decline in the number of competitive districts. To put it another way, between 1990 and 2002, 38 percent of the reduction in the number of competitive districts within the 45–55 percent range and 78 percent within the 48–52 percent range can be attributed directly to redistricting.[13]

13. The measure of district competition for the 1990–92 redistricting cycle is the 1988 presidential vote in the pre- and post-redistricted districts; for the 2000–2002 redistricting cycle it is the 2000 presidential election. The mid-decade change in competitiveness described

These findings comport with other recent studies. Swain, Borrelli, and Reed found a decrease of seventeen competitive districts within a 48–52 percent range during the 1990–92 redistricting.[14] Using a similar metric, Jacobson found a decrease of thirty-eight "at-risk" or "competitive" districts across the 2000–02 redistricting.[15] Since 1990 there has been a decrease in the number of competitive districts following redistricting, resulting in low levels of competition following the 2000–02 redistricting.

Redistricting Process and Motivations

An understanding of the motivations of those engaged in redistricting and the processes that they use illuminates why redistricting results in few competitive districts and the direction redistricting reform might take. Article 1, section 4 of the U.S. Constitution places the authority of conducting elections squarely with state governments, although the federal government has the right to pass legislation to regulate elections. The federal government and courts have set important criteria governing redistricting, but states have a wide array of their own criteria and processes. Within this context, three important interests play a role: incumbents, political parties, and racial groups.

Criteria and Processes

General criteria for drawing congressional and state legislative districts are found in federal and state law. Currently, by federal law, districts that elect members to the House of Representatives are single-member districts.[16] The U.S. Supreme Court ruled that districts must be of equal population size.[17] All districts must adhere to the federal Voting Rights Act, and the Court has articulated, with regard to racial redistricting, that districts cannot have bizarre shapes unless there is a compelling state interest in drawing such districts, such as rectifying a history of discrimination.[18] Generally districts must

---

here therefore more accurately captures the underlying change in the distribution of partisans (without redistricting) from 1988 to 2000 than from 1992 to 2000.

14. Swain, Borelli, and Reed (1998) used a more sophisticated statistical approach to measuring the number of competitive districts, which accounts for the difference between their results and the results presented here.

15. Jacobson (2003).

16. U.S. Code, Title 2, Chapter 1 § 2c.

17. *Wesberry v. Sanders*, 376 U.S. 1 (1964); and *Reynolds v. Sims*, 377 U.S. 533 (1964). The Court has generally allowed up to a 1 percent population deviation for congressional districts and 10 percent for state legislative districts.

18. *Miller v. Johnson*, 515 U.S. 900 (1995).

be contiguous, though there are recent examples of districts that are contiguous at only one point or that are of questionable contiguity because they stretch over water with no connecting bridge in the district.[19] These federal districting requirements overlay state requirements that govern the congressional and state legislative districting processes. States may require specific compactness formulas, such as those respecting political boundaries and communities; they may forbid the use of the knowledge of the location of a candidate's home; and they may even call for the drawing of competitive districts, as in Arizona and Washington.

Redistricting rules and processes vary from state to state, and even state legislative and congressional redistricting can vary within a state. Table 10-1 provides an overview of the processes used in the post-2000 census round of redistricting. While the regular legislative process is the most frequent choice, the states have experimented with an array of redistricting institutions. Second in usage to the legislative process are commissions, which take many forms. In some states, commissions take over the redistricting process only if the legislative process fails, while in other states commissions are the sole authority. Commissions operate under different rules for the selection of members and for the adoption of plans (by a majority or supermajority vote, for example). Also important are the roles of the courts, which can step into redistricting to balance the population of the districts if the commission cannot agree on a plan, or to resolve constitutional issues such as violations of the Voting Rights Act or state requirements. Some states are also covered under special provisions of section 5 of the Voting Rights Act, which requires districts to be cleared with the Department of Justice or the District Court of the District of Columbia before taking effect.

Incumbent Protection Gerrymanders

David Mayhew argued that incumbents structure their behavior in order to secure their reelection,[20] a goal that can be furthered by having safe districts to run in. Incumbents seek to maintain their reelection constituency by jettisoning voters least likely and incorporating those most likely to support their candidacy.[21] Incumbents of different parties in adjacent districts who find themselves with shared interests may be willing to trade supporters of their respective parties to increase their collective margin of victory. The ideal

19. Altman (1998).
20. Mayhew (1974).
21. For example, Robert Boatright (2004) details the lobbying efforts of members of North Carolina's congressional delegation during the state's turbulent 1990s litigation.

Table 10-1. Redistricting Processes Used in the United States, 2001–03

Type of process	States
Legislative process	
Congressional (38 states)	Alabama, Alaska, Arkansas, California, Colorado, Delaware, Florida, Georgia, Illinois, Kansas, Kentucky, Louisiana, Massachusetts, Michigan, Minnesota, Mississippi, Missouri, Nebraska, Nevada, New Hampshire, New Mexico, New York, North Dakota, Ohio, Oklahoma, Oregon, Pennsylvania, Rhode Island, South Carolina, South Dakota, Tennessee, Texas, Utah, Vermont, Virginia, West Virginia, Wisconsin, Wyoming
State legislative (26)	Alabama, California, Delaware, Georgia, Indiana, Kentucky, Louisiana, Massachusetts, Michigan, Minnesota, Nebraska, Nevada, New Hampshire, New Mexico, New York, North Dakota, Rhode Island, South Carolina, South Dakota, Tennessee, Utah, Vermont, Virginia, West Virginia, Wisconsin, Wyoming
Legislative process/commission	
Congressional (2)	Connecticut,[a] Indiana
State legislative (7)	Connecticut,[a] Illinois, Mississippi,[b] Ohio, Oklahoma, Oregon,[c] Texas
Commission	
Congressional (7)	Arizona, Hawaii, Idaho, Maine,[d] Montana, New Jersey, Washington
State legislative (12)	Alaska, Arizona, Arkansas, Colorado, Hawaii, Idaho, Maine,[d] Missouri,[e] Montana, New Jersey, Pennsylvania, Washington
Other	
Congressional (3)	Iowa,[f] Maryland,[g] North Carolina[b]
State legislative (5)	Florida,[h] Iowa,[f] Kansas,[h] Maryland,[g] North Carolina[b]
No congressional redistricting (7)[i]	Alaska, Delaware, Montana, North Dakota, South Dakota, Vermont, Wyoming

Source: Compiled by the author; this table first appeared in McDonald (2004).

a. In Connecticut, the legislature must adopt a districting plan with a two-thirds vote. If this vote cannot be achieved, a commission convenes to propose districts to the legislature that can be adopted with only a majority vote. If the commission fails to produce a plan that wins a majority vote, the state Supreme Court draws the districts.

b. In Mississippi and North Carolina, the governor does not have a veto over the redistricting plan.

c. In Oregon, the commission consists solely of the secretary of state. The state Supreme Court must approve any redistricting plan.

d. In Maine, a commission proposes a districting plan to the legislature, where it must be approved by a two-thirds vote, followed by the governor's approval. If this fails, the state Supreme Court draws the districts.

e. Missouri uses two separate commissions for its Senate and House state legislative redistricting. The House commission has twenty members and the Senate ten, with equal numbers selected by each party. Maps are adopted by a seven-tenths vote of the commission. If it fails to adopt a plan, the state Supreme Court forms a commission to draw a plan of its own.

f. In Iowa, nonpartisan staff in the Legislative Service Bureau propose districting plans to the legislature. The legislature is offered three plans in succession, any of which may be adopted by majority vote of the legislature, thus ending the process. If all three plans fail to receive majority support, the regular legislative process is used.

g. In Maryland, the governor proposes a districting plan to the legislature, which can approve it on a majority vote. The legislature may adopt a different plan on a two-thirds vote. If the legislature fails to act, the governor's plan becomes law.

h. In Florida and Kansas, the legislature adopts a plan that it then proposes to the state Supreme Court. The court may reject the legislature's map and draw its own plan.

i. For the seven states with no congressional redistricting, the process that would be used if the state had more than one district is listed in the table.

bipartisan incumbent protection gerrymander protects the reelection of incumbents of both political parties by creating safe, uncompetitive districts for them to run in, what Issacharoff calls a "bilateral cartelization of political markets."[22]

Bipartisan incumbent protection deals arise when the two political parties are forced to negotiate with each other. For states that use the legislative process this happens when there is divided control of the state legislature or there is a governor of a different party from the legislature. In some states, legislatures must adopt a map recommended by an outside entity by a supermajority vote. The type of plan likely to be adopted by a commission is dependent on the voting rules for commission action and the commission membership. Bipartisan compromises can be forged where there are supermajority rules for commission action or when tie-breaking members are appointed by a supermajority vote. If legislatures and commissions cannot reach a compromise, gridlock may force redistricting to the courts.[23] It is also possible for forces outside the normal redistricting process to structure a compromise, as Democratic legislative leaders did in California by negotiating with Republicans who threatened to place a redistricting reform initiative on the ballot if the Democrats did not compromise.[24]

Whether or not the districts are congressional or state legislative also structures the compromise forged in states that use the legislative process. Members of Congress do not play a formal role in redistricting but often propose districts to redistricting authorities, which are adopted out of respect for the widely followed norm that legislative bodies have the right to redistrict themselves. This power of incumbency is observed in adopted bipartisan compromises negotiated among the members of a state's congressional delegation, as happened in Illinois in 2001.[25] Bipartisan compromises favoring incumbents in state legislatures take another form and typically happen when there is divided control of the state government. In these circumstances, the opposing chambers draw partisan gerrymanders for their chamber's districts with the approval of the other chamber in the form of a bipartisan logroll. Minority-party members have some protection in these situations as they can appeal to their cross-chamber majority-party colleagues.

---

22. Issacharoff (2002).
23. Cox and Katz (2002).
24. McDonald (2004).
25. McDonald (2004, p. 380).

Partisan Gerrymanders

Partisan gerrymanders occur where one party controls the redistricting process. For states that use the legislative process, "control" means control of the legislature and the governor's office. In the nine states where commissions have the sole authority to oversee the congressional or state legislative redistricting, a majority of commissioners are selected by one party and a majority voting rule is used for commission action.[26]

Where the legislative process is used and there is a divided government, the parties may balk at compromise in the hope that a court will adopt a partisan map. A perusal of *Congressional Quarterly Weekly*'s redistricting synopses reveals that since 1970 only ten of the thirty-five court-approved congressional maps were drawn without favoring a party or incumbents. More often courts adopted or modified maps proposed by party leaders during the redistricting process. Still, perhaps with the advent of new technology, courts have approved neutral maps with increasing frequency (five of ten opportunities in 2001).

Whether partisan gerrymanders produce competitive districts is a matter of academic dispute. Map drawers of the party with redistricting control seek to maximize the expected number of districts that they can win by inefficiently distributing the voters of the other party. Owen and Grofman formally show how the optimal partisan gerrymander, in terms of maximization of expected seats, produces no competitive districts.[27] Burnham, in contrast, argues that "partisan gerrymandering is the best producer of competitive districts" because parties may act suboptimally in their quest to maximize seats, inadvertently shave their margins too close, and thereby create competitive districts.[28] Burnham offers the unsuccessful Republican gerrymander of New York's congressional seats in 1961 as an example, and others have occurred since. Other scholars have argued that, compared to incumbent protection gerrymanders, partisan gerrymanders result in a greater level of competition within districts.[29]

26. McDonald (2004, p. 382).
27. Owen and Grofman (1988).
28. See Burnham (1971). However, Burnham (1971, p. 276) notes that "comparable efforts have been resoundingly successful" and provides analysis of successful partisan gerrymanders in eight states.
29. See Gopoian and West (1984); Glazer, Grofman, and Robbins (1987); and Gelman and King (1994).

Figure 10-2. Three Configurations of Four Equi-Populous Districts in a Hypothetical Evenly Partisan Jurisdiction

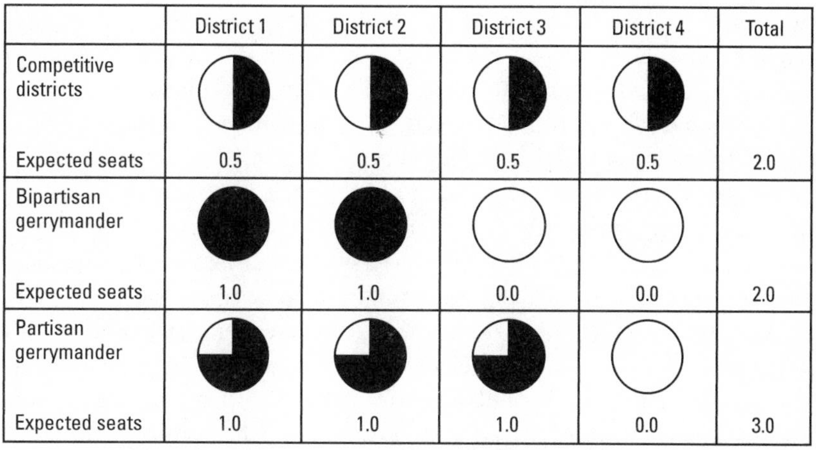

	District 1	District 2	District 3	District 4	Total
Competitive districts					
Expected seats	0.5	0.5	0.5	0.5	2.0
Bipartisan gerrymander					
Expected seats	1.0	1.0	0.0	0.0	2.0
Partisan gerrymander					
Expected seats	1.0	1.0	1.0	0.0	3.0

Surprisingly, both arguments are correct. Districts drawn for members of the gerrymandering party in a partisan gerrymander are relatively more competitive than the ideal incumbent protection gerrymander, but they do not fall within a competitive range. To understand the dynamics involved, consider a hypothetical state in which partisanship is evenly divided. Figure 10-2 shows three ways of distributing partisans into four equal-population districts. A perfectly competitive districting plan, presented in the top row of figure 10-2, would draw every district as a mirror of the state, resulting in four evenly divided districts, each with a 50 percent chance of electing a party member. With each district a toss-up, a party would expect to win "half" a seat on average within each district, for a total of two expected seats across all four districts. If the two parties colluded, they could create two very safe seats for their respective parties, as shown in the middle row, also producing (with a higher certainty) two seats for each party. A party seeking to maximize winning seats can do better. The bottom row of figure 10-2 shows an allocation of partisans that wins three districts for one party. The strategy here is to waste the other party's votes by inefficiently distributing them by "stacking" the other party's supporters into one extremely safe district and "cracking" their remaining supporters across the three remaining districts in which they have little chance of winning.

The first row of figure 10-2 is only meant to illustrate that partisan gerry-manders do not necessarily lead to competitive districts. As I describe in the concluding discussion, there are normative reasons why a competitive-maximization districting plan as represented in the first row of figure 10-2 might be undesirable. In the real world, too, many other factors come into play that constrain manipulating lines to effect a political purpose: for exam-ple, partisan loyalties among the electorate may be unknown; there are usu-ally more than four districts at play; and geography may constrain district boundaries. The same general results presented in figure 10-2 hold as long as there are some reasonable beliefs about how the underlying partisan support within a district translates into how competitive a district is. If the level of competitiveness does not change much in the range of 50–52 percent support for a party, decreases dramatically in the 52–55 percent range, and then does not change much in a range 55 percent and above (much like the bell-shaped normal curve), then parties will want to create districts at what Bruce Cain calls an "efficient level of partisan strength" somewhere around 55 percent.[30] The exact percentage can be determined by statistical analysis of election re-sults. Indeed, I have observed firsthand party leaders setting target levels of partisan support for districts, none of which were competitive, and I set tar-get partisan strength to draw competitive districts as a consultant to the Ari-zona Independent Redistricting Commission.

From this example, we can see why it is simultaneously true that incum-bents of a gerrymandering party are less secure in their reelection under a partisan map than under an incumbent protection map *and* why optimal incumbent protection and partisan gerrymanders produce no competitive districts. Incumbents of the gerrymandering party may find their margin in extremely safe districts shaved down to increase the number of seats the party will win. However, as Glazer, Grofman, and Robbins argue, such a decline in security is "more apparent than real" since the margin of the districts will not be drawn down to a point to make them competitive.[31]

Racial Gerrymanders

The Voting Rights Act (VRA) and minority representation case law place important constraints on redistricting, with effects on district competitive-ness. In certain circumstances the VRA mandates drawing special "minority-majority" districts, so-called because they contain within their borders a majority of minority persons. Minorities often participate at low rates owing

30. Cain (1984).
31. Glazer, Grofman, and Robbins (1987, p. 683).

to their lower socioeconomic status and (for Hispanics) rates of citizenship. Minority-majority districts must often contain a supermajority of minorities to provide a chance for minorities to elect a candidate of their choice.[32] A spirited scholarly debate has been joined as to the exact percentage of minorities to place within minority-majority districts to further their descriptive and substantive representation.[33] Regardless, minority-majority districts tend to be the most Democratic and least competitive. The ninety-two districts with a majority-minority total population of either Hispanics or another race gave an average of 67.2 percent of their votes to Al Gore in 2000, as a percentage of the Gore and Bush vote.[34]

Summary

Despite the motivations to reduce the number of competitive districts during redistricting, electoral competition usually increases in redistricting's wake. Incumbents can be displaced from their core reelection constituency and thus need to establish their name recognition and other intangibles that make up the incumbency advantage.[35] Strategic strong candidates emerge to challenge the temporarily vulnerable incumbents.[36] A pattern evident in *Congressional Quarterly Weekly*'s handicapping of congressional elections is for electoral competition to gradually decline throughout the redistricting decade as incumbents in unfriendly districts are defeated and others establish ties and name recognition with their new constituencies.[37]

Something odd happened in the period 2000–2002: the number of competitive elections declined when we might otherwise have expected an increase. Some have blamed computerized redistricting for providing the tools necessary for parties and incumbents to fine-tune their maps for a political purpose. For example, Supreme Court Justice Stephen Breyer stated, "The availability of enhanced computer technology allows the parties to redraw boundaries in ways that target individual neighborhoods and homes, carving out safe but slim victory margins in the maximum number of districts, with little risk of cutting their margins too thin."[38] My coauthors and I investigated this claim; we found that "improved tools can provide a greater set of possible

---

32. Brace, Grofman, Handley, and Niemi (1988).

33. See Cameron, Epstein, and O'Halloran (1996) and Lublin's (1999) critique.

34. Note that this measure includes the Cuban-American congressional districts in Florida and Republican-leaning districts with sizable noncitizen populations in states like Texas.

35. See Ansolabehere, Snyder, and Stewart (2000) and Desposato and Petrocik (2003).

36. See Cox and Katz (2002) and Hetherington, Larson, and Globetti (2003).

37. See Grofman and Jacobson (2003).

38. *Vieth v. Jubelirer*, 541 U.S. 267 (2004).

redistricting plans, but that does not mean that those in charge of redistricting will necessarily choose the plans that suffer perceived defects."[39] Sophisticated computerized redistricting databases are valuable but not essential to achieve redistricting goals, since political operatives with intimate knowledge of their state often have such a database locked away in their brains.[40] Before condemning computers, one might consider their beneficial effects, such as the relatively cheap technologies that have opened redistricting to a greater number of participants, including courts, which can fashion their own maps rather than choose among competing maps proposed by the political parties during litigation.

A more mundane explanation for the current situation is that redistricting goals aligned in 2001 to reduce district and electoral competition. Jacobson finds "three quarters of the marginal districts were made safer by redistricting" and that the redistricting musical chairs sat a net of nineteen incumbents with districts leaning toward the other party in new seats leaning toward their party.[41] More incumbents were protected in this redistricting because a greater number of districts were drawn under bipartisan incumbent protection compromises, from 147 in 1990–92 to 233 in 2000–2002. Counterintuitively, the increase in the number of districts exposed to incumbent protection gerrymanders was not a consequence of more bipartisan compromises, as nineteen redistricting plans in 1992 and twenty in 2002 had been. Rather, the increase of districts exposed to bipartisan plans was the result of the adoption of such maps by larger states, most notably California and Texas (Ohio and New York also had bipartisan plans in both redistricting cycles).[42]

Reform Efforts

The Supreme Court has been reluctant to formulate a partisan gerrymandering standard with any teeth, so redistricting reform, if it is to come, must come through state politics.[43] Unfortunately, redistricting reform is perceived by

---

39. Altman, Mac Donald, and McDonald (2005).

40. Bruce Cain (1984) relates the encyclopedic knowledge of Phil Burton, the former U.S. representative from California. Political gurus reside in other states. For example, in a personal communication (February 15, 2006) with an Arkansas Apportionment Board lawyer, I was told that the board did not need to match census and election data because Arkansas is a small state and those drawing the lines know which precinct everyone lives in.

41. Jacobson (2003, p. 10).

42. McDonald (2004) and Cain, Mac Donald, and McDonald (2005).

43. In *Davis* v. *Bandemer*, 478 U.S. 109 (1986) the Supreme Court found that partisan gerrymandering was justiciable. However, the Court set a high standard, that a party must be

some to be a partisan issue. In 2000, Republicans gained control of redistricting processes in key states leading into redistricting.[44] The post-2000 redistricting gave Republicans a strong structural advantage in House of Representatives elections, resulting in a majority that Democrats will find difficult to overcome "without the help of a sizable national tide in their favor."[45] But while redistricting reform may benefit Democrats nationally, it could benefit Republicans within some states. Republican governor Arnold Schwarzenegger's backing of a 2005 reform ballot initiative in California, and Ohio Republican legislative leaders' 2006 reform efforts, indicate that state politics can provide conditions where Republicans favor redistricting reform.[46]

In 2005, redistricting reform ballot initiatives failed miserably, being rejected by voters by nearly 20 percentage points in California and nearly 40 percentage points in Ohio. From this one might incorrectly conclude that the public is opposed to redistricting reform. Despite the defeats, post-election polling by Lake Research Partners found broad support for the principles of redistricting reform within California and Ohio, with over 70 percent agreeing that it is a conflict of interest for state legislators to draw their own districts. Redistricting reform was recently successful in other states: Alaska, Arizona, and Idaho adopted redistricting reform ballot initiatives leading into the 2000–2002 round of redistricting. To reiterate that redistricting reform is not simply a Democratic issue, note that all three states gave a vote majority to George W. Bush in 2000 and 2004.

So why did redistricting reform fail in 2005? Post-election polling points to three factors: an unpopular mid-decade redistricting component that was perceived, in the wake of the re-redistricting in Texas, to be an unfair power play; the combination of an energized opposition and a fragmented coalition in support (in California, conservative Republicans opposed reform; in Ohio, minorities opposed it); and a complicated reform proposal that was packaged with other ballot initiatives. The failures provide some lessons for future efforts. First, build a coalition early to generate broad support, ideally bipartisan support. Second, support will more likely come if a reform effort is not

---

effectively shut out of all politics by the partisan gerrymandering. In the case at hand, the Court did not overturn Indiana's state legislative districts. To my knowledge, only the adoption of at-large judicial districts in North Carolina has been overturned under the *Bandemer* standard; see *Republican Party of North Carolina* v. *Martin*, 980 F.2d 943 (4th Cir. 1992).

44. Hirsch (2003).

45. Jacobson (2003, p. 21).

46. "Ohio Redistricting Issue Nears Compromise: Legislators Aiming to Have Amendment on Nov. Ballot," *Toledo Blade*, March 3, 2006.

perceived to be overtly partisan; and as a corollary, partisan leaders are more likely to support reform if they are uncertain who will control future redistricting. Finally, keep it simple, because complicated initiatives are notoriously prone to rejection by voters.

Despite the defeats in California and Ohio, redistricting reform has been successful elsewhere. Twenty states have chosen a commission system for some stage of either state legislative or congressional redistricting. Redistricting reform by commission is not a modern idea. The first redistricting commission in the United States was established in Ohio by an 1850 constitutional convention convened to address, among other issues, a debate over state legislative apportionment in the rapidly growing state. The new constitution resolved the issue by removing control of state legislative redistricting from the state legislature and placing it in the hands of three statewide elected officials and four officials appointed by legislative leaders, a system that remains in effect today.[47]

The issue of apportionment continued to motivate the creation of redistricting commissions, though the rise in the number of states adopting commissions would occur roughly a century later and largely coincide with the equal population mandate for legislative districts handed down by the courts in the 1960s. Entering the 1960s, because many states had not redistricted for decades, there were districts with severely unequal populations between rapidly growing urban areas and rural areas. Following the new court standard, states suddenly found themselves needing to draw equal population districts to abide by the equal population mandate. Some were able to do so, but others did so only as a result of court action.

Since redistricting authority is often found in state constitutions, many states held constitutional conventions during the 1960s and early 1970s specifically to rectify the failure of state legislatures to redistrict, sometimes adopting redistricting commissions as a solution. The details of their operation vary, but they generally follow two models, those of Ohio and Texas. The Ohio model centralizes redistricting in the hands of a commission that avoids the possibility of gridlock between legislative chambers or among legislative members. The Texas model, adopted in 1948, allows the state legislature to act first and then hands redistricting to a commission if the legislature gridlocks. It was not necessarily the intent of these constitutional conventions to remove politics from the redistricting process, but rather to make sure that redistricting would occur. Commission members selected under both models tend

47. Barber (1981).

to be highly partisan; they are either elected partisan officials or handpicked by party leadership. Maps are adopted either by a simple majority vote, typically leading to a partisan gerrymander, or by a supermajority vote, typically leading to a bipartisan gerrymander.[48]

In recent years, redistricting commissions have been established via a different mechanism, the initiative process. Initiatives establishing redistricting commissions have been adopted beginning with Washington in 1983, and followed by Idaho in 1994, Alaska by referendum in 1998,[49] and Arizona in 2000. Good-government organizations such as the League of Women Voters and Common Cause have often supported these reforms. The newer redistricting commissions tend to place more constraints on what constitutes a permissible district in order to ostensibly remove politics from the redistricting process. A handful of states have experimented with redistricting standards that attempt to explicitly divorce politics from the process. Hawaii's constitutional convention in 1968 put three amendments related to redistricting before Hawaii's voters, including a standard now enshrined in article 4, section 6 of the Hawaii constitution, that "No district shall be so drawn as to unduly favor a person or faction." Idaho, Iowa, and Washington subsequently adopted similar language in state statutes.[50] Washington goes further to encourage electoral competition: "The commission shall exercise its powers to provide fair and effective representation and to encourage electoral competition," and a similar standard can be found in the Arizona constitution.[51] To prevent partisan considerations from entering into redistricting decisions, Arizona and Iowa forbid by constitution or statute the use of election results and voter registration records when maps are drawn. Arizona and Iowa also prevent incumbent interests from entering into redistricting decisions by drawing districts that are blind to the location of individuals' homes.

Another approach to limiting political mischief during redistricting is through qualifications and restrictions on commissioners. The 1960 Alaska constitution was the first to require of redistricting commission members that "none . . . may be public employees or officials."[52] However, these commissioners were direct appointees of the governor, so their political independence

48. McDonald (2004).

49. Alaska's 1998 initiative was backed by Republican leaders as a way to shift power away from the governor who, under a commission devised in the 1960 constitution, selected all commissioners.

50. See Idaho Code 72-1506; Iowa Code § 42.4; and Revised Code of Washington § 44.05.090.

51. Arizona Constitution, article 4, part 2, section 1.

52. Alaska Constitution, article 6, § 6.

was limited. Hawaii was the first to restrict the political ambitions of commission members by forbidding them from running for state legislative or congressional districts in the two elections following redistricting.[53] Idaho in 1994, and later Alaska in 1998, combined the two approaches.[54] Arizona adds to these qualifications a vetting process for prospective commission members by the state's Commission on Appellate Court Appointments.[55]

Despite these limited efforts, there are few truly neutral redistricting processes on which to base reform. Iowa's method of handing redistricting authority to nonpartisan legislative support staff is often heralded as the model for reform, but a close examination of the procedures suggests that its method would be difficult to export to another state and that it might not always produce a nonpartisan outcome. Legislative support staffers can be former partisan operatives; and even if staff in another state were nonpartisan, there is no guarantee that politically motivated personnel decisions would not corrupt the staff. Furthermore, the Iowa procedure has escape mechanisms that give the legislature some control over line drawing and enable it to entirely reclaim control if the staffers do not produce a map to the legislature's liking. But there is a limited amount of mischief political interests could play in Iowa with redistricting: the state's population is fairly politically balanced, without concentrated partisan strongholds. Thus, no matter how one slices Iowa, you get back Iowa.

Rather than handing over redistricting control and hoping for the best, reformers favor redistricting institutions formally structured to encourage a nonpartisan outcome. Arizona's commission is a model for a commission-style reform: a combination of weak partisan attachments of commissioners encouraged through a complex vetting and selection procedure, a specific set of criteria to apply to the designing of districts, sunshine through public hearings, and public map submissions. One criterion highlighted during the campaign for the Arizona ballot initiative is that the commission must draw competitive districts where practicable and where they do not conflict with the other criteria. My experience as a consultant to the Arizona Independent Redistricting Commission on issues of competition demonstrates that it is possible to devise a working definition of a competitive district that will foster competitive elections.[56] However, reformers designed a redistricting commission largely on intuition, and the outcome of the commission fell well short of their expectations.

53. Hawaii Constitution, article 4, § 2.
54. See Alaska Constitution, article 6, § 8, and Idaho Code 72-1502.
55. Arizona Constitution, article 4, part 2, section 1(3).
56. McDonald (2006a).

Although sold as a vehicle to increase competition, the congressional and state legislative maps produced by the Arizona commission had only a modest number of competitive districts. Some limitations are structural, beyond state reform. Arizona is a Republican-leaning state subject to Section 5 of the Voting Rights Act, requiring the drawing of a substantial number of uncompetitive, Democratic minority-majority districts. Once these districts were accounted for, there were few Democrats to spread around to build competitive districts.

Some limitations were found in the commission's criteria and the commission's interpretation of those criteria. Compactness and respect for political boundaries took precedence over competitiveness, which meant that shoestring districts could not be created to generate competitive districts. However, a greater number of competitive districts of a pleasing appearance could have been drawn, except for a criterion respecting communities of interest, which are almost by definition politically homogeneous communities sharing similar interests. Communities of interest defined by the commission, such as the foothill communities north of Tucson, reduced the possibilities for drawing competitive districts, in this case squeezing the Democratic areas around the University of Arizona between the foothills to the north and minority-majority districts to the south and west. Furthermore, the commission interpreted respecting communities of interest to mean not placing dissimilar communities together, in this case the University of Arizona with a Republican-leaning retirement community on the east side of town. Where three compact and competitive state legislative districts were possible, none were viable given the commission's interpretation of protecting communities of interest.

As Nobel laureate Herbert Simon noted, it is difficult, if not impossible, for administrators to simultaneously maximize multiple criteria.[57] Still, reformers learned from the Arizona experience that the rules a commission operates under can affect the desired outcomes. Reformers in Ohio, desiring greater competition for their congressional and state legislative districts, elevated competitiveness in the rank ordering of their proposed commission's criteria. Taking redistricting out of the hands of political interests, absent a laundry list of criteria, might also be sufficient to produce more competitive districts, too. Separate analysis of California's 2005 redistricting reform ballot initiative, Proposition 77, by UC Berkeley's Institute of Governmental Studies and Claremont McKenna College's Rose Institute found that the proposed redistricting

57. Simon (1948).

institution would result in a greater number of competitive districts.[58] Given the paucity of neutral redistricting processes and the structural factors peculiar to those states, simulating redistricting under proposed criteria may be the best method of predicting the effects of a proposed reform.

Conclusion

Critics of drawing competitive districts claim that maximizing the number of competitive districts will result in spaghetti-like districts splattered over a state. It is true that maximizing any political goal tends to produce stringy districts: Illinois's current incumbent protection congressional map has districts that stretch hundreds of miles across the state, and North Carolina's much litigated 1990s minority-majority district followed the median of a freeway. At one stage of litigation in Arizona, I created a competitiveness-maximization plan with many odd shapes, but I also drew compact competitive districts. Similar analysis in California and Ohio demonstrated that a greater number of reasonably compact and competitive districts could be drawn in those states. Maximizing the number of competitive districts might very well have the claimed effect; but creating a modestly larger number of competitive districts while balancing against other goals such as compactness likely would not.

There are normative reasons why maximizing the number of competitive districts may produce negative outcomes. In the abstract, if every district were competitive, the number of seats a party won would be highly sensitive to national or state swing toward either party. In the extreme, a small swing in the vote from 49 to 51 percent would result in one party winning all or an inordinately large number of the seats, shutting out minority voices in the deliberative policymaking process. A mix of competitive and uncompetitive districts is desirable to facilitate representation of a minority, be it racial or political, and to promote accountability among some legislators and the party in the majority.

The racial minority community is wary of reforms aimed to increase the number of competitive districts. Minority-majority districts are drawn because there remains a significant amount of racially polarized voting, where whites and minorities will not cross over to vote for candidates of another

---

58. See separate reports by Cain, Mac Donald, and Hui (2006) and by Johnson, Lampe, Levitt, and Lee (2005).

race. Creating competitive minority-majority districts might adversely affect minority representation if the minority-majority districts were made too competitive; because of racially polarized voting the districts would never elect a minority candidate. However, minority representation is not furthered by packing minorities into districts they win by overwhelming margins, and notable minority leaders such as Senator Barack Obama (D-Ill.) have indicated support for creating more competitive minority-majority districts that would "reduce the number of guaranteed African American districts, but might also force the kinds of dialogue and parties actively seeking support from not-so-easily-identified racial groups."[59]

The debate over racial redistricting and representation is relevant to re-forms designed to increase the number of competitive districts. The tension is between "descriptive" representation and "substantive" representation. Descriptive representation is having someone like you represent you, and people generally prefer having a representative who is similar to them.[60] Substantive representation is having a legislature that is more likely to make policy closer to your preferred position. While the two are not mutually exclusive, uncompetitive districts maximize descriptive representation to the detriment of substantive representation for the party in the minority and for voters in the middle who do not have strong partisan attachments.

There is also a greater issue of accountability. A legislature composed solely of uncompetitive districts is not accountable to the people. Because there are so few competitive districts and competitive elections, even in the best of circumstances in 2006, it is uncertain, perhaps unlikely, that Democrats can win fifteen seats to give them a majority following the 2006 midterm election. The same can be said for Republicans in states like California and Massachusetts, where Democrats dominate, and nationally Republicans could find themselves disadvantaged after the 2011 redistricting if they do not control as many redistricting processes as they did in 2001. Without the fear of defeat, majority legislative parties are not responsive to the needs of the nation or their state; they are at best responsive to their base. Restoring accountability of incumbent members through competition within their districts will encourage accountability of national and state parties, and thus uphold the principles of voter choice that are necessary for a functioning democracy to work.

59. Comments of Senator Barack Obama at the AEI-Brookings Election Reform Launch Project, February 8, 2006.
60. Brunell (2006).

References

Abramowitz, Alan, Brad Alexander, and Matthew Gunning. 2006a. "Don't Blame Redistricting for Uncompetitive Elections." *PS: Political Science and Politics* 39 (1): 87–90.
———. 2006b. "Drawing the Line on District Competition: A Rejoinder." *PS: Political Science and Politics* 39 (1): 95–98.

Altman, Micah. 1998. "Traditional Districting Principles: Judicial Myths vs. Reality." *Social Science History* 22 (2): 159–200.

Altman, Micah, Karin Mac Donald, and Michael P. McDonald. 2005. "Pushbutton Gerrymanders? How Computing Has Changed Redistricting." In *Party Lines: Competition, Partisanship, and Congressional Redistricting*, edited by Bruce Cain and Thomas Mann. Brookings.

Ansolabehere, Stephen, James M. Snyder Jr., and Charles Stewart III. 2000. "Old Voters, New Voters, and the Personal Vote: Using Redistricting to Measure the Incumbency Advantage." *American Journal of Political Science* 44 (1): 17–34.

———. 2001. "Candidate Positioning in House Elections." *American Journal of Political Science* 45 (1): 136–59.

Barber, Kathleen L. 1981. "Ohio." In *Reapportionment Politics: The History of Redistricting in the 50 States*, edited by Leroy Hardt, Alan Heslop, and Stuart Anderson. Beverly Hills, Calif.: Sage.

Boatright, Robert. 2004. "Static Ambition in a Changing World: Legislators' Preparations for and Responses to Redistricting." *State Politics and Policy Quarterly* 4 (4): 436–54.

Box-Steffensmeier, Janet M., and Jay K. Dow. 1992. "Campaign Contributions in an Unregulated Setting: An Analysis of the 1984 and 1986 California Assembly Elections." *Western Political Quarterly* 45 (3): 609–28.

Brace, Kimball, Bernard Grofman, Lisa Handley, and Richard Niemi. 1988. "Minority Voting Equality: The 65 Percent Rule in Theory and Practice." *Law and Policy* 10 (1): 43–62.

Brunell, Thomas. 2006. "How Drawing Uncompetitive Districts Eliminates Gerrymanders, Enhances Representation, and Improves Attitudes towards Congress." *PS: Political Science and Politics* 39 (1): 77–86.

Burnham, Walter Dean. 1971. "Congressional Representation: Theory and Practice of Drawing the Districts." In *Reapportionment in the 1970s*, edited by Nelson W. Polsby. University of California Press.

Cain, Bruce E. 1984. *The Reapportionment Puzzle*. University of California Press.

Cain, Bruce, Karin Mac Donald, and Michael P. McDonald. 2005. "From Equality to Fairness: The Path of Political Reform since Baker v. Carr." In *Party Lines: Competition, Partisanship, and Congressional Redistricting*, edited by Bruce Cain and Thomas Mann. Brookings.

Cain, Bruce, Karin Mac Donald, and Iris Hui. 2006. "Competition and Redistricting in California: Lesson for Reform." Berkeley, Calif.: Institute for Governmental Studies.

Cameron, Charles, David Epstein, and Sharyn O'Halloran. 1996. "Do Majority-Minority Districts Maximize Substantive Black Representation in Congress?" *American Political Science Review* 90 (4): 794–812.

Cox, Gary W., and Jonathan N. Katz. 2002. *Elbridge Gerry's Salamander: The Electoral Consequences of the Reapportionment Revolution*. Cambridge University Press.

Desposato, Scott W., and John R. Petrocik. 2003. "The Variable Incumbency Advantage: New Voters, Redistricting, and the Personal Vote." *American Journal of Political Science* 47 (1): 18–33.

Erikson, Robert S., and Gerald C. Wright. 2001. "Voters, Candidates, and Issues in Congressional Elections." In *Congress Reconsidered*, 7th ed., edited by Lawrence C. Dodd and Bruce I. Oppenheimer. Washington: CQ Press.

Gelman, Andrew, and Gary King. 1994. "A Unified Method of Evaluating Electoral Systems and Redistricting Plans." *American Journal of Political Science* 38 (2): 514–54.

Glazer, Amihai, Bernard Grofman, and Marc Robbins. 1987. "Partisan and Incumbency Effects of 1970 Redistricting." *American Journal of Political Science* 31 (3): 680–707.

Gopoian, J. David, and Darrell M. West. 1984. "Trading Security for Seats: Strategic Considerations in the Redistricting Process." *Journal of Politics* 46 (4): 1080–96.

Grenzke, Janet. 1988. "Candidate Attributes and PAC Contributions." *Western Political Quarterly* 42 (2): 245–64.

Grofman, Bernard, and Gary Jacobson. 2003. *Vieth v. Jubelirer*, Brief as *Amici Curiae* in Support of Neither Party, no. 02–1580.

Hetherington, Marc J., Bruce A. Larson, and Suzanne Globetti. 2003. "The Redistricting Cycle and Strategic Candidate Decisions in U.S. House Races." *Journal of Politics* 65 (4): 1221–35.

Hirsch, Sam. 2003. "The United States House of Unrepresentatives: What Went Wrong in the Latest Round of Congressional Redistricting." *Election Law Journal* 2 (2): 179–216.

Issacharoff, Samuel. 2002. "Gerrymandering and Political Cartels." *Harvard Law Review* 116 (2): 601–48.

Jacobson, Gary C. 2001. *The Politics of Congressional Elections*. 5th ed. Washington: CQ Press.

———. 2003. "Terror, Terrain, and Turnout: Explaining the 2002 Midterm Elections." *Political Science Quarterly* 118 (1): 1–22.

Johnson, Douglas, Elise Lampe, Justin Levitt, and Andrew Lee. 2005. "Restoring the Competitive Edge." The Rose Institute of State and Local Government, Claremont McKenna College.

Lublin, David. 1999. "Racial Redistricting and African-American Representation: A Critique of 'Do Majority-Minority Districts Maximize Substantive Black Representation in Congress?'" *American Political Science Review* 93 (1): 183–86.

Maisel, L. Sandy, and Walter J. Stone. 1997. "Determinants of Candidate Emergence in U.S. House Elections: An Exploratory Study." *Legislative Studies Quarterly* 22 (1): 79–96.

Mayhew, David R. 1974. *Congress: The Electoral Connection*. Yale University Press.

McDonald, Michael P. 2004. "A Comparative Analysis of U.S. State Redistricting Institutions." *State Politics and Policy Quarterly* 4 (4): 371–96.

———. 2006a. "Drawing the Line on District Competition." *PS: Political Science and Politics* 39 (1): 91–94.

———. 2006b. "Re-Drawing the Line on District Competition." *PS: Political Science and Politics* 39 (1): 99–102.

Niemi, Richard G., and John Deegan Jr. 1978. "A Theory of Political Districting." *American Political Science Review* 72 (4): 1304–23.

Owen, Guillermo, and Bernard N. Grofman. 1988. "Optimal Partisan Gerrymandering." *Political Geography Quarterly* 7 (1): 5–22.

Simon, Herbert A. 1948. *Administrative Behavior: A Study of Decision-Making Processes in Administrative Organization.* New York: Macmillan.

Swain, John W., Stephen A. Borrelli, and Brian C. Reed. 1998. "Partisan Consequences of the Post-1990 Redistricting for the U.S. House of Representatives." *Political Research Quarterly* 51 (4): 945–67.

11 Do Public Funding Programs Enhance Electoral Competition?

Kenneth R. Mayer, Timothy Werner, and Amanda Williams

Advocates of public funding offer four main arguments about the consequences of taxpayer-financed elections.[1] First, public funding can help potential candidates overcome the barriers that might deter them from running. In a vicious cycle, potential candidates who lack the ability to raise campaign funds are not taken seriously, and candidates who are not taken seriously cannot raise campaign funds. The cost of a campaign, even at the state legislative level, prevents potentially qualified candidates from even entering. A system of public grants can give candidates the seed money necessary to launch broader fundraising efforts, or even provide them all the resources they need to run credible campaigns. By reducing the campaign funding barrier, public funding systems might encourage candidates to emerge. Grants can be especially crucial for challengers, who face particularly daunting prospects in taking on an incumbent.

A corollary advantage to public financing is that it can encourage the emergence of candidates who lack substantial personal resources. Because

1. See for example, "Clean Money Campaign Reform," a brochure produced by Public Campaign (www.publiccampaign.org/publications/factsheets/CleanMoneyCampaign Reform.pdf); and Arizona Clean Elections Institute, *Clean Elections Works!* (www.azclean.org/documents/PositiveImpactofCleanElections.doc).

campaigning is so expensive, candidates (especially challengers) routinely put thousands of dollars of their own money—sometimes millions—into their campaigns. Candidates without deep pockets have more difficulty persuading potential contributors (and political parties) to take them seriously. Public funding lowers this barrier, and therefore might increase the ideological and demographic diversity of candidates, as well as the range of policy positions that are put before the electorate.

Second, public grants can make elections more competitive. By reducing the fundraising advantages that, in particular, incumbents have over challengers, public funding systems can "level the playing field" and reduce the number of landslide victories.

Third, public funding can reduce the influence of private contributions on both candidates and officeholders. By replacing individual, corporate, labor, or political action committee contributions with public funds not tied to any particular interest, public funding can, in theory, refocus attention away from parochial concerns to those of the broader public.

A fourth argument put forth by advocates is that public financing can control campaign costs. Since candidates who accept public grants must, as a general rule, agree to abide by spending limits, higher participation in public funding programs can prevent further escalation in the spiral of campaign spending.

Does public financing achieve any of these goals? The short answer is that nobody knows because there has been no comprehensive evaluation of public finance systems to identify what conditions and program elements lead to successful outcomes. The conventional wisdom is based on either a limited amount of data or anecdotal impression. Consequently, the elements of clean elections programs—funding amounts, eligibility rules, spending limits, and other regulations—are based more on guesswork than on solid evidence. The clean elections movement is in part motivated by axioms about the political process: that the need to raise funds deters many candidates from emerging; that candidates need protection against independent expenditures and issue ads; and that incumbents are as a rule unbeatable. While these are reasonable conclusions, they have not been subjected to rigorous analysis and testing. "The justifications normally offered for public funding," wrote Michael Malbin and Thomas Gais, "all rest on long strings of difficult assumptions."[2]

The question was also uninteresting, since only a handful of states had public funding programs. That changed, though, when Arizona and Maine

2. Malbin and Gais (1998, p. 70).

adopted full public funding (dubbed "clean elections" by proponents) beginning with the 2000 cycle. For the first time, public grants would pay the full cost of a state legislative campaign.[3] Hawaii changed its public funding law in 1995, raising grant size from what had been a trivial amount ($50 for State House candidates) to several thousand dollars, depending on the number of registered voters in each district. New York City changed its public funding program for city council candidates to a four-to-one matching formula, in which each $1 raised in qualifying contributions is matched by a public grant of $4 (in December 2004, the city council raised the maximum matching rate to six-to-one). We summarize provisions of the state legislative programs in table 11-1.

This combination of major change and continuity presents an unusually favorable opportunity to see if public funding has made any difference or achieved the goals that it was intended to achieve. We are particularly interested in how public funding affects legislative elections. With legislatures, because multiple elections occur at precisely the same time, we have a much larger set of races to analyze (than, for example, after a single gubernatorial or attorney general election). We also believe a plausible case can be made that public funding is more likely to affect legislative elections, since statewide races are more likely to attract well-known and experienced candidates who may be less influenced by the existence of a public funding program. For legislative candidates, especially first-time challengers, public funding is more likely to make a difference in their decision to run.

There has been some research on the consequences of these reforms, but these initial evaluations are incomplete. Some reports, especially those produced by advocacy groups that strongly support public funding, overstate the effect of the new law and ignore other factors, such as term limits or redistricting, that have without question shaped outcomes.[4] Others, including the General Accounting Office's evaluation of the Maine and Arizona programs, understate the reforms' impact.[5] We will navigate between these two edges and make an effort to specify the conditional nature of our conclusions, which can be summarized as follows:

—Public funding programs increase the pool of candidates willing and able to run for state legislative office. This effect is most pronounced for challengers, who were far more likely than incumbents to accept public funding.

---

3. To qualify for the grants, candidates had to raise a small amount of seed money and had to agree to spending limits.

4. Clean Elections Institute (2002); Breslow, Groat, and Saba (2002).

5. General Accounting Office (2003).

Table 11-1. Characteristics of Public Funding Programs in Five States

Characteristic	Arizona 2000	Maine 2000	Wisconsin 1978	Minnesota 1976	Hawaii 1996
			State and date effective		
Qualification	Raise $1,050 in qualifying contributions ($5 each)	Raise $250 (House) or $750 (Senate) in qualifying contributions ($5 each)	Win primary with at least 6 percent of total vote for office Raise threshold amount in $100 contributions ($1,725 for Assembly, $3,450 for Senate)	Raise $1,500 (House) or $3,000 (Senate) in qualifying contributions ($100 each)	Raise $1,500 (House) or $2,500 (Senate)
Maximum grant	Up to spending limit Bonus provisions against privately funded candidates and independent expenditures	Up to spending limit Bonus provisions against privately funded candidates and independent expenditures	$15,525 for Senate (2002) $7,763 for Assembly (2002) Grants for general election only	Up to 50 percent of spending limit Small contribution refund program reimburses individuals up to $50 for contribution to participating candidate	Amount of grant restricted to 15 percent of spending limit
Spending limit (2004)	$28,300 for primary/general in House and Senate elections	$4,406 for primary/general in House $23,278 for primary/general in Senate	$17,250 for Assembly $34,500 for Senate Limits unchanged since 1986	$34,100 for House (2004) $64,866 for Senate (2002) Separate spending limits for election and non-election years	$1.40 x number of registered voters in district 2004 ranges (approx.): House: $14,000–19,000 Senate: $23,000–45,000
Special conditions	Unopposed candidates not eligible for public funds beyond qualifying contributions	Nonparticipating candidates face additional reporting requirements	Spending limits apply only if all candidates accept public funds	Spending limits increase by 10 percent for first-time candidates and by 20 percent for candidates running in competitive primary Spending limits waived when nonparticipating opponent exceeds threshold expenditures	

Source: Compiled by authors.

—Public funding increases the likelihood that an incumbent will have a competitive race.

—Public funding has reduced the incumbency reelection rates in Arizona and Maine, although the effects are marginal. We can say with certainty, though, that public funding has *not* made incumbents safer. Fears that public funding would amount to an incumbency protection act are unfounded.

—Public funding programs have a threshold effect: if grant sizes and spending limits do not have a realistic connection to what candidates actually need, programs will have no effect.

In the end, we conclude that public funding programs—particularly the full "clean elections" systems in Arizona and Maine—increase the competitiveness of state legislative elections.

Why Worry about Competition at All?

Meaningful political competition is the foundation of democratic legitimacy. The ability to freely choose among realistic alternatives, especially at the ballot box, is a prerequisite to the exercise and protection of most other political rights. To create even a token degree of accountability, elections "must occur in circumstances that involve an appropriate degree of genuine competition."[6] At some point, a minimum level of competition is essential "for legislatures to be responsive to electoral change."[7]

This should not to be a controversial assertion. To be sure, competition is not the only important aspect of legitimacy, and it does not by itself guarantee justice, or fairness, or rational deliberation, or individual autonomy. It is possible, as well, to have too much competition, and at least two pathologies—instability and perverse antimajoritarian outcomes—can result from too many choices.[8] If incumbents are always running scared, they may be unwilling to do anything even remotely unpopular, transforming government into the direct democracy that the Framers feared.[9] Competition is a

6. Pildes (2004, p. 686).
7. Cain, Mac Donald, and McDonald (2005, p. 20).
8. An excess of competition can lead to outcomes that a large majority opposes, or to the success of extremist positions (Saari 2000, 2003; Gulati 2004). A hypercompetitive environment can also, in theory, make it harder for officeholders to establish relationships with constituents. Constant turnover can diminish the expertise of public officials.
9. Thompson (2002, p. 201, n. 16) identified an example of the tension between justice and competitiveness, noting that because of high levels of electoral competition in the post–Civil War Congress, members who feared retribution at the polls were unwilling to compromise on racial issues.

necessary, but not sufficient, condition. And finally, a lack of competition might stem from stable preferences, or from the wisdom of the initial choices that put competent people into office. If an incumbent runs unopposed because potential challengers know she is unbeatable, and she is unbeatable because a majority thinks she is doing an outstanding job, where is the harm?

Perhaps there is too much emphasis on competition in the first place. Many of the institutional structures of contemporary politics are designed to insulate decisionmakers from public opinion, and by inference, challenges to their leadership. Complicated procedural rules, lengthy Senate terms, multiple opportunities for position-taking, diffusion of responsibility, even the dominance of the two major parties, all serve to temper public wrath and make it possible for elected officials to serve—temporarily at least—at the displeasure of the electorate.[10] "Competitiveness" is not synonymous with "immediate reaction to every change in public opinion."

Most people, however, would agree that a surfeit of electoral competition is not a problem that afflicts contemporary politics. Incumbent legislators win reelection nearly 100 percent of the time, and many face no opposition at all. In 2004 the House incumbent reelection rate was 99 percent, and only a handful of districts were even remotely competitive. In the states, 93 percent of all state legislators who ran for reelection won,[11] and the major parties have *given up* on over a third of the legislative seats, contesting only 65 percent of races.[12] In California, every incumbent legislator—in the State Assembly, State Senate, U.S. House of Representatives, and U.S. Senate—won in 2004.

Stephen Ansolabehere and James Snyder find that the incumbency advantage has grown for every office in the past half-century.[13] Whether the cause is campaign finance disparities, polarization of the electorate, redistricting, pork, the franking privilege, or a reluctance of potential challengers to subject themselves to the sharp elbows of the campaign environment, incumbents have a virtual lock on their seats. About the only time that incumbents lose is when they are "paired" with other incumbents by hostile cartographers and must run against each other, or when they attract the attention of the district attorney.

---

10. For a positive view of the major party duopoly, see Cain (2000–01). Lizzeri and Persico (2002) offer a theoretical rationale for limiting the number of parties that appear on the ballot.

11. Authors' calculations, from data provided by the National Institute on Money in State Politics.

12. National Conference on State Legislatures (www.ncsl.org/programs/press/2004/unopposed_2004.htm).

13. Ansolabehere and Snyder (2002).

Even if we agree that the electoral system could use more competition, there is little consensus on the best methods of producing it. There is no way to know a priori how much competition there ought to be, no guarantee that any particular policy would succeed, and not even an agreement on how anyone would recognize the right balance among the competing normative values in play.[14] Tinkering with the electoral process to generate outcomes that are fair assumes that procedural changes will resolve the underlying political disputes that, having not been resolved, led to the belief that procedural changes were needed in the first place. In doing so, conflict is not resolved, but is simply moved from the political process itself (which is unable to produce "good" decisions), to making decisions about how the political process will operate (in order to make that process more likely to produce good decisions). That is a snake eating its own tail.

One way that public policies can affect political competition is by forcefully redistributing political power toward or away from particular groups. Policies that give advantages in ballot access to the two major political parties, or require district lines to be drawn by nonpartisan bodies, are two examples. In the first instance, third parties are intentionally hindered in their ability to get on the ballot; in the second, incumbents and the major parties are prevented from using the redistricting process to create safe seats or punish the opposition. Term limits are another option. Barring incumbents from running past their fourth term (or whatever limit is imposed) automatically creates open seats, which at least guarantee new faces, if not changes in party control.

But these top-down reforms, which fundamentally restructure political relationships, can be questioned in that they grant or deny political power on the basis of a prior decision about how that power should be allocated. Not only does this assume prior knowledge about what the proper distribution of power *should* be; it also presumes that reform efforts will lead to the expected results. Sometimes this works—nobody denies that Minnesota's antifusion law (which precludes a political candidate from being listed on a ballot under more than one party for one office) does precisely what it was intended to do, which is to make life more difficult for third parties—but the history of campaign finance reform demands caution in the face of the law of unanticipated consequences.[15]

14. Pildes (1999, p. 1612) argues that this does not matter; we do not need a complete theory of competition, nor do we have to know what the optimal level is, to know that some outcomes are "troublingly unfair."

15. Here, term limits are an instructive and cautionary example. A popular anti-incumbent reform, term limits were designed, in part, to force a return to the "citizen legislator" who

Public funding programs offer a way to resolve these difficulties, by increasing the opportunities to run for office and enhancing voter choice, rather than imposing constraints. There are, of course, many ways to measure the efficacy or responsiveness of a political system or election system: citizen engagement, turnout, partisan balance, levels of corruption, openness, to give a few possibilities. But competitiveness has been a focus of past research on state politics, beginning with V. O. Key's pathbreaking studies of southern states.[16] It is difficult to argue with the position that, other things being equal, more competition is preferable to less. Our view is that in a state with truly competitive elections, many other problems—whether corruption, insulation, or undue interest group influence—will take care of themselves.

Does It Work? The GAO Report and Beyond

Past work on public funding has come to a mixed result: some studies find evidence that grant programs increase election competitiveness, while others find no effect. As we noted earlier, the significant recent changes in Arizona and Maine make another round of investigation worthwhile. Until recently, any analysis of public funding was confined to a comparison of Wisconsin and Minnesota, since Hawaii's program offered only trivial grants to candidates until 1996.[17] As recently as 1998, Malcom E. Jewell and William E. Cassie concluded that since Wisconsin and Minnesota were the "only two states that provide for public financing of legislative elections . . . it [is] difficult to assess the impact of public financing as it could apply to other states."[18] In one of the few studies to even attempt to measure the impact, across states, of public funding on competitiveness, Malbin and Gais concluded that "there

---

resumed private life after a short stint as a public servant. But, as Kousser (2005) documents, a consequence has instead been a concentrated hypercareerism, as term-limited legislators immediately begin thinking about what they'll do next, and often run for another office, become lobbyists, or accept political appointments upon retirement. Moreover, the new incoming classes are more likely to have political experience under term limits than before, at least in California. Finally, Kousser demonstrates that term-limited legislatures are less innovative and show more deference to the executive branch. Whether these are positive or negative consequences is debatable, but what is clear is that term limits by themselves have not transformed politics as much as advocates hoped.

16. See Holbrook and Van Dunk (1993).

17. Mayer and Wood (1995); Mayer (1998); Donnay and Ramsden (1995).

18. Jewell and Cassie (1998, p. 225).

is no evidence to support the claim that programs combining public funding with spending limits have leveled the playing field, countered the effects of incumbency, and made elections more competitive."[19] However, this study, of necessity, was again limited to a focus on Wisconsin and Minnesota; other research has concluded that public funding can indeed make a difference.[20] More recent work has begun to challenge the efficacy of New York City's public funding program, noting that it has not done much to make municipal elections more competitive.[21] Through the 2000 election cycle, public funding did not have a good track record in creating competitive electoral environments, and a comprehensive study of state-level programs concluded that "full-blown public funding programs with spending limits do not seem to do much for competition.[22]

Section 310 of the Bipartisan Campaign Reform Act (BCRA)—more commonly known as McCain-Feingold—directed the General Accounting Office to study the Maine and Arizona public funding systems in the 2000 and 2002 election cycles. The GAO's cautious May 2003 report offered some support for the clean elections programs, but concluded that "it is too soon to determine the extent to which the goals of Maine's and Arizona's public financing programs are being met."[23] The report found that more candidates in both states were running and winning with public funding, and that funding differences between incumbents and challengers had narrowed. But it also found no evidence that elections had become more competitive, or that interest group influence had diminished.[24]

The GAO report received scant press attention, with no major mentions in the national media, perhaps in part because of its tentative nature (a Lexis-Nexis search did not result in a single mention in any national newspaper). The reform group Public Campaign, which supports public funding, criticized the report as "too cautious in [its] analysis" and argued that the GAO's own evidence could have supported stronger conclusions.[25] The publisher of the trade newsletter *Political Finance* argued that the authorizing language

---

19. Malbin and Gais (1998, p. 136).
20. Mayer (1998).
21. Kraus (2006).
22. Malbin and Gais (1998, p. 158).
23. GAO (2003, p. 5).
24. GAO (2003, pp. 3–6).
25. Public Campaign, *A Critical Reading*, May 20, 2003 (www.publiccampaign.org/pressroom/pressreleases/release2003/release05-21-03.htm).

resulted in a report that intentionally overstated the impact of the clean elections law, attributing to public funding outcomes that actually resulted from term limits.[26]

A review of the GAO's methods reveals that the office did significantly underestimate most measures of electoral competitiveness, in large part because the authors performed many of their calculations using unorthodox measures. Many of these choices were justified as necessary because of some unusual features of Arizona's political landscape, but there are perfectly adequate and commonly accepted alternative methods that take advantage of data that the GAO discarded.

The GAO's analysis, in fact, should be viewed with some caution. The analysis of "contestedness"—the likelihood that a candidate would have an opponent—looked only at primary elections. The GAO's justification for this was that candidates were much more likely to run unopposed in primary than in general elections. Primary competition, though, is not a good measure of political competitiveness. There are good reasons, having nothing to do with campaign finance, why primary elections are less likely to be contested than general elections. Particularly when an incumbent is running for reelection, state and local party organizations may actively discourage—and potential candidates may be reluctant to take on—primary challenges that might weaken the party's eventual candidate in the general election. No sensible political party, moreover, will encourage primary challenges if doing so risks losing the seat to the other major party. Potential challengers may decline to run simply because of deference or party discipline, or because running against an incumbent of one's own party is a poor career move. Of course, contested primaries are more likely for the out-party, for open seats, and when an incumbent is vulnerable. But in these cases, primary competitiveness is only a rough proxy for overall district competitiveness.

Further, the GAO's calculation of incumbent reelection rates looks only at general elections and does not include incumbents who lost in the primary. Including incumbent primary losses can have a dramatic effect on reelection rates; to give one example, the GAO report calculates an incumbent reelection rate of 90 percent for the Arizona House in 2002, based on thirty incumbents running in the general election and twenty-seven winning.[27] But forty incumbents ran that year, with nine losing in primary contests.[28] The overall

26. Zuckerman (2003).
27. GAO (2003, p. 38).
28. In our calculations we counted Representative Joe Hart (R., 3rd district) as an incumbent because he was a state senator prevented by term limits from running for office again.

reelection rate in 2002 was 70 percent (twenty-eight out of forty), not 90 percent. Even if we remove from this calculation incumbents who had to run against each other because of redistricting, the reelection rate was 75.6 percent (twenty-eight out of thirty-seven).

Finally, the GAO report did not take into account the impact of redistricting in its analysis of the 2002 elections. Redistricting can affect elections in several ways. Redrawn districts can often put incumbents in difficult political situations, especially if population shifts have been extensive or boundaries have been radically changed. Incumbents can also be paired after redistricting, if district boundaries change in a way that pits two or more incumbents against each other in a single new district (this also means that an open seat has been created somewhere else). In an election with paired incumbents, by definition at least one incumbent will lose, even though this will have nothing to do with campaign finance. A failure to correct for this will understate the true incumbent reelection rate.

Our intention in noting these criticisms is not to bash the GAO, which operated under the constraints of both a statutory mandate and the difficulties of addressing an overtly political question in the context of a broader policy analysis. Rather, our intent is to highlight some of the difficulties in sorting through an extraordinarily complex set of causal mechanisms (and we make no claim that we have had the final word on the question). We now turn to our own analysis of electoral competition, which offers a somewhat clearer picture of the impact of the Maine and Arizona reforms.

Data on Electoral Competition

To measure the extent to which public funding has affected electoral competition, we calculated the following indicators, from 1990–2004, for elections to the lower house in the state legislatures in Arizona, Hawaii, Maine, Minnesota, and Wisconsin:

—the percentage of incumbents who faced a major-party opponent (contestedness)

—the percentage of incumbents who were in a competitive race, defined as one in which the winner received less than 60 percent of the two-party vote (competitiveness)

Since House and Senate districts are identical in Arizona, we concluded that Hart's Senate incumbency gave him the same advantages that House incumbency would have.

—the percentage of incumbents who ran for and were reelected to office (reelection rate)

For the first and third indicators, we controlled for the presence of paired incumbents in the 2002 elections.[29] We did not count a race as contested if the two (or more) major-party candidates were paired through redistricting, and we removed losing paired incumbents from our calculations of incumbent reelection rates.

For comparison, we also calculated these figures for states that do not offer public funding.

Assessing the effect of the clean elections law in Arizona is more difficult since its implementation coincided with two other significant changes to state election law. In 1992, Arizona enacted term limits for state legislators, limiting them to four consecutive terms. The 2000 elections were the first in which members were "termed out," and fifteen legislators (nine representatives and six senators) were ineligible for reelection in 2002. Second, in 2000 voters opted to conduct the decennial reapportionment process using an Independent Redistricting Commission (IRC), rather than allow state legislators to draw district lines. Advocates of the independent commission approach hoped that the new method would produce districts less tied to incumbent interests (indeed, the law prohibited the commission from identifying or taking into account incumbents' residency when drawing the new districts). The near simultaneous effects of these three major reforms—public funding, term limits, and a new approach to redistricting—produced significant turnover in both chambers, and it is not immediately apparent how the effects should be allocated.

In addition, the 2004 election cycle was unusually tumultuous because of legal disputes surrounding the new legislative districts that the IRC created for the 2002 elections. In January 2004, a state court rejected the redistricting plan in a lawsuit challenging the constitutionality of the proposed districts. Holding that the commission did not comply with the constitutional language requiring it to create competitive districts, a State Superior Court judge ordered the IRC to draw up a new plan for the 2004 elections.[30] The commission complied, and in April 2004 submitted a map to the U.S. Department

---

29. Arizona, Hawaii, Minnesota, and Wisconsin had completed their redistricting processes in time for the 2002 elections, although Arizona is now making some changes to its new districts in response to a court order. Maine redistricts on a different schedule, with new districts put in place for the 1994 and 2004 elections.

30. *Arizona Minority Coalition for Fair Redistricting* v. *Independent Redistricting Commission*, Maricopa County Superior Court, CV 2002-004380, January 19, 2004.

of Justice for preclearance under section 5 of the Voting Rights Act.[31] But the filing deadline for state office passed before the DOJ had approved the new plan, so state officials were forced to use a version of the 2002 plan for the upcoming 2004 elections. The uncertainty over the district maps meant that some prospective candidates had no idea which district they lived in, and some of these may have chosen to stay out of the ring until 2006.

A final problem is that Arizona's House elects its members from multi-member districts, which do not translate into head-to-head campaigns. We address some of these methodological difficulties, and describe our application of an existing method of measuring competitiveness in multicandidate systems, in the appendix.

In figure 11-1, we report contestedness from 1990 to 2004. The key to this and subsequent figures is the change in the period 2000–04 in Maine and Arizona, when the full public funding system was in place. Several patterns emerge from this graph. Arizona experienced a significant jump in the number of contested races in 2002 and 2004, increasing from under 40 percent in 2000 to over 50 percent in 2002 and 2004. This increase was not only large; it also reversed the previous trend of uniformly fewer contested elections between 1994 and 2000. While we cannot attribute this shift entirely to public funding (which was also in place in 2000), it is likely to have played a key role. Of the twenty-five major-party challengers who took on an incumbent in the general election in 2002, twelve were publicly funded. Given that these races present poor electoral odds for the challenger—incumbents are difficult to beat except in unusual circumstances—it is a defensible inference that some of these candidates would have stayed away without the existence of public funding.

The patterns for Maine and Hawaii are murkier, though in the expected direction. Both saw the percentage of contested incumbents increase in 2002, and again in 2004. Maine's contested rate in 2004 (98 percent) was higher than it was at any point since 1990.

Wisconsin and Minnesota show a continuation of patterns that existed throughout the 1990s. Minnesota's public funding program, which combines direct grants with refunds of small individual contributions, is generally regarded as effective in both encouraging candidate participation and in fostering a competitive environment. Wisconsin, which provides grants that

---

31. As a covered jurisdiction under the act, Arizona may not make any changes to its voting procedures or practices without obtaining prior approval (or preclearance) from the Department of Justice.

Figure 11-1. Incumbents Facing Major-Party Challengers in General
State House/Assembly Elections, Excluding Incumbent Pairings, 1990–2004[a]

Percent incumbents in contested races

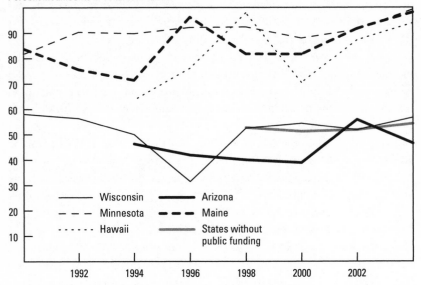

a. Incumbent pairings refer to incumbents running against each other.

have not changed since 1986, is at the other end of the spectrum, with low
candidate participation rates and a program generally considered close to
irrelevant. In Minnesota, uncontested House elections are rare, with contested rates almost always higher than 90 percent. In Wisconsin, uncontested
incumbents are almost the norm, with just over half of incumbents facing a
major-party opponent.

For comparison, we also show the contested rate for states that do not
have public funding programs, using data from the Institute on Money in
State Politics (IMSP).[32] In these states, incumbents face major-party challenges about 50 percent of the time; that figure changed little from 1998
through 2004.

32. We excluded Louisiana (which elects candidates in primary elections as long as the
winner receives more than 50 percent of the vote); states with multimember districts;
Nebraska (which holds nonpartisan elections to a unicameral legislature); and states that hold
off-year elections.

Figure 11-2. Incumbents in Competitive Races in General and State Assembly/House Elections, 1990–2004[a]

Percent incumbents in contested races

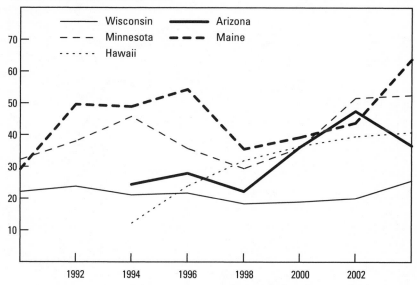

a. A competitive race is defined here as one in which the winner received less than 60 percent of the two-party vote.

In figure 11-2 we report on the competitiveness of elections when an incumbent is running. We defined a competitive race as one in which the incumbent received less than 60 percent of the two-party vote. This is not a universally accepted threshold—many political professionals would consider a 60–40 race something of a blowout—but we regard it as an acceptable minimum baseline of competitiveness, especially given the advantages that incumbents have in these low-visibility races.

Figure 11-2 shows that the percentage of competitive races went up in Hawaii, Maine, and Minnesota between 1998 and 2004. In Maine, 64 percent of incumbents were in competitive races in 2004, nearly double the 1998 rate (35 percent), and higher than the rate in Minnesota. The increase in Hawaii was much more modest, with only a slight improvement over the 2002 and 2000 rates.

The 2004 Arizona House elections proved something of a disappointment to campaign finance reformers: the percentage of incumbents in competitive races in 2004 was the same as it was in 2000 (about 36 percent), declining

Figure 11-3. Incumbent Reelection Rates in the State Assembly/House, Excluding Incumbent Pairings

Percent incumbents who run and win

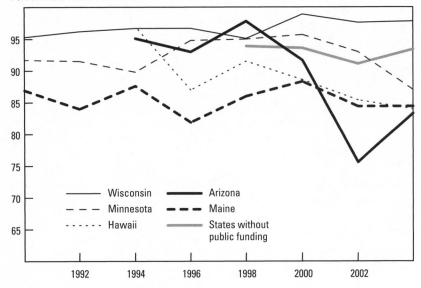

Source: Wisconsin Campaign Finance Project.

from a post-1990 record of 47 percent in 2002. At the same time, in Arizona this measure of competition remained higher than it had been during the pre-public-funding era (1998 and earlier).

In 2004, Minnesota continued its pattern of close races, with over half of its House incumbents facing competitive challengers. Wisconsin trails the pack, with only one incumbent in four having faced a competitive race in 2004.

Figure 11-3 shows the incumbent reelection rate—that is, the percentage of incumbents who run and are reelected to another term. This represents what many would consider to be the payoff measure. Opponents of public funding often argue that it is nothing but an incumbent protection act: since incumbents have formidable advantages in name recognition, experience, and ability to mobilize supporters, the spending limits that always accompany public grants could, in this view, simply institutionalize the inability of challengers to overcome the incumbency advantage. But this has not happened. In Arizona, the incumbent reelection rate dropped from a Congress-like 98 percent in 1998 to 75 percent in 2002 (even after controlling for incumbency pairings), and remained low in 2004, at 83 percent. In comparison with 1998, incumbent reelection rates in 2004 were also lower in Maine, Hawaii, and Minnesota. The changes in these states, though, appear to be within normal limits and are not radically different from levels that existed throughout the 1990s.

Wisconsin, making a three-for-three sweep, again holds the record for the least competitive elections. Ninety-eight percent of unpaired incumbents won reelection in 2004 (eighty-eight out of ninety won).

We also include a measure of incumbency reelection for the states that do not have public funding, again using IMSP data. These data are not fully comparable to the lines for publicly funded states, both because they do not control for pairings and because they consider as incumbents lower House members running for Senate seats. This is one reason why the incumbency reelection rate dipped in 2002, after redistricting had occurred in most states. However, we calculated reelection rates using several different methods, and all were within a percentage point of the others. In the states without public funding, the incumbency reelection rate has remained stable, at about 93 percent.

What accounts for these results? Obviously, they cannot be attributed entirely to changes in campaign finance law, but all of the trends are in the expected direction. The dramatic changes in Arizona cannot be attributed to term limits, since we are focusing on incumbents who are running for reelection; nor can the Maine results be the result of redistricting, since the state did not begin the process until 2003. And the stark lack of electoral competition in Wisconsin clearly sets it apart from the other states in this group—even from Hawaii, which has been dominated by the Democratic Party for decades.

One difference among these states is the varying amounts of money available to candidates through the public funding programs. We can distinguish between the full public funding systems (Arizona and Maine), those that provide multiple sources of public grants (Minnesota), and those that provide relatively small grants (Hawaii and Wisconsin). Table 11-2 shows our calculation of the overall percentage of candidate spending in the 2002 and 2004 state legislative elections made up by public funds.

These data suggest a clear explanation for why public funding has apparently made so little difference in Wisconsin, as public grants make up only a tiny and shrinking share of overall campaign spending. During the 1980s, public funds made up as much as one-third of candidate spending. But in 1986, grant levels and spending limits were fixed and have not changed since then. When a candidate has to raise $80,000 or more to run a competitive Assembly campaign, and $250,000 or more for the Senate, the maximum

Table 11-2. Public Contribution to Campaign Spending in Five States

State	Year	Total candidate campaign spending (dollars)	Aggregate public funds (dollars)	Percent of public funds
Maine	2002	2,927,454	2,062,762	70.5
	2004	3,665,839	2,789,250	76.1
Arizona	2002	5,737,227	3,084,298	53.8
	2004	5,196,413	3,668,455	70.6
Minnesota	2002	12,370,369	6,049,863	48.9
	2004	7,573,816	4,123,662	54.4
Wisconsin	2002	8,449,888	449,684	5.3
	2004	8,969,369	283,846	3.2
Hawaii	2002	5,872,989	34,498	0.6
	2004	5,406,837	26,268	0.5

Source: Compiled by authors.

grants—$15,525 for a Senate candidate, $7,763 for the Assembly—are hardly worth the bother.[33]

The data also confirm that public funding could not possibly have had any effect in Hawaii, since grants continue to make up only a trivial fraction of overall campaign spending. This is a limiting case which shows that campaign finance is not the only factor that affects election competition.

Hawaii's experience with public funding—minimal grants, but a trend toward increased electoral competitiveness—highlights some of the limits of public funding as a comprehensive reform strategy. Although the evidence from Maine and Arizona, in particular, points to a significant improvement in electoral competition, even dramatic changes in campaign finance practices do not by themselves uproot electoral systems or produce fundamental rearrangements of political influence (at least none that we can detect so far). More to the point, when the political context does change, it may be the result of broader political forces, or even idiosyncratic events.

Although Hawaii was considered a Republican state in its early years of statehood, the Democratic Party ascended in the early 1960s to dominate state politics, with a coalition of labor unions and minority groups organized into a powerful majority by skilled politicians like Daniel Inouye and John Burns.[34]

33. In addition, perpetual funding shortfalls mean that the actual grants are smaller than the statutory maximum. In 2004, Assembly candidates received at most $5,574, Senate candidates $13,958.

34. See Coffman (2003) for an analysis of Hawaiian political history.

But the Democratic hold on state elections began to waver in the mid-1990s because of a combination of stagnant economic growth, ethics scandals, and efforts to organize in response to a 1993 state Supreme Court decision opening the door to same-sex marriages.[35] Republicans held only seven of fifty-one State House seats in 1995, but won nineteen of fifty-one in the 2000 elections (Democrats now have a 41–10 majority). And although the state GOP has failed to cut into the Democratic legislative lock, in 2002 Hawaii elected its first Republican governor since 1962, and was considered competitive—for a time, at least—during the 2004 presidential election.[36]

Conclusion: Does Public Funding Make Elections More Competitive?

We are left with something of a mixed picture. There is compelling evidence that Arizona and Maine have become much more competitive states in the wake of the 1998 clean elections programs. The fact that indicators of competitiveness in Arizona remained stable through the 2002 and 2004 cycles is evidence that the electoral dynamic has indeed changed. We have revised our view of the impact of Maine's program: based on the 2002 elections, we concluded that it was too early to tell whether public funding had changed the electoral landscape. With the 2004 results in hand, we can say that public funding appears to have significantly increased the competitiveness of State House elections, based on the percentage of incumbents who face major-party opponents and run in reasonably close races. Minnesota's program continues to show a high degree of efficacy.

Not everyone agrees with our conclusions. Elsewhere in this volume, Primo, Milyo, and Groseclose argue that "the jury is still very much out on clean elections laws," observing that the changes we noted here may be fleeting. In particular, they note that the decline in incumbency reelection rates may be the result of a culling effect, in which the best and most experienced incumbents are the first to be forced out by term limits. The incumbents who are left are, by definition, the ones with less experience. It is possible, then, that the incumbents we are observing in 2002 and 2004—that is, post-reform—are less experienced and of lower quality than those who stayed in

35. John M. Broder, "Death and Scandal Leaving Democrats in Chaos in Hawaii," *New York Times*, October 19, 2002; Rohter (1997).

36. Bush lost the state to John Kerry, receiving 45.3 percent of the vote. This was an improvement over his 2000 total, however (35.5 percent).

office before term limits. If this is true, these incumbents would have wound up in closer races (because they are less experienced and skilled, or because term limits reduced the incumbency advantage in some other way) even without clean elections.

It is of course possible that the effects we have observed will ebb. Everyone who studies elections will concede that the environment is complex, with many interactions, simultaneous relationships, and causal chains that are hard to pin down. Even so, we are confident in our results, because while we cannot claim to have controlled for every possible alternative explanation, we have eliminated the most obvious ones. Moreover, a growing literature suggests that term limits may *decrease* electoral competition by giving potential challengers a reason to bide their time until a seat opens up. In any case, we expect that a few more election cycles will clear up disagreement over the public funding effect.[37]

Hawaii and Wisconsin are states with ineffective programs; the key characteristic in both states is that public funds make up only a fraction of what candidates raise and spend. Although there is some evidence from Hawaii that elections have become slightly more competitive, this has more to do with long-term changes in the political composition of the electorate than with campaign finance law (and in any event, Hawaii Republicans have yet to seriously challenge the Democratic Party's hold on the legislature, even as they have achieved some statewide successes).

One significant inference that we draw is that there is no merit in the argument that public funding programs amount to an incumbent protection act. The fear that spending limits would put challengers in an impossible strategic situation and make incumbents even more unbeatable has simply not been realized.

There are limits to what these data can tell us, in any event. We do not yet have evidence that public funding has altered roll-call voting patterns or legislative coalitions, as might be expected if interest group influence or party influence has declined as legislators utilize their newfound independence. But the evidence points strongly to the conclusion that, under the right set

---

37. Early data from 2006, while not definitive, are consistent with our argument. In Maine, 321 candidates have filed for the 151 House seats, with 81 percent stating an intention to accept public funding. One hundred forty-six of the 151 seats are contested. In the Senate, all thirty-five seats are contested by the major parties, with 71 percent of candidates accepting public funding. These figures will change, since Maine ballot laws are flexible. But they suggest that the competitive effects observed have not yet dissipated. See Maine Commission on Governmental Ethics and Election Practices (www.state.me.us/ethics/candidate-list.htm).

of circumstances, public grants can significantly increase the level of election competition.

Appendix 11A. Assessing Competitiveness in Arizona House Elections

Calculating margins of victory and competitiveness in multicandidate districts poses some challenges; it is not immediately obvious how to translate the typical definition of competitiveness—say, a winning margin of 55–45 percent in a two-candidate race. Moreover, some districts might be fully contested—with each party running as many candidates as seats—while others might be partially contested, with, say, one party running only a single candidate in a two-slot election. The GAO, in noting these difficulties, skirted the problem by simply not including Arizona House races in its analysis. But this is not an ideal solution, since it requires jettisoning valuable data. Niemi, Jackman, and Winsky (1991) offer a few possible metrics: proportion of races fully contested, partially contested, or uncontested; incumbent success rates; the number of districts that elect candidates from both major parties. These authors offer as well an innovative method of creating "pseudo-single-member districts" in fully contested districts, by pairing the candidates against each other in ways that simulate two-candidate races. In this method, the top Democratic (or Republican) vote getter is paired with the weakest Republican (or Democratic) vote getter; the Democrat (Republican) with the second most votes is paired with the Republican (Democrat) with the most votes. Each of these pairings is analyzed as if it were a single election.

For elections that are not fully contested—meaning that one party runs two general election candidates, the other only one—we count the highest vote getter of the fully contesting party as unopposed.

Example: consider the result from the 2000 Arizona House election in district 4:

Candidate	Party	Votes won
Jake Flake	R	26,806
Debra Brimhall	R	23,836
Claudia Maestas	D	19,997
M. Phil Martin	D	17,908

To create two pseudo-pairs, we match Flake against Martin and Brimhall against Maestas, yielding the following:

Candidate / party	Votes won	Percent
Flake / R	26,806	59.9
Martin / D	17,908	40.1
Brimhall / R	23,836	54.4
Maestas / D	19,997	45.6

Under our definition of competitive—a winning total under 60 percent—both races would count as competitive, the first comfortably so, and the second by a narrow margin.

We use this method to create pseudo-pairs for each election, and count these as the equivalent of single-member results.

References

Ansolabehere, Stephen, and James M. Snyder Jr. 2000. "The Incumbency Advantage in U.S. Elections: An Analysis of State and Federal Offices, 1942–2000." *Election Law Journal* 1 (3): 315–38.

Breslow, Marc, Janet Groat, and Paul Saba. 2002. *Revitalizing Democracy: Clean Election Reform Shows the Way Forward*. Northeast Action Coalition. Money and Politics Implementation Project (January).

Cain, Bruce E. 2000–01. "Party Autonomy and Two-Party Electoral Competition." *University of Pennsylvania Law Review* 149: 793–814.

Cain, Bruce E., Karin Mac Donald, and Michael McDonald. 2005. "From Equality to Fairness: The Path of Political Reform since *Baker v. Carr.*" In *Party Lines: Competition, Partisanship, and Congressional Redistricting*, edited by Thomas E. Mann and Bruce E. Cain. Brookings.

Clean Elections Institute (Arizona). 2002. *The Road to Victory: Clean Elections Shapes 2002 Arizona Elections* (December).

Coffman, Tom. 2003. *The Island Edge of America: A Political History of Hawai'i*. Honolulu: University of Hawai'i Press.

Donnay, Patrick D., and Graham P. Ramsden. 1995. "Public Financing of Legislative Elections: Lessons from Minnesota." *Legislative Studies Quarterly* 20 (3): 351–64.

General Accounting Office. 2003. *Campaign Finance Reform: Early Experiences of Two States That Offer Full Public Funding for Political Candidates*. GAO-03-453, May 2003.

Gulati, Girish J. 2004. "Revisiting the Link between Electoral Competition and Policy Extremism in the U.S. Congress." *American Politics Research* 32 (5): 495–520.

Holbrook, Thomas M., and Emily Van Dunk. 1993. "Electoral Competition in the American States." *American Political Science Review* 87 (4): 955–62.

Jewell, Malcom E., and William E. Cassie. 1998. "Can the Legislative Campaign Finance System Be Reformed?" In *Campaign Finance in State Legislative Elections*, edited by Joel A. Thompson and Gary E. Moncrief. Washington: CQ Press.

Kousser, Thad. 2005. *Term Limits and the Dismantling of State Legislative Professionalism*. New York: Cambridge University Press.

Kraus, Jeffrey. 2006. "Campaign Finance Reform Reconsidered: New York City's Public Finance Program after Fifteen Years." *The Forum* 3 (4). www.bepress.com/forum/vol3/iss4/art6/.

La Raja, Raymond J., and Matthew Saradjian. 2004. "Maine Clean Elections: An Evaluation of Public Funding for Legislative Elections." University of Massachusetts Policy Center, January 19, 2004.

Lizzeri, Alessandro, and Nicola Persico. 2002. "The Drawbacks of Electoral Competition." Paper WP2003-6. Berkeley, Calif.: Institute for Governmental Studies, UC Berkeley.

Malbin, Michael J., and Thomas L. Gais. 1998. *The Day after Reform: Sobering Campaign Finance Lessons from the American States.* New York: Rockefeller Institute Press.

Mayer, Kenneth R. 1998. *Public Financing and Electoral Competition in Minnesota and Wisconsin.* Citizens' Research Foundation, University of Southern California (April).

Mayer, Kenneth R., and John M. Wood. 1995. "The Impact of Public Financing on Electoral Competitiveness: Evidence from Wisconsin, 1964–1990." *Legislative Studies Quarterly* 20: 69–88.

Niemi, Richard G., Simon Jackman, and Laura R. Winsky. 1991. "Candidacies and Competitiveness in Multimember Districts." *Legislative Studies Quarterly* 16 (1): 91–109.

Pildes, Richard H. 1999. "The Theory of Political Competition." *Virginia Law Review* 85: 1605–26.

———. 2004. "Book Review: Competitive, Deliberative, and Rights-Oriented Democracy." *Election Law Journal* 3 (4): 685–97.

Rohter, Ira. 1997. "Right to Rule." *Honolulu Advertiser*, July 13.

Saari, Donald G. 2000. *Chaotic Elections! A Mathematician Looks at Voting.* Providence, R.I.: American Mathematical Society.

———. 2003. "Unsettling Aspects of Voting Theory." *Economic Theory* 22 (3): 529–55.

Stanley, Harold W., and Richard G. Niemi. 2003. *Vital Statistics on American Politics, 2003–2004.* Washington: CQ Press.

Thompson, Dennis F. 2002. *Just Elections: Creating a Fair Electoral Process in the United States.* Chicago: University of Chicago Press.

Zuckerman, Edward. 2003. "GAO Looks through Flawed Prism, and Finds No Evidence of Success." *Political Finance* (June).

12

State Campaign Finance Reform, Competitiveness, and Party Advantage in Gubernatorial Elections

David M. Primo, Jeffrey Milyo, and Tim Groseclose

Electoral competition is thought to be the cornerstone of democratic rule, yet many policymakers, scholars, and concerned citizens perceive the existence of a competitiveness crisis in the United States today. As the introductory chapter to this volume notes, U.S. House races are becoming increasingly uncompetitive; this is no mean feat, as reelection rates for House incumbents have been in the 90 percent range for much of the postwar era. If the dearth of electoral competition is a problem, what is the solution? One popular remedy among "good government" groups and policymakers is campaign finance reform, especially partial or complete public funding of campaigns.

Campaign finance reform addresses what many perceive to be the central problem with elections: money. It can easily cost a million dollars to run a competitive House race these days, and upwards of $5 million to do the same in the Senate. Races for governor far exceed these figures and sometimes cost in excess of $100 million. The high cost of campaigning is thought to be a barrier for challengers, who have relatively more difficulty raising funds,

We thank Matt Jacobsmeier for research assistance. We also thank Michael Bailey, Jim Snyder, and the editors for helpful comments. Jeffrey Milyo gratefully acknowledges financial support from the Hanna Family Fellowship and the Center for Applied Economics at the University of Kansas School of Business.

especially from political action committees (PACs) and other organizations that tend to give primarily to incumbents. Given these hurdles, campaign finance reform that aids challengers in raising money, or in leveling the playing field with incumbents, has the potential to increase electoral competition if implemented properly.

Perhaps the most straightforward way to increase competitiveness via campaign finance laws, constitutional issues aside, would be to set the size of campaign spending exogenously and provide both incumbents and challengers with a set amount of funds. There is, after all, ample evidence that the marginal impact of an additional dollar of campaign spending is close to zero or, at best, small but positive.[1] Once a challenger spends "enough," more money has little impact on vote share. The problem for policymakers is determining what "enough" is—that amount will vary from race to race, district to district, state to state. In addition, much as reformers might like, the politics cannot be taken out of reform. Most campaign finance rules are implemented through the legislative process. Incumbents may have an incentive to set artificially low limits, and Democrats and Republicans may favor campaign finance rules that are likely to give their party an advantage.

In short, in addition to constitutional constraints, which prevent the implementation of policies such as mandatory expenditure limits, there are three obstacles to other potentially effective reforms—informational limits, incentives for incumbent protection, and partisan battles. In the realm of the possible, the current menu of constitutional campaign reforms that plausibly relate to competition are limits on contributions by organizations, limits on contributions by individuals, and full or partial public funding of campaigns tied to voluntary expenditure limits. We explore all of these reforms in this chapter.

Despite the attention given to electoral competitiveness and campaign money, and the assertions made by both proponents and opponents of campaign finance reform in court cases and other public debates, we know surprisingly little about the impact of campaign finance laws on electoral outcomes. The following comment was made in 1981, but is still applicable, with few exceptions, today: "Although the impact of public funding on the electoral process is a popular topic of speculation for political journalists and pundits and a source of practical concern for political parties and candidates, neither they nor the research community has had adequate information

---

1. Recent work includes Levitt (1994); Gerber (1998); and Milyo (1998); but compare Erikson and Palfrey (1998, 2000). A related literature examines the electoral consequences of campaign war chests (for example, Goodliffe 2001) and candidate wealth (for example, Milyo and Groseclose 1999).

about campaign financing in general and information about public financing at the state level in particular."[2]

Most empirical research linking campaign finance and competitiveness has focused on the marginal impact of spending at the federal level. There is some work at the state level linking spending and competitiveness,[3] but extant state-level research typically does not address a fundamental endogeneity problem. Namely, spending both influences and is influenced by the competitiveness of a race.

In this chapter, we take a different tack. Rather than wandering into the spending-competitiveness thicket, we estimate the *net* effect of campaign finance laws on competitiveness and party advantage (which can be thought of as something like "party competition") in gubernatorial elections. Because campaign finance laws vary greatly across states, the U.S. states are an ideal arena for exploration. Yet surprisingly, there is a limited amount of systematic empirical work in this area that does not suffer from the same endogeneity problem described above.[4]

In fact, we know of only one such study, by Thomas Stratmann and Francisco Aparicio-Castillo, who examine competitiveness in state legislative elections.[5] These authors advance the previous literature in two important ways. First, they examine a more comprehensive set of state legislative elections over a longer time period (twenty years) than any previous study. Second, the authors control for unobserved state effects that might influence both electoral outcomes and the presence of state campaign finance laws. Previous studies of legislative elections have not addressed the potentially confounding effects of unobserved heterogeneity across states. Stratmann and Aparicio-Castillo find that contribution limits do appear to help challengers in legislative elections; such regulations are associated with both an increase in the number of challengers and a decrease in incumbents' reelection margins.

In this chapter, we focus on gubernatorial elections from 1978 to 2004, the era following a landmark Supreme Court decision, *Buckley* v. *Valeo*, which altered the landscape of campaign finance reform.[6] Like Stratmann and Aparicio-

2. Jones (1981, p. 344).
3. For example, see Gross and Goidel (2003).
4. The limited work that has been done (for example, Gross and Goidel 2003; Bardwell 2003; Gross, Goidel, and Shields 2002) fails to address the interrelationships among challenger spending, incumbent spending, competitiveness, and campaign finance laws. For a summary of research at the state level, see Ramsden (2002). For a more general review of the literature, see Stratmann (2005).
5. Stratmann and Aparicio-Castillo (2006).
6. *Buckley* v. *Valeo*, 424 U.S. 1 (1976).

Castillo, we employ state fixed effects in our analysis in order to control for unobserved state-specific heterogeneity. In addition, unlike previous studies of gubernatorial campaign finance that rely on ad hoc models and questionable identification strategies, we estimate the reduced-form effects of state campaign finance laws. For the most part, we find that only limits on individual contributions to candidates have statistically and substantively significant effects on the winning margins in gubernatorial races, narrowing such margins. However, these effects are not driven by an impact on close races. In contrast, limits on organizational contributions and public financing regimes have small but statistically insignificant effects on winning vote margins. Finally, we also examine whether state campaign finance reforms confer any electoral advantage to one party over the other, and we find that campaign finance laws have no effect on party advantage in gubernatorial races. In the discussion section, we address the implications of these findings for future reform efforts.

Linking Campaign Finance Laws and Election Outcomes

We think about the impact of campaign finance laws on competitiveness and party advantage as part of a system of relationships. Campaign finance laws have an indirect effect on election outcomes via spending, turnout, and challenger quality. These variables are in turn interrelated. See figure 12-1 for a visual description of these relationships, assuming that an incumbent is in the race. Statistical identification and estimation of the causal pathways within this system require strong assumptions about the structure of the related processes in the system; sometimes such assumptions are untenable, and so unbiased estimation of even some of the direct causal relationships within the larger system is not possible. Specifically, we are concerned with "endogeneity bias," which occurs when there is reciprocal causality, as in figure 12-1, or when there are important unobserved phenomena present in such a system (for example, unobserved state-specific heterogeneity).

Fortunately, in order to understand the *net* effects of these laws on competitiveness and party advantage, we do not need to estimate the full set of causal relationships. Instead, we model the process depicted in figure 12-1 as a system of equations, then solve the system for the one dependent variable of interest in terms of only exogenous variables (that is, all determinants within the larger system that are not themselves caused by either competitiveness or unobserved determinants of competitiveness). Regression analysis of the "reduced-form" equation yields unbiased estimates of the net effects of state campaign finance laws on competitiveness, thereby offering policymakers and

Figure 12-1. The Complex Web of Campaign Finance Laws and Election Outcomes

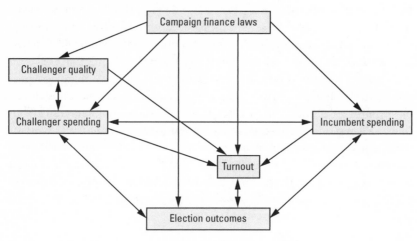

scholars a "bottom-line" estimate of the impact of reform that does not suffer from an endogeneity bias.[7]

One disadvantage of a reduced-form approach is that it does not enable us to determine the specific pathways by which campaign finance laws affect competitiveness.[8] For instance, we cannot identify and estimate the direct effects of challenger versus incumbent spending on competitiveness. However, since it is state campaign finance laws that are the relevant policy lever for policymakers, we are able to answer an important question in this study—namely, what is the *net* impact of laws on competitiveness?

We examine the effects of three distinct types of laws that occur in the states and that have been the focus of reformers and scholars alike: restric-

---

7. Primo and Milyo (2006a, 2006b) estimate the reduced-form effects of state campaign finance reforms on voter turnout and political efficacy.

8. One implication of a reduced form is that the laws may affect both challenger and incumbent spending, but if the effects work in equal but opposite directions, a reduced form will find that the laws have zero effect. For instance, public funding may have large effects on certain aspects of the process—for instance, an incumbent may redouble efforts to raise money in response to a publicly funded challenger—but on net have no effect on competitiveness. Such a situation merely underscores the importance of reduced-form analysis, since this procedure avoids the problems that might occur by focusing on just one aspect of a larger system. Namely, one might find a large effect at one stage of the process, but miss an equally large (unmodeled) effect that moves the dependent variable in the opposite direction.

tions on campaign contributions form organized interests, restrictions on contributions from individuals, and public financing of political campaigns. Starting with limits on organizations, we expect these to have a modest positive effect on competitiveness, since organizations are more likely to contribute to an incumbent than to a challenger. Consequently, these limits are unlikely to help either party systematically. Limits on individuals may also decrease winning margins, since incumbents are more likely to be successful at fundraising in general (since, after all, incumbents have already succeeded in the previous election). However, we expect that limits on individual contributions may advantage Democrats, who in general do not have as deep a donor pool as Republicans.

Things get more interesting when we turn to public funding. First, we follow the convention of using the term "public funding" to describe any state subsidy for qualifying candidates who agree to limit their campaign spending. We do not have a strong expectation about the likely impact of public financing in gubernatorial elections, in part because the literature is somewhat mixed. For example, Gross, Goidel, and Shields, as well as Gross and Goidel, find no effect of public funding on competitiveness in state elections, while Mayer and Wood argue that public funding in Wisconsin has had little impact on legislative election outcomes, in part because grants were too small and recruiting quality challengers still proved difficult.[9]

In contrast, Donnay and Ramsden find that public financing of legislative elections in Minnesota increased competitiveness.[10] And in another chapter of this volume, Mayer, Werner, and Williams argue that properly funded public funding programs will increase competitiveness in legislative races. They base these findings on recent reforms in Maine and Arizona, although the long-term effect of these laws remains to be seen. More important, none of these authors adequately address the concerns about endogeneity bias described above. For example, none of these studies employ state fixed effects in order to control for unobserved state-specific heterogeneity. Our study addresses these limitations.

In theory, public funding could be expected to help challengers, provided that expenditure limits are set high enough and contribution limits are not so restrictive as to prevent the challenger from raising funds. However, public funding, which is often enacted or amended through the legislative process, may be crafted so as to aid incumbents over challengers, via either a small

9. Gross, Goidel, and Shields (2002); Gross and Goidel (2003); Mayer and Wood (1995).
10. Donnay and Ramsden (1995).

matching component or artificially low limits. Ultimately, it is an empirical question whether the net effects of public financing in state elections increase competitiveness.

The impact of public funding on party advantage is also open. In a pioneering 1981 study, Jones found that the money advantage of the majority party (at the time typically Democrats) in states with public funding varied according to the types of laws in place, but that typically the advantage was not much different than the electoral advantage the majority party already enjoyed.[11] Since that article was written, divided government has come to dominate the states, but the larger lesson still applies: the net effect of incumbents battling over the design of public funding laws may result in a wash, maintaining the existing political equilibrium.

Data and Method

We analyze the determinants of competitiveness and party advantage in gubernatorial elections from 1978 to 2004, or the post-*Buckley* era. We include every state gubernatorial election from this period; data on election outcomes were obtained from *America Votes*.[12] We measure competitiveness by the winning candidate's percentage vote margin over that of the closest competitor, which can range from 0 to 100. Similarly, we measure party advantage by the Democratic candidate's percentage margin over the top Republican candidate, which can range from −100 to 100. Descriptive statistics for the key variables in this analysis are found in table 12-1; the rest are listed in table 12A-1 in the appendix.

Several previous studies of electoral competitiveness examine open-seat races separately from races that include an incumbent. But because term limits on governors' terms of service are so common, there are simply too few cases of gubernatorial incumbents running for reelection to follow this precedent. Further, given our reduced-form estimation strategy, it would be inappropriate to do so. This is because the choice of a non-term-limited

---

11. Jones (1981).

12. Because Louisiana's open primary system is unique, we check whether our results change when we drop Louisiana elections from the analysis. The only result that is affected is the impact of individual contribution limits on the log of margin, which is statistically significant at the .10 level when Louisiana is omitted. Throughout, whenever we discuss robustness checks like this, we will only mention noteworthy deviations from our reported results. Finally, for all sensitivity results mentioned in this paper, further details are available from the authors upon request.

Table 12-1. Descriptive Statistics for Key Variables in Gubernatorial Elections, 1978–2004

$N = 370$

Variable	Mean	Standard deviation	Minimum	Maximum
Winning margin (percent)	15.84	13.45	0.00	64.74
Democratic margin over Republicans				
(percent)	1.34	20.78	−58.34	64.74
Limits on organizational contributions	.76	.42	0	1
Limits on individual contributions	.59	.49	0	1
Public funding of gubernatorial candidates	.15	.36	0	1
Term limits for governor	.61	.49	0	1

incumbent to run for reelection or not is itself a function of the electoral environment, including state campaign finance regulations. And while in principle we could examine open-seat races that occur because the incumbent is term-limited, there are even fewer of these. Consequently, we pool all gubernatorial elections and estimate a common specification, and we do not include controls for instances in which incumbents run for reelection (since the incumbency indicator is endogenous and does not appear in the reduced form).

We estimate least squares regressions with robust standard errors; in addition, we adjust the standard errors to account for the clustering of errors by state, since multiple observations over time within the same state may not be independent.[13] Our primary specifications also include fixed effects for states and each two-year electoral cycle;[14] these fixed effects serve as a proxy for unobserved heterogeneity in the data, and also serve to mitigate any concerns about the possible endogeneity of state campaign finance laws.

We code campaign finance laws as being present if they apply to gubernatorial elections and were put into effect before the election in question. Three dichotomous campaign finance variables represent the laws in each state.[15] These are indicators for the presence of:

13. Bertrand, Duflo, and Mullainathan (2004).

14. An odd-year election at time t was coded as part of the even-year electoral cycle at time $t + 1$. We do not include an indicator to control for odd-year elections; such a variable is collinear with the set of state fixed effects, since it does not vary over time.

15. We do not create an index of laws because we do not expect their effects to be additive. Also, in this analysis, we do not examine the effects of different types of public financing regulations (that is, full versus partial public funding) due to a lack of variation in our data.

Table 12-2. State Campaign Finance Laws, 1976–2004[a]

Number

Laws	1976	1980	1990	2000	2004
Limits on organizational contributions	34	35	36	44	45
Limits on individual contributions	23	25	27	36	37
Public funding of gubernatorial candidates	1	5	6	14	13

a. Cell entries indicate the number of states with each type of law.

—limits on contributions by organizations (for example, corporations);
—limits on contributions by individuals; and
—public subsidies to candidates who abide by expenditure limits.

Campaign finance laws have changed dramatically in the states in recent decades. In 1976 few states had restrictions on campaign contributions by individuals, but by 2004 such limits were the norm. Similarly, the number of states that limit contributions from both organizations (corporations, unions, and PACs) and individuals has increased substantially over the past thirty years. State campaign finance reforms were particularly frequent in the 1990s, with more than one-third of states altering their laws during this period.[16] We are currently in what might be called an era of "mature" campaign finance regulation, since most states have some restrictions on contributions (see table 12-2).[17]

As noted above, we consider contribution limits on organizations, contribution limits on individuals, and the presence of public financing tied to voluntary expenditure limits. While there are several ways to categorize and measure state-level laws, in this case simpler is better. We measure the presence or absence of particular types of laws, such as contribution limits and public financing. Using specific dollar amounts leads one into a morass, in part because states differ greatly in many respects, including cost of living, wealth, and the cost of media markets. Put concretely, does a $1,000 limit on individual contributions to a candidate mean the same thing in Arkansas as it does in California? If not, how would one compare specific limits across states? Other aspects of campaign finance law, such as enforcement quality, suffer from similar problems. In contrast, the pres-

16. Malbin and Gais (1998).
17. In table 12-2, we include Maryland among the states with public funding for gubernatorial elections and treat it as such in our statistical analyses. However, because few candidates have taken public funds in Maryland, some observers do not consider this state to have an effective public funding program. An alternate construction of the public funding variable, treating Maryland as not having such a law, attenuates the estimated impact of public funding in every model that we examine.

ence or absence of particular laws can be clearly measured and is directly comparable across states.

In addition to these key independent variables of interest, we include several control variables in our analysis. First, in every specification, we control for competitiveness or party advantage in the lower chamber of the state legislature, as a proxy for party strength.[18] That is, when estimating the determinants of the winning margin, we include a control variable that describes the "seat margin" enjoyed by the party to which the governor belongs. Similarly, when estimating the Democratic margin, we include a control for the Democratic seat margin in the lower chamber of the state legislature. In addition, we include the margin in the most recent or concurrent presidential vote as a second proxy for party strength.

We also examine the effects of several other institutional control variables, including the presence of term limits for governors, the length of gubernatorial terms, and the ease of voter registration (same-day registration or registration not required). Finally, we examine the impact of controlling for several state demographic control variables: the log of real per capita income, percent black, percent Hispanic, the percentage of voters age 21 and up, and the percentage of voters age 65 and up. Data on political institutions are taken from *The Book of the States* and *Campaign Finance Law*, while demographic and income data are taken from the *Statistical Abstract of the United States*. Missing years for state-level demographic variables are linearly interpolated from adjacent years.

Results

In table 12-3 we present the main results for the impact of campaign finance laws on winning vote margins. In the first column, we present our key estimates for only a sparse model with few control variables; in the second column, we present estimates for the same key variables when a richer set of controls is included in the model (estimation results for the remaining variables are shown in table 12A-2 in the appendix). Regardless of the specification, there are several noteworthy findings. First, merely having organizational contribution limits in place has no impact on competitiveness. In

18. This variable takes the value of zero for Nebraska, which has a nonpartisan legislature. Our results are little changed by dropping Nebraska from the analysis, so we work with all fifty states. In cases where an independent candidate is victorious, we also code party strength as zero. We have checked our findings by dropping races where independents were victorious from our analysis; this also does not change the reported results in any noteworthy way.

Table 12-3. Least Squares Regression Estimates of the Winning Margin in Gubernatorial Elections, 1978–2004[a]

N = 370

Variable	(1)	(2)
Limits on contributions from organizations	0.10	−1.82
	(3.78)	(3.73)
Limits on contributions from individuals	−9.70***	−7.57**
	(3.46)	(3.43)
Public funding of gubernatorial candidates	−5.02	−4.01
	(3.49)	(3.36)
Term limits for governor	−1.73	−3.32
	(3.30)	(4.02)
Other institutional controls	No	Yes
Demographic controls	No	Yes
R^2	.26	.28

a. Heteroscedastic-consistent standard errors in parentheses (White's method); all standard errors are also adjusted for clustering within states. The dependent variable is the difference between the winner's vote percentage and that of the next highest finisher. All regressions include controls for electoral cycle and state fixed effects, and the strength of the winning candidate's party (see table 12A-2 for complete results).
*** $p < .01$.
** $p < .05$.

contrast, individual contribution limits have a large, statistically significant, and negative effect on the size of the winning vote margin, implying an increase in competitiveness. However, moving beyond individual limits appears to do little to improve competitiveness. Public funding has only a modest and statistically insignificant effect on winning margins. Finally, another law thought to affect competitiveness, term limits, has a small (pro-competitive) effect, albeit one that is also not statistically significant.

One potential disadvantage of focusing on winning margins in this analysis is that some laws may not affect races in which the winner routs the opposition, but may nevertheless have an important impact in more competitive races. For this reason, we checked the sensitivity of our findings by examining whether state campaign finance laws have a different effect on the natural log of competitiveness. In this model, no campaign finance laws achieve statistical significance. We also ran the same specification for the square of margin—this captures whether the impact of the laws is larger for uncompetitive races; here individual limits are statistically significant. These results suggest that campaign finance laws do not affect close races more than lopsided races, and that in fact the reverse may be true.

Table 12-4. Least Squares Regression Estimates of the Democratic Margin in Gubernatorial Elections, 1978–2004[a]

$N = 370$

Variable	(1)	(2)
Limits on contributions from organizations	−13.46**	−6.77
	(5.99)	(6.88)
Limits on contributions from individuals	4.93	−0.30
	(5.59)	(5.77)
Public funding of gubernatorial candidates	−3.97	−1.74
	(6.64)	(6.44)
Term limits for governor	−9.59*	−11.67*
	(4.90)	(5.85)
Other institutional controls	No	Yes
Demographic controls	No	Yes
R^2	.29	.32

a. Heteroscedastic-consistent standard errors in parentheses (White's method); all standard errors are also adjusted for clustering within states. The dependent variable is the difference between the Democratic candidate's vote percentage and that of the Republican candidate. All regressions include controls for electoral cycle and state fixed effects, and for the strength of the Democratic party (see table 12A-3 for complete results).
** $p < .05$.
* $p < .10$.

The winning margin is one way to characterize competitiveness, but another important measure of competitiveness is the difference between the vote percentages of the major-party candidates, or "party advantage." We are particularly interested in this dependent variable, since Democrats and Republicans alike may oppose campaign finance reform out of perceived party interest.

In table 12-4 we present the key results from a similar analysis as above, except this time looking at party advantage (the remaining estimates associated with this specification are presented in table 12A-3). The results here may offer solace to partisans who are concerned that particular reforms will harm their party. In the sparse specification, limits on contributions from organizations are associated with a lower Democratic vote margin, while individual limits have the opposite effect (only the former is significant). However, with the addition of more control variables, these estimated effects do not hold up (see column 2 in table 12-4); in fact, none of the state campaign finance laws are significant.

Overall, the observed effect of public financing on competitiveness is unimpressive. However, one concern may be that in this analysis we do not control for whether a candidate actually accepts public funding. So it might be argued that if candidates choose not to accept public funding, then that election should not be counted as being conducted under a public funding system. However, a candidate's decision whether to accept public funding depends on other exogenous variables in the larger structural system that motivated our reduced-form model. Therefore, an individual candidate's choice to take public funds or not should not be controlled for in our estimation models. This is because the inclusion of variables that do not belong in the reduced form may bias the coefficients of interest in our analysis.

Discussion

Though campaign finance laws are often heralded as the cure for what ails elections in the United States, such optimism must be tempered by statistical reality. In an examination of gubernatorial races from 1978 to 2004, we find evidence that only contribution limits on individuals benefit electoral competition, and that this effect is not driven by an impact on close races. We also find that none of the laws confer an advantage on either political party. Most notably, we find no statistically or substantively significant impact of public funding on electoral competitiveness. Given that public funding is where most reform is headed today, our results suggest caution in this regard.

One possible reason why state campaign finance laws have a limited impact on competitiveness is that these rules are typically designed by elected officials who have either incumbent- or party-based reasons for desiring ineffectual reforms. While we cannot test whether an "incumbent protection" scheme is at work in the states, the absence of a strong and consistent impact on competitiveness suggests that state reforms at least do not give challengers a significant leg up.

What does this mean for future reform efforts? The Supreme Court decision in *Randall v. Sorrell*, which dealt with a reform law in Vermont, reaffirmed the unconstitutionality of spending limits and for the first time struck down contribution limits as too low. This decision has galvanized reformers who continue to push for "clean money" or "clean elections" reforms that provide for full public funding of campaigns. As they do so, we hope that our findings are taken into account. Also, we want to be clear that our findings do not suggest that contribution limits cannot have deleterious effects on competition if set too low; our findings here suggest that contribution limits, as enacted in the states, have on net had a modest positive impact on competitiveness. Still, very low limits like those in Vermont, which raised concerns even for pro-reform Supreme Court Justice Stephen Breyer, merit caution. Reformers sometimes learn this the hard way. A successful 1997 campaign to limit contributions to $100 per donor in Austin, Texas, has by all accounts been an utter failure. As one of the reform leaders said, "The point of it was to increase the competitiveness of elections. It hasn't done that."[19] Again, since we are in a mature era of regulation, with most states having some reforms in place, imposing stricter limits or additional reforms may do more harm than good.

To be sure, some might think us overly pessimistic. After all, "clean elections" reforms are often passed by direct democracy, which insulates them to some degree from incumbents who may want to stack the deck against challengers. Though direct democracy may offer more hope for effective reform, it is unclear that many states would be able to adopt reforms via this method. More significantly, the jury is very much still out on clean elections laws. Mayer, Werner, and Williams's findings in this volume suggest that, at least initially, reforms in Arizona and Maine have been net positives for competition, but our results suggest that the historical experience of reform is not in accord. One explanation for these disparate findings is that campaign reform limits may have different consequences for legislative elections than they do for gubernatorial elections. However, it is also possible that Mayer and his coauthors' positive findings would be attenuated if their data were analyzed using the same methodological approach adopted in this study.

Finally, large short-term effects of a law may dissipate over time for a variety of reasons. For instance, there is a great deal of uncertainty when a new law takes effect. Once political actors have adjusted to the new law, the effects are likely to be dampened. Also, there may be a "culling" phenomenon associated with campaign reforms: incumbents on the fence regarding retirement may choose to retire rather than confront an uncertain electoral environment. However, once this cohort has been replaced, it is quite possible that incumbent reelection rates will return to their customary levels.

The evidence presented here suggests that only limits on individual contributions have an appreciable impact on electoral competitiveness, albeit less so in close races. This, together with recent studies that find state campaign finance reforms have little to no impact on either voter turnout or citizens' perceptions of government,[20] suggests that such reforms do not appear to

19. Sarah Coppola, "Campaign Donation Plan May Not Work, Critics Say," *Austin American-Statesman*, March 21, 2006, p. A1.

20. Primo and Milyo (2006a, 2006b).

achieve their stated goals. Even so, the desirability of reform rests on normative judgments, but such subjective opinions should nevertheless be informed by objective analysis of the actual effects of reform. Therefore, we present these statistical findings to better inform the debates over reform that will undoubtedly ensue in coming years.

Table 12A-1. Descriptive Statistics for Key Variables in Gubernatorial Elections, 1978–2004 (continuation of table 12-1)

N = 370

Variable	Mean	Standard deviation	Minimum	Maximum
Seat margin in lower chamber of legislature (winning candidate's party)	6.15	37.28	−88.00	94.34
Vote margin in most recent presidential election (winning candidate's party)	−0.75	19.27	−62.75	49.00
Democratic seat margin in lower chamber of legislature	14.26	35.50	−74.29	94.34
Democratic vote margin in most recent presidential election	0.72	19.72	−62.75	46.36
Two-year term for governor	0.11	0.32	0	1
Easy voter registration	0.09	0.29	0	1
Log of real per capita income	10.09	0.18	9.60	10.61
Percent with high school education	76.31	9.06	41.30	91.90
Percent with college education	20.41	5.13	9.08	35.50
Percent black	9.26	9.25	0.12	36.82
Percent Hispanic	5.43	7.44	0.41	43.07
Percent age 65+	12.06	2.14	2.58	18.54
Percent age 21+	68.08	3.68	40.14	74.84

Table 12A-2. Least Squares Regression Estimates of the Winning Margin in Gubernatorial Elections, 1978–2004 (continuation of table 12-3)[a]

Variable	(1)	(2)
Seat margin in lower chamber of legislature (winning candidate's party)	0.09*** (0.02)	0.08*** (0.02)
Vote margin in most recent presidential election (winning candidate's party)	0.00 (0.06)	–0.01 (0.05)
Two-year term for governor		4.76 (4.08)
Easy voter registration		–0.81 (2.75)
Log of real per capita income		1.53 (17.50)
Percent with high school education		–0.38 (0.27)
Percent with college education		–0.92 (0.85)
Percent black		–0.58 (1.23)
Percent Hispanic		–0.05 (0.26)
Percent age 65+		–0.72 (1.35)
Percent age 21+		–0.60 (0.36)
R^2	.26	.28

a. Heteroscedastic-consistent standard errors in parentheses (White's method); all standard errors are also adjusted for clustering within states. The dependent variable is the difference between the winner's vote percentage and that of the next highest finisher. All regressions include controls for electoral cycle and state fixed effects.
*** $p < .01$.

Table 12A-3. Least Squares Regression Estimates of the Democratic Margin in Gubernatorial Elections, 1978–2004 (continuation of table 12-4)[a]

$N = 370$

Variable	(1)	(2)
Democratic seat margin in lower chamber of legislature	0.09	0.10
	(0.12)	(0.12)
Democratic vote margin in most recent presidential election	0.19	0.17
	(0.17)	(0.15)
Two-year term for governor		−1.37
		(4.26)
Easy voter registration		−5.66
		(4.89)
Log of real per capita income		−48.09
		(28.73)
Percent with high school education		−0.42
		(0.52)
Percent with college education		−0.61
		(1.47)
Percent black		−0.85
		(0.84)
Percent Hispanic		−0.85
		(0.67)
Percent age 65+		−2.69
		(2.84)
Percent age 21+		1.37***
		(0.33)
R^2	.29	.32

a. Heteroscedastic-consistent standard errors in parentheses (White's method); all standard errors are also adjusted for clustering within states. The dependent variable is the difference between the winner's vote percentage and that of the next highest finisher. All regressions include controls for electoral cycle and state fixed effects.

***$p < .01$.

References

Bardwell, Kedron. 2003. "Campaign Finance Laws and Competition for Spending in Gubernatorial Elections." *Social Science Quarterly* 84: 811–25.

Bertrand, Marianne, Esther Duflo, and Sendhil Mullainathan. 2004. "How Much Should We Trust Differences-in-Differences Estimates?" *Quarterly Journal of Economics* 119 (1): 249–75.

Book of the States. Various years. Lexington, Ky.: Council of State Governments.

Congressional Research Service. Various years. *Campaign Finance Law.* Washington: National Clearinghouse on Election Administration.

Donnay, Patrick D., and Graham P. Ramsden. 1995. "Public Financing of Legislative Elections: Lessons from Minnesota." *Legislative Studies Quarterly* 20: 351–64.

Erikson, Robert S., and Thomas R. Palfrey. 1998. "Campaign Spending and Incumbency: An Alternative Simultaneous Equations Approach." *Journal of Politics* 60: 355–73.

———. 2000. "Equilibrium in Campaign Spending Games: Theory and Data." *American Political Science Review* 94: 595–609.

Gerber, Alan. 1998. "Estimating the Effect of Campaign Spending on Senate Election Outcomes Using Instrumental Variables." *American Political Science Review* 92 (2): 401–11.

Goodliffe, Jay. 2001. "The Effect of War Chests on Challenger Entry in U.S. House Elections." *American Journal of Political Science* 45: 830–44.

Gross, Donald A., and Robert K. Goidel. 2003. *The States of Campaign Finance Reform.* Ohio State University Press.

Gross, Donald A., Robert K. Goidel, and Todd G. Shields. 2002. "State Campaign Finance Regulations and Electoral Competition." *American Politics Research* 30 (2): 143–65.

Jones, Ruth S. 1981. "State Public Campaign Finance: Implications for Partisan Politics." *American Journal of Political Science* 25: 342–61.

Levitt, Steven. 1994. "Using Repeat Challengers to Estimate the Effects of Campaign Spending on Election Outcomes in the U.S. House." *Journal of Political Economy* 102: 777–98.

Malbin, Michael J., and Thomas L. Gais. 1998. *The Day after Reform: Sobering Campaign Finance Lessons from the American States.* Albany, N.Y.: Rockefeller Institute Press.

Mayer, Kenneth R., and John M. Wood. 1995. "The Impact of Public Financing on Electoral Competitiveness: Evidence from Wisconsin, 1964–1990." *Legislative Studies Quarterly* 20 (1): 69–88.

Milyo, Jeffrey. 1998. *The Electoral Effects of Campaign Spending in House Elections.* Los Angeles: Citizens' Research Foundation.

Milyo, Jeffrey, and Timothy Groseclose. 1999. "The Electoral Effects of Incumbent Wealth." *Journal of Law and Economics* 42: 699–722.

Primo, David M., and Jeffrey Milyo. 2006a. "Campaign Finance Laws and Political Efficacy: Evidence from the States." *Election Law Journal* 5: 23–39.

———. 2006b. "The Effects of Campaign Finance Laws on Turnout, 1950–2000." Working Paper. University of Rochester and University of Missouri.

Ramsden, Graham P. 2002. "State Legislative Campaign Finance Research: A Review Essay." *State Politics and Policy Quarterly* 2 (2): 176–98.

Stratmann, Thomas. 2005. "Some Talk: Money in Politics. A (Partial) Review of the Literature." *Public Choice* 124: 135–56.

Stratmann, Thomas, and Francisco Aparicio-Castillo. 2006. "Competition Policy for Elections: Do Campaign Contribution Limits Matter?" *Public Choice* 127: 177–206.

United States Census Bureau. Various years. *Statistical Abstract of the United States.* Washington: GPO.

13 | The Perfect Electoral Marketplace: "If Men Were Angels …"

Michael P. McDonald and John Samples

This volume brings together high-quality research on the state of electoral competition in American politics in the early twenty-first century. While we know a great deal about the decline of competition in congressional elections, the contributors to this volume advance our knowledge of state legislative general elections and congressional and statewide primaries. Presidential elections are important too, and the close elections in 2000 and 2004 belie a competitive national battlefield narrowed to a few key states. At all levels of government, competition has diminished.

Changes beget explanations, particularly among those who care about the harm diminished electoral competition might do to democracy. The explanations explored here center on legislative and statewide elections. The large number of elections provides a large number of cases from which to draw statistically meaningful conclusions. Article I, section 4 of the Constitution gives states primary regulatory authority over elections. The states are laboratories of electoral reform seeking enhanced electoral competition. A true patchwork of electoral laws governs elections within states, providing the necessary variation to test hypotheses concerning the effect of electoral laws on competition. The contributors find that reform efforts can affect electoral competition, though the effects are sometimes small, and even significant impacts can be short-lived as political actors adapt to the new political environment.

Evidence of Low Competition

A number of the contributors to this volume provide basic facts about electoral competition for many offices, in addition to other analyses. While we know much about the decline in competition for congressional races, important contributions here add to our knowledge of statewide elections, state legislative elections, and primary elections, as well as competition fostered by minor-party candidates and the competition for money in presidential campaigns.

House of Representatives

Perhaps the most commented on and visible decline in electoral competition is in races for the House of Representatives. Jacobson finds declining competition in congressional general elections over the past thirty years on multiple measures of turnover, incumbent reelection rates, margin of victory, and expert handicapping. He finds that current levels of competition are exceedingly low, that "on average in the four most recent elections (1998–2004), a mere fifteen of the 435 seats changed party hands, and only five incumbents lost to challengers." Senate elections tend to be more competitive than House elections because states tend to be more heterogeneous than House districts and the more prestigious Senate seats tend to attract higher-quality candidates even when an incumbent is present. Jacobson notes that although a "substantial proportion of Senate races remain competitive" the number of competitive Senate elections has also declined.

Party Primaries

American elections include primary elections, in which party nominees are selected, followed by the general election, in which elected officials are selected. Even if general election competition has declined, it would be possible for overall levels of competition to remain constant or even rise if general election competition has shifted to primary elections. In the first comprehensive study of primary election competition for the House of Representatives since the adoption of the direct primary in the early 1900s, Ansolabehere, Hansen, Hirano, and Snyder find that primary competition has declined as well and is at historically low levels. This comports with a limited analysis of primary competition in state legislative elections by Cain, Hanley, and Kousser in term-limited states. It might be possible to recover competition if primary and general election competition were increasingly negatively correlated, but even here Ansolabehere and his colleagues find that "primary competition is not a substitute for general election competition." Not only are primary and general election competition independently decreasing, combined levels of primary and general competition are decreasing, too.

State Elections

The study of and concern about elections has been largely centered on congressional elections, arguably the most important legislative body in the United States. Because of its importance, data collection efforts have been focused on the institution. Ansolabehere and his colleagues also find, as does Jacobson, that electoral competition is higher in statewide elections, such as those for U.S. senator, governor, lieutenant governor, and attorney general. Ansolabehere and his colleagues offer a more comprehensive analysis of statewide races, which finds, contrary to Jacobson, a slight rise in general election competition for statewide offices, from 48.7 percent of races in the period 1910–38 to 59.2 percent in the period 1960–2000. The different findings are likely due to changes in competition among statewide constitutional offices unexamined by Jacobson. As in their study of House elections, Ansolabehere and his colleagues find steep declines in primary competition among statewide offices and as a result, 26.8 percent of candidates faced neither a competitive primary nor a general election race in the early period, while 33.1 percent of candidates faced neither in modern elections. The rise in general election competition in statewide offices observed by Ansolabehere and his colleagues is more than offset by a lower level of primary competition.

State elections also have little competition. Niemi, Powell, Berry, Carsey, and Snyder engage in a collaborative effort to update an important collection of state legislative election results to include the most recent elections. Examining multiple measures of competition, such as incumbent reelection rates, turnover, and margin of victory, these authors find that electoral competition in current state legislative elections is low. We are grateful to have their preliminary analysis in this volume, and we expect future analysis to examine historical trends in competition to see if levels of competition are decreasing or whether state legislative elections have been generally uncompetitive.

Minor Parties

Electoral competition is usually conceptualized as that between Democratic and Republican candidates. Where a major-party candidate chooses not to contest an election to the House of Representatives, Herrnson shows that "minor-party candidates provided voters with an alternative choice on the ballot in every 2002 House race where two-party competition was absent." But while these candidates provide choice, few voters will vote for minor-party candidates, even where the contest is solely between a major- and a minor-party candidate. The average margin of victory for the major-party candidate where there was no major-party opposition was 79 percent in 2002. Minor-party candidates face significant ballot access and campaign financing barriers as well as public indifference in the voting booth. Minor-party candidates can be "spoilers" in a limited number of House elections. In three 2002 House races, all minor-party candidates combined received more votes than the winner's margin of victory.

Fundraising

Gimpel and Lee provide a silver lining to these clouds of declining competition. They contrast the electoral battle for presidential votes with the fundraising battle. While the electoral battle is waged on the familiar, narrowed territory where close outcomes are expected in the battleground states, the battle for money is waged, not surprisingly, where the money is. The two are not the same, but perhaps surprisingly, as in the battleground states, the two major-party presidential candidates compete for money in the same regions, particularly the large and electorally uncompetitive states of California, New York, and Texas. Although a much smaller segment of the electorate contributes money than votes, because the two battlegrounds do not overlap, presidential campaign outreach for support, more broadly conceptualized, occurs among a broader audience. We suspect that similar patterns exist among the other offices examined by other contributors to this volume. However, there is an important point that deserves future research: we do not know how patterns of giving have changed over time; thus we do not know if competition for money has narrowed or expanded.

Summary

The inescapable conclusion from these authors is that electoral competition across many offices is low and has generally declined. The level of the office seems to matter, with statewide elections for governor and senator usually attracting more competition than lower offices in the House of Representatives and state legislatures. Indeed, there has been a slight increase in general election competition for statewide constitutional offices, though combined primary and general election competition has declined. Overall, the picture painted by the experts here is not pretty: electoral competition is weaker than in the past, and the objective reader may well wonder if American democracy is the worse for it.

Reform Efforts

What can be done to improve electoral competition in America? Rational responses to public problems begin with an analysis of the factors that contribute to shortcomings in our politics. Policymakers can use their knowledge of these factors to design innovations that deal with the problems and improve the society. We turn first in this section to the factors that have led to the decline in electoral competition and then set forth some conclusions drawn from the work of our contributors.

A Framework for Assessing Reform

Faced with the clear decline in electoral competition in the nation, we might be tempted to conclude that a single factor—say, incumbent misbehavior—accounts for the dearth of challengers. After all, incumbents benefited the most from the decline in competition, and they have in some measure the ability to control who challenges them and on what terms. But we should also keep in mind that any large change in politics or society that slowly emerges is likely to have several causes. That reality should temper the way we evaluate reforms. If the problems came from several causes, any one reform—even if it is well designed and effective—is likely to have a relatively small marginal effect on enhancing electoral competition.

This is all the more true because not all declining competition is caused by government policy, or factors helping incumbents may have large benefits in their own right, the decline in competition notwithstanding. For example, the United States has enjoyed improved and more stable economic growth in recent years; since 1982 the nation has experienced only two mild recessions, after a period of greater, more virulent economic instability from the late 1960s to 1982. Several political economy scholars have shown how strong economic performance affects presidential and congressional elections. Generally, a better economy leads to fewer votes against the political status quo and thus to greater rates of reelection for incumbents. It is not hard to imagine backlashes against or rallies for incumbents or the party in power in other contexts, such as an attack on the United States or a major scandal. Of course, no one hopes for war or economic decline only in order to affect electoral competition.

The advantages of office have also helped incumbents win more than in the past. In part, such advantages are part of the way the world must be. Members of Congress should stay in touch with their constituents and keep them informed of what Congress is doing (or failing to do). But these vital aspects of representation also help create the "personal vote" and brand name recognition that make incumbents so hard to beat. Finally, Jacobson argues in this volume that the decline in competition arises in large part from the partisan realignment of the South. Districts that once offered close partisan fights have now become safely Republican for reasons of ideology and history. That may be good or bad, depending on one's views. It is not a change aptly addressed by public policy.

Such caution about causality and the effects of reforms are not counsels of despair. In fact, just the opposite. If we have false expectations about the causes of declining competition, we can easily expect too much from any one reform and dismiss small changes as failures. But if we are aware of the complexity of the issue, we look at reforms differently: a reform that changes the competition picture at all may actually be judged a success. With all this in mind, we turn to the effects of several reforms.

Ballot Initiatives

A popular reform today is a Progressive era innovation, the amending of a state constitution through the ballot initiative. Not all states allow for the ballot initiative. Perhaps surprisingly for reformers, Matsusaka finds that, except for term-limits reforms, there is weak evidence that the initiative process is related to the adoption of reform, even as a means of forcing an otherwise ignored issue onto the legislative agenda. Still, with these caveats in mind, Matsusaka finds that the presence of the initiative makes policy more responsive to a majority of the voters' preferences. If electoral majorities favor reform, then legislatures within initiative states will be more disposed to enact reform policies, perhaps in an attempt to retain some policy control. Directly or indirectly, the initiative may prove to be a useful tool of reform if citizens in the relevant states come to see a competition problem and if activists offer attractive proposals.

Term Limits

Ballot initiatives bring to mind the electoral success of term limits in the 1990s. Cain and his colleagues note, like Matsusaka, that over just a few years more than twenty states limited the terms of their state legislators. This success through the initiative process suggests that voters do respond favorably and strongly to a reform that promises to end the advantages of incumbency. The appeal of term limits was twofold. If nothing else, limiting terms would promote turnover in office. Second, voters could expect that limiting terms would create open seats, thereby fostering greater electoral competition since open seats traditionally saw closer races.

Two contributions to this volume look at the effects of term limits. Both conclude, somewhat predictably, that term limits have increased turnover.[1] The question of competition turns on a methodological question. Niemi and his colleagues measure competition by the percentage of districts with close votes. They find, with qualifications, that term limits increased both the number of open seats and electoral competition. Cain and his colleagues, in contrast, understand competition through the metric of average margin of victory. They find that term limits have not increased electoral competition. Remarkably, they find that the margin of victory increased in open-seat contests. Cain and his colleagues argue that term limits may have changed the calculations of challengers: those who would have stood against an incumbent in a particular year now simply wait until the term limit takes effect. Some elections would thereby have higher margins of victory than they would have had in the absence of term limits. Cain and his coauthors also note that term limits remove all incumbents, creating open seats everywhere. Many of those seats, however, may not be competitive for some reason (for example, because they are safe seats for one of the major parties). Before term limits, challengers had to take on incumbents, and might have done so on average only when victory seemed possible. This difference in open seats may explain the unexpected rise in the margin of victory in contests without an incumbent.

Here again we would be well advised to keep in mind the difficulty of enhancing electoral competition. Term limits may or may not have increased

---

1. Yet a data collection that included states and localities that rescinded term limits might have reached a different or weaker conclusion on turnover. The elections that would have not had an incumbent on the ballot had term limits not been rescinded would then count as a failure of turnover.

electoral competition, depending on the measure the reader finds most useful. However, term limits have led to greater turnover in the states where they were adopted. That may not be a surprising change, but it should count as an accomplishment, particularly in comparison with the small average effects of other reforms. Here as elsewhere, more research will reveal whether term limits have opened up the political system or fallen victim to the law of unintended consequences.

Public Financing

Critics have often argued that many campaign finance reforms erect barriers such as spending limits to challengers against incumbent legislators. Public financing of candidates, however, seemed different. By giving qualified candidates the means to contest an election, it seemed likely that public financing would increase electoral competition, assuming that a lack of money was an important reason why incumbents were so rarely challenged. As noted in the contributions to this volume, the evidence to date has not shown much increase of competition in states with public financing.

Arizona is a test bed of three major reform efforts that took effect simultaneously: term limits, public financing, and redistricting reform. The first year in which state legislative incumbents were term-limited out of their seats was 2000; a redistricting commission drew the maps for 2002 (though ultimately a court-ordered plan took effect); and full public financing took effect in 1998. Kenneth Mayer and his colleagues find that the number of contested seats increased between 2000 and 2002, as might be expected where there are more open seats due to term limits and shuffling of incumbents due to redistricting and there is public financing for candidates who might not otherwise be able to raise enough money to run a competitive campaign. Yet three of this volume's chapters (those by Mayer, Niemi, and Cain along with their colleagues) agree that electoral competition as measured by margin of victory decreased in Arizona between 2000 and 2002. Mayer and his colleagues, however, do find decreases in incumbent reelection rates in the first few elections after public financing began in Arizona. The effects in Maine are weaker but in the same direction. In contrast, Milyo and Primo studied a large number of gubernatorial races and found no effect of public financing on electoral competition. As always, we need to observe more elections, and in the best circumstances in more states, before we can more definitively link electoral competition with a particular reform. It could be that unusual circumstances in the 2002 Arizona election temporarily increased candidates' margins of victory. At this point, the reader may be wishing, as President Truman once did, for a "one-handed" analyst, but the best analysis suggests a mixed picture for public financing and competition.

 ## Redistricting Reform

Arizona is a hotbed of electoral reform and its redistricting commission has become a model for those wishing to reform redistricting, which McDonald shows has had a negative effect on electoral competition in recent House of Representatives elections. The reform model is one of a nonpartisan commission operating under a set of explicit criteria in public view with full public participation. This model contrasts with other established "independent" redistricting commissions that are designed to centralize power in the hands of a few and operate in secrecy.

McDonald demonstrates that political parties and incumbents have little incentive to increase competition through redistricting. Transferring at least some power away from these political actors may increase competition, as studies of California's redistricting reform initiative found. Another method is to explicitly require competition as a goal of the redistricting process. Such is the approach in Arizona and Washington, whose criteria include a specific statement favoring competition. Yet, to the disappointment of Arizona reformers, the newly configured districts produced by the commission did not result in a great increase in competition. Reformers elsewhere have not been deterred by this outcome and have tinkered with the sometimes conflicting redistricting criteria, such as those in Ohio, by elevating the competitiveness criterion. Despite ballot initiative losses in 2005 in California and Ohio, reformers continue to push ahead and have been greeted by serious legislative deliberations in these states.

 ## The Judiciary

From the beginning of the Republic and especially since 1941, the U.S. Supreme Court has served as the guardian of the democratic process. The guarantees in the First Amendment and the Equal Protection Clause of the Fourteenth Amendment have provided textual foundations for protecting aspects of political speech and association as well as of voting rights. The U.S. Constitution, however, does not guarantee competitive elections or limits on the advantages of incumbency. Not surprisingly, as Nathaniel Persily's article makes clear, the American judiciary has not generally applied the markets metaphor in constitutional jurisprudence. This is hardly surprising. The Supreme Court avoids conflicts with Congress, a co-equal and elected branch of government. Yet, as Persily also shows, the Court has acted incrementally to constrain legislatures that go "too far" in reducing competition. This incremental approach may both restrain some anti-competitive practices and over time foster a more coherent and comprehensive judicial approach to political competition. In that sense, Persily may be correct that the best hope for reform lies with the courts.

Summary

Those who are concerned about the decline in electoral competition may be disappointed by the findings in this volume about the consequences of reforms. We too are surprised in some ways that the reforms have not had more robust positive effects on electoral competition. However, we reiterate the difficulties of changing a political equilibrium that is deeply rooted in many factors. In that light, our average expectation might have reasonably been that the reforms would have little or no effect on competition. The reforms studied here have probably done better than that, and the final judgment must await the passage of time.

If behavior observed in the wake of longer-standing reforms such as direct primaries and term limits is a guide, significant effects may be observed in the short term, only to dissipate over time as politicians adapt to a new reform regime. That does not mean that small effects will not linger; certainly even low levels of primary competition provide more competition than if there were no primaries. There is also the possibility that reforms will have unintended consequences, such as perverse effects on competition. Because of public financing, money may be provided to candidates who have little chance of winning, thereby decreasing overall competition in contested elections. Because of term limits, otherwise vulnerable candidates may go unchallenged as viable candidates bide their time until the incumbent is forced out of office.

Conclusion

The authors of the studies in this volume agree that levels of competition are low; moreover, the evidence from primary and term-limits reforms suggests that political actors will adjust their behavior to the reform, weakening the effect of the reform on electoral competition in the long run. We are not that pessimistic. The states continue to make policy innovations, and it may be that the right campaign financing or redistricting reform, tailored to the political culture in a state, will have the desired effect in the short and the long term.

We also note that levels of competition vary among offices. Statewide offices tend to be more prestigious and powerful, attracting a greater number of high-quality candidates. Logically, reform efforts may have different effects for different offices. For example, candidates for governor and for the Senate may be more capable of raising sufficient amounts of money to be competitive than their legislative counterparts; thus campaign finance regulation or public financing may have a greater effect on races lower on the ballot. Certainly, redistricting reform is relevant to legislative offices. Reform efforts need to be narrowly tailored to the office they seek to affect.

Finally, this collection of works is focused on the issue of electoral competition. There is no perfect electoral system. As James Madison wrote, "If men were angels, no government would be necessary. If angels were to govern men, neither external nor internal controls on government would be necessary."[2] Our motivation for producing this volume is our belief that competitive elections are an external control citizens can exercise over their government. While some electoral reforms might be explicitly designed to increase competition, the contributors to this volume allude to other goals, such as removing corruption or increasing diversity. If a reform fails to have a significant effect on electoral competition, it does not mean that the reform fails to achieve other goals.

Because there is no perfect electoral system, any system implicitly represents a trade-off between competing values. Any reform produces a new electoral system and therefore changes the relative weights of the competing values. For example, campaign finance reform may be perceived to increase electoral competition, but it may also be perceived to decrease freedom of speech. Since reforms tap into core values, it is not surprising to find passionate support and opposition crystallizing around a reform effort. In these debates is easy to caricature one's opposition, though we hope that deliberative minds will thoughtfully weigh the pros and cons of a given reform.

2. James Madison, *Federalist* 51.

Contributors

Stephen Ansolabehere
Massachusetts Institute of Technology

William D. Berry
Florida State University

Bruce Cain
University of California–Berkeley

Thomas M. Carsey
Florida State University

James G. Gimpel
University of Maryland–College Park

Tim Groseclose
University of California–Los Angeles

John Hanley
University of California–Berkeley

John Mark Hansen
University of Chicago

Paul S. Herrnson
University of Maryland–College Park

Shigeo Hirano
Columbia University

Gary C. Jacobson
University of California–San Diego

Thad Kousser
University of California–San Diego

Frances E. Lee
University of Maryland–College Park

John G. Matsusaka
University of Southern California

Kenneth R. Mayer
University of Wisconsin–Madison

Michael P. McDonald
George Mason University

Jeffrey Milyo
University of Missouri–Columbia

Richard G. Niemi
Rochester University

Nathaniel Persily
University of Pennsylvania Law School

Lynda W. Powell
Rochester University

David Primo
University of Rochester

John Samples
Cato Institute

James M. Snyder Jr.
Massachusetts Institute of Technology

Timothy Werner
University of Wisconsin–Madison

Amanda Williams
University of Wisconsin–Madison

Index